# Fashioning Bollyw(

# Fashioning Bollywood

## The Making and Meaning of Hindi Film Costume

Clare M. Wilkinson-Weber

B L O O M S B U R Y

LONDON • NEW DELHI • NEW YORK • SYDNEY

**Bloomsbury Academic**

An imprint of Bloomsbury Publishing Plc

50 Bedford Square
London
WC1B 3DP
UK

1385 Broadway
New York
NY 10018
USA

**www.bloomsbury.com**

**Bloomsbury is a registered trade mark of Bloomsbury Publishing Plc**

First published 2014

**British Library Cataloguing-in-Publication Data**
A catalogue record for this book is available from the British Library.

ISBN:   HB: 978-1-8478-8698-9
PB: 978-1-8478-8697-2
ePDF: 978-0-8578-5296-0
ePub: 978-0-8578-5297-7

**Library of Congress Cataloging-in-Publication Data**
Wilkinson-Weber, Clare M.
Fashioning Bollywood : the making and meaning of Hindi film
costume / Clare Wilkinson-Weber.
pages cm
Includes bibliographical references and index.
Includes filmography.
ISBN 978-1-84788-697-2 (pbk. : alk. paper) —
ISBN 978-1-84788-698-9 (hardback : alk. paper) —
ISBN 978-0-85785-296-0 (epdf) —
ISBN 978-0-85785-297-7 (epub)
1. Costume—India.   2. Clothing and dress in motion pictures.
3. Fashion in motion pictures.   4. Clothing and dress—India—
Social aspects.   I. Title.
PN1995.9.C56W55 2014
791.4302'6—dc23        2013039561

Typeset by Apex CoVantage, LLC, Madison, WI
Printed and bound in Great Britain

# Contents

# List of Figures

# Acknowledgments

Over the many years it has taken to produce this book, many people have given freely of their time and their support, and I would like to acknowledge them here. My research in India has been funded by the American Institute of Indian Studies (AIIS) and Washington State University (WSU), with considerable logistical and scholarly support from the Research Centre for Women's Studies (RCWS) at SNDT Women's University in Juhu, Mumbai. In particular, I want to recognize Veena Poonacha and Usha Lalwani at RCWS, Amy Wharton, Candice Goucher and Carolyn Long at WSU Vancouver, and Elise Auerbach and Purnima Mehta at AIIS for their untiring efforts on my behalf. In India, my research was enormously blessed by my associations with Monalisa Sata and Rinki Roy Bhattacharya, both of whom have given time, hospitality, and reflection on the issues and problems presented by my research. Colleagues Laurie Drapela, Zafreen Jaffrey, and Sudhir Mahadevan have helped me in the tedious and difficult process of writing. Other individuals have helped in numerous large and small ways, all much appreciated. These people include Arjun Appadurai, Aditya Bhattacharya, Kaushik Bhaumik, Aseem Chandaver, Leena Daru, Jigna Desai, Rachel Dwyer, Teja Ganti, Emmanuel Grimaud, Doug Haynes, Ravi Indulkar, Sunil Khanna, Stuart Kirsch, Priyanjali Lahiri, Amruta Lovekar, Heather Lehman, Sudhir Mahadevan, Anthea Mallinson, Henry Martis of the Cine Costume, Make-up Artistes and Hair Dressers Association, Ranjani Mazumdar, Monika Mehta, Vinta Nanda, Judith Okely, Vaidehi Padhye, Sanjeev Puri, Shobhna Sagar, Aditi Sen, Maria Sharma and Rachana Sharma, Rosie Thomas, U. N. Umesh, Ravi Vasudevan, Ranga Venkatacharya, and Anita Weiss. I am grateful to many others from the film industry, including those cited (pseudonymously or otherwise) in the text, as well as Mala Dey, Sunil Indulkar, Shabina Khan, Shail Kriplani, Manish Malhotra, Dilshad Pastakia, Mani Rabadi, Naresh Rohira, Rocky S. and Sunetraa. The YWCA was a wonderful place to stay during my first research trip in 2002. During the analysis and writing stages, the South Asia Center at the University of Washington and the Whiteley Center at Friday Harbor Laboratories were welcoming and productive places to work as a visiting scholar. At Bloomsbury, Anna Wright, Emily

Roessler, and Hannah Crump have been supportive and patient during the preparation of the manuscript. Various anonymous readers and reviewers of manuscripts based on my research helped me develop more incisive and interesting theses about the industry and dress. Last but not least, I thank my family: my parents, Jack and Gwyneth Wilkinson, who encouraged me to pursue the life of the mind as a goal in itself, and Steve Weber, my husband, and my children, Ceri and Evan Weber, who have shared my life during this research and this book's gestation.

# Introduction

This is a book about popular Hindi film as viewed through its costume. More than this, it is about the social environment in the city of Mumbai from which film costume comes and to which it speaks, as well as the people who make film costume possible.[1] Anthropological and sociological studies tell us that what clothes reveal—and what they conceal—have been sources of speculation and concern across time and across cultures (e.g., Barnes and Eicher 1992; Eicher, Evenson, and Lutz 2000; Entwistle and Wilson 2001; Hansen 2004). If this is the case for clothes in everyday life, how much more true is it of clothing in performance, where the desires and the capacities of beings (human or otherwise) to control the world around them are infused with added emotional and moral significance? Of the various tools at the dramatist's disposal, film costume brims with powerful narrative, symbolic, and sensory possibilities (e.g., Berry 2000; Gaines and Herzog 1990; Street 2001). In India, film costume ventures have distinct historical and social foundations, most of them dealing with the persistent dilemmas of how to balance integrity and authenticity with modernity. While the kinds of challenges that film costume presents only partly overlap with those that beset ordinary Indians trying to decide "what to wear" (Tarlo 1996), they are no less indicative of how clothes crystallize core questions of identity and belonging.

In this book, I have chosen to approach these issues by examining actual practice in the planning and making of costume. Paying attention to the processes by which costumes come to the screen, and what these processes reveal about important aspects of urban and industrial life over the past several decades, reminds us that there are no singular geniuses presiding over the look or the meaning of a film. Costume flows from the ideas, opinions, skills, and toil of many people, all with a claim of some kind on its authorship. For my analysis, I use insights from film studies and anthropology. From anthropology, my home discipline, I draw on findings from the study of dress, craft and production, material culture, and, more recently, the body. From the study of film and fashion, there is a wealth of insight into making and meaning in media texts and fashion products. Like most anthropologists, I see the value of objects—and in the case of clothing, the bodies they are associated with—emerging from their insertion into social life. In the following sections,

I describe the scope of my interest in the making and meaning of the book's subtitle—the significance of stardom and fashion—and my methods for this study.

## MAKING

As a material item, a costume starts life as uncut fabric ready for the various embellishments and decorations it will receive. The fabric is converted into a carefully crafted garment, or—if a ready-made item is being repurposed as costume—it becomes a mass-manufactured commodity. The next step in the costume's career is to become an instrument of production of the film itself, as the clothing the actor wears on set. Then, it goes on to a bifurcated existence as, on the one hand, a physical garment that may end up as a celebrity auction item or just another piece of cloth tossed and locked into a trunk, and on the other, the filmed image, seamlessly joined with the body that wears it. At all stages, there are cultural, political, and economic issues at stake, so that costume is never simply about "fashion" or about a form of signaling behavior, but about labor, commodity consumption, enactment, and audience appropriation.

So who are the people responsible for making and managing costume? What do they think? Why do they do what they do? One can ask these questions of the people who are formally given credit for costume design. But this tactic is insufficient, due largely to its obviousness: for what is obvious is usually maximally contingent. In other words, in being steered toward an authoritative source, one is being diverted from other, equally valid ones: the men (but not women) employed to manage the wardrobe on set, known as dressmen, the tailors, the costume supply shops and their proprietors (both referred to as *dresswalas*), and so on. Howard Becker argued in his influential book *Art Worlds* (1982) that in order to understand art, one had to stop treating it as an exceptional activity and instead treat it like work. Further, Pierre Bourdieu in his work on art as a social field argues for the necessity of keeping texts grounded in the social relations that produce them (Bourdieu 1993). These are especially salutary injunctions given that much of the work that goes into the "glamour" industries of film and advertising is either painstakingly concealed or as astutely "handled" as the commodities and bodies that are the industries' primary products. Scholars who have now turned toward the study of production in the American film and TV industries are acutely aware of this problem, and their work is a carefully crafted response to Hollywood's appetite for consuming all forms of representation and self-representation, so that nothing evades the domain of spin. Years of interviewing and working with media professionals in Hollywood led John Caldwell (2008, 3) to propose the truism that candor varies in inverse proportion to power. By this reckoning, those lower in the media food chain are less likely to offer calculated responses to a researcher's questions.

But we should be careful not to assume that technicians and craftspeople in the Hollywood or Bollywood industries are always conduits of simple facts, any more than are company heads: "insider knowledge," Caldwell (2008, 2) cautions, "is *always* managed." While film workers may appear to be more artless in their conversations as compared to their industry superiors, they do have their own discursive strategies to deploy. As a result, careful attention to the cross-talk of work narratives alongside film analysis and ethnography can reveal the sociopolitical fissures that run through the costume section of the industry.

## MEANING

Film costume has many things to do in a film: it communicates, via the use of well-understood tropes, about moral character; it instigates actions and responses in the characters who wear and witness it; and it is the very substance of spectacle. Via its fascination with the material accoutrements of status and power, Hindi film generates its own "symbolic economy" (see Berry 2000, xiii), in which appearance is tantamount to a moral statement about self in a society rife with class, caste, religious, and gender differences. These meanings do not emerge only upon viewing of the film; instead meaning is anticipated and negotiated from the moment a film is first conceived. The same social actors described above encounter presumptions about clothes, propriety, style, and desire that circumscribe their productive activities. Neither the meaning of a costume nor its material details—how it is cut, how it is sewn, what style and silhouette it possesses, how it makes a character tangible—are decided unilaterally by designer, tailor, producer, actor, or viewer. Each is bound by the presumptions and habits of the others, so that the costume is both the outcome of a set of interconnected social practices and a singular sample of prevailing material and sartorial norms in society at large.

This last point about film costume's partial character is important to bear in mind. Film costume belongs conditionally within a wider "fashion system" (Barthes 1990), but it is not a microcosm of that system. Film never shows the complete range of dress that people in the world actually wear, only a selection from the great variety of dress that exists or can be imagined, a selection guided by both explicit and implicit considerations and constrained by time and resources. It is both a pastiche of the life to which it refers and the outcome of specific, sequential acts of "wearing" that are part of the actor's performance. Then, there are the costumes that mediate history or fantasy, or costumes that seem to exist in a world by themselves. I refer here to what is termed in India *filmi*—that is, a dress that is flashy, excessive, or revealing, and frequently all three. Not everyone in the cast is dressed in a *filmi* way, of course: in fact, *filmi* clothes derive much of their impact from being set beside the costume of mothers, fathers, and other less ostentatious and non-transgressive figures.

It is this intensification of the kinds of cultural processes that clothed human beings engage in every day—choosing what to wear, assessing its impact on others, reflecting on its effects on oneself—that makes performance in costume particularly compelling. In a riposte to the view that dress, as an external covering of the body, may be dismissed as a mere veneer to what is essential and true, Dani Cavallaro and Alexandra Warwick (1998, xxiii) have proposed that dress constitutes a "deep surface" that is there not so much to conceal as to act as the location for the "fashioning of subjectivity" (see also Miller 2005, 3). As a deep surface that is part of and yet not part of the body, dress speaks to who we are and where we belong, and it is, at the same time, a sensual form that connects the knowing, desiring body to the social order (Hansen 2004, 372). Because film costume is composed of clothes, it may seem that costume shares the same characteristics with them. But in a very clear sense, costumes are quite different. Above all, a costume is deliberately engineered to be simultaneously depth and surface: depth in its heightened salience, or how it signifies mood, personhood, and status in ways more deliberative and purposeful than in real life (Entwistle and Wilson 2001, 91); surface in the choices and treatments of fabric, color, and embellishment that turn dress into spectacle.

Nevertheless, film costume as a factor in a film production starts and ends as clothing, becoming costume as the actor (or arguably the director) uses it as a professional tool in the performance. It is difficult to generalize about the precise moment when one turns into the other, and the fact that two-dimensional films show clothes sutured to bodies in ways not encountered in life makes things harder. What I mean by this last remark is that, on the surface of the film, clothes and bodies are continuous; and in addition, film costume acquires heightened semiotic significance from the fact that viewers know that it isn't simply the character wearing certain clothes, but the actor playing that character as well. In other words, the practical, psychological, and cultural detachability from our clothes that we take for granted in real life does not operate in the same way on screen. The second phenomenon—perceiving both the character and the actor in the position of the wearer—is a distinct component of stardom and underscores the centrality of dress to a star's allure.

## STARDOM AND FASHION

Comparing the experience of filmgoing with models of everyday religiosity in India, scholars have argued that star and audience encounter each other via a powerful, mutual gaze (Lutgendorf 2006). Offering themselves to be seen and appreciated by humans is a particular favor of the deities; likewise, stars bestow on the audience the privilege of viewing them, and this view invariably includes sight of the costume in which the star is dressed.[2] Writers on costume in the European and American industries have made the case that stardom is intrinsically wrapped up in the clothes that help define it (Church Gibson 2012; Moseley 2005). Given Hindi cinema's reputation for excess, with "costumes rather than clothes, sets and exotic settings, and lavish song and dance" (Virdi 2003, 2), star costumes are particularly demonstrative. In fact, film stars have long been regarded as cultural brokers par excellence of innovations in appearance and behavior, alert to the constantly revolving door of fresh or reinvented styles and helping to market them to the young and the affluent. In Hindi film, stars and fashion are effortlessly elided.

Stars are consumers of fashion in all aspects of their professional and everyday lives. Acting in films is one among several activities to which stars devote themselves; others include advertising, lending their charisma to public events, and modeling. All of these require that stars show some awareness of and facility with fashion and, in the present day, serve as opportunities for label-clothing companies and fashion designers to leverage star power to their advantage. Scrutiny of stars' tastes and preferences even extends into their private lives. Yet, few people realize how much stars draw on the exclusivity of brands and top designers to steer choices in certain directions and not others in their film costuming. Even away from the glare of the media spotlight, fashion judgments are woven into the practices of filmmaking, affirming both the actor's distinction and his or her value as an industry asset.

It is important to recognize, however, that even as stars facilitate the encounter of the new, they also help underscore the rules of dress and demeanor against which each new fashion outing must be evaluated. Contemporary scholars prefer to define fashion broadly, mindful of the way in which we all craft our appearance in such a way that "clothing, body, and performance come together in dress as embodied practice" (Hansen 2004, 373). In such a view, fashion is understood as literally a kind of making, both of the assemblage of things and ideas that comprise a fashionable or even simply an agreeable appearance, and of the person as a social being. Without dress, the body cannot present itself as meaningful, whether in the public domain, domestic space, or the most intimate settings of personal life (Eicher 2001, 234). Film, as I noted above, does not exactly mirror dress in the real world, but it exploits familiarity with shared conventions when it leads viewers to make sense of people they do not know engaged in behaviors that would otherwise be unseen by outsiders (the secret plotting of villains, furtive embraces between lovers, or angry recriminations among family members). Stars (lead actors and, on occasion, well-known character actors) do not simply test the boundaries of what is acceptable dress; they help organize the fashion system across multiple contexts.

In India, self-fashioning has taken on renewed significance in the wake of the country's economic transformation of the past twenty years or so, leading to a flood of consumer goods landing on India's shores (Mazumdar 2007, xxi; Vedwan 2007, 665; Virdi 2003, 201). Starting in the 1980s, and reaching a critical point in the early 1990s, the government embarked on a new economic course, permitting overseas investment and lightening regulation of private enterprise. By 2012, India's economy had grown to the point of being the world's fourth-largest in purchasing power parity terms, according to the World Bank (2011). Film marks this transition in its portrayal of the lives of the young, fashionable, and affluent. But it is shaped by it too, as production processes, aesthetics, and a commodity environment that provides the ingredients from which costumes are made shift unalterably from the sparer and more limited dress landscape of the past. The profound importance of this shift is evident in the case of costume designers and actors, but its effects are equally great on other, less recognized members of the costume-production world. In order to understand why I have chosen to look at the opinions and practices of costume personnel in addition to designers (and other "creative" figures), it is important to know more about the Hindi film industry's history and organization. The remainder of this introduction gives just such an overview and finishes with an account of the way I went about my project.

## INDIAN FILM AND ITS INVESTIGATION

Studies of Indian film have multiplied in the past decade, with the lion's share of attention paid to the Hindi-language industry based in Mumbai. The accessibility of the industry to Hindi speakers is an element in this apparent favoritism, but the primary reasons why the industry widely known as Bollywood captures academic attention are the same as those that reap it such widespread appeal. There is its sheer reach, extending throughout India and overseas into the Indian diaspora, as well as into parts of the world without significant Indian expatriate presence—West Africa and the former Soviet Union, for example. And there is its continued grappling with the dilemmas of modern living, whether material, psychological, or political.

By the 1920s, filmmaking was done in large studio set-ups—Kohinoor, Imperial, Ranjit Movietone, and Sagar Film Company—modeled on Hollywood equivalents (Barnouw and Krishnaswamy 1980, 117; Rajadhyaksha 1996a, 403).[3] Studio fortunes were volatile, however, and in the aftermath of World War II and Independence the studio era came to an end. The oldest of my interviewees could describe their early years in the industry in the late 1940s and 1950s, the point at which studios were giving way to smaller, independent production houses. Despite its hold on the popular imagination (or because of it), film was only grudgingly acknowledged by the state in the post-Independence era, and its national and international success came without benefit of many of the kinds of incentives that other film industries around the world came to enjoy. Indian film has had recurrent periods of crisis, and at one point became notorious for securing funding from illicit sources. Accounts of costume production in the 1980s gave a sense of an industry at the limits of what it could do with the systems it had. The scale of production was frenetic, with stars doing multiple movies at once. Some films took years to complete, either because they lacked a reliable source of funding or the stars could not commit themselves to sufficient consecutive dates to finish them.

Madhav Prasad (1998, 49) notes that the trope of imminent improvement has featured in the industry for decades, and to hear a claim that professionalization was on the horizon at the end of the chaotic 1980s would have come as no great surprise. Only something was different this time, in that when the call for improvement came, the means to alter the industry in far-reaching ways was truly about to be established courtesy of economic liberalization. At the time of writing this book, multinational global entertainment companies such as Sony and Viacom have dipped their feet into the media waters of India, and computer-generated effects, improved camera equipment, and increasingly rational industry practices are making their impact felt. There are plenty of films made with the coarse sensibilities and haphazard tactics that are so disparaged by the leading filmmakers of today; but the big-banner films are rapidly incorporating the structures and procedures of what is considered proper filmmaking.

Paying attention to the full range of practitioners is important to understanding exactly what is at stake in transforming filmmaking practice (or alternatively, sticking to the tried and true). It is helpful here to think in terms of a "field of cultural production," in which all positions are interdependent and change in one invariably implicates others (Bourdieu 1993). Film workers constitute a pool of skilled, urban labor with its own habitus, or set of dispositions that directs interpretation and action. Technicians and those in what is termed (in the United States) the craft sector of filmmaking guide the production of media just as more powerful agents do, albeit not as obviously or singlehandedly. Film production proceeds upon the basis of cultural and practical conventions that workers uphold (Becker 1982, 28–34), and designers, directors, producers, and so on are compelled to operate within the frameworks of the industry as they find them. To say that worker conservatism represents a negative constraint upon what can or cannot be done in a film certainly falls in with what many at the top of the hierarchy like to argue. There are as many occasions, though, when the resourcefulness and tactical thinking of dressmen, tailors, or hairdressers generate solutions to problems that are unseen and unnoted by their superiors. Singularly and cumulatively, these everyday acts become part of the film as it is made and, by extension, the film as it is experienced by viewers.

Changes in the ways of working, as well as the justifications that are given for them, rarely take account of all of the constitutive processes of making a film. In fact, the inequality of positions within a cultural field means that the habitual, restorative, and compensatory practices that, on a daily basis, ensure that a film actually gets made are either underestimated or routinely disregarded. The truth of this observation can as easily be confirmed in industries outside India as inside, but its poignancy in the Hindi film industry comes from the frequent, almost relentless emphasis upon its disorganization and disarray, without regard to the fact that despite all the problems, somehow films do get made. Thus, a senior producer, moments after repeating to me the standard line about the chaos of filmmaking, made the point that the chaos was, in fact, a kind of coping:

> How does a street dog cross the road? He somehow does it. How does he do it? He doesn't know; it's impossible to know. How do we dress a film? We don't know: we just do it. It's like a mother who comes up with a dish from a few things in the refrigerator and gets 100 percent marks for it. It is a dish dictated by need, and the person consuming it knows it.

The fatalistic, even cynical tone here is commonly encountered among industry veterans, although not all of them express themselves this eloquently.

The point they want to press home is that exigency and constraint have characterized the industry for decades, and one simply figures out a way to work with that fact. There is no mention, however, of the people upon whom falls much of the job of working around, adapting, and making do.

For Tejaswini Ganti, claims and counterclaims by filmmakers in the 1990s and 2000s about being at the leading edge of the much-anticipated reform of filmmaking constitute some of the most pointed and revealing discourse in the industry (Ganti 2012, 7–9). My own explorations turned up a similar disdain on the part of contemporary designers, assistant directors, and producers for their fellow filmmakers and much of the filmgoing public. What I found particularly striking, however, was that the friction between succeeding generations of designers coexisted with a widening gulf between English speaking, "creative" agents in filmmaking, and technicians and craftspeople who feel that the areas of autonomy they used to enjoy are shrinking. Scorn among dressmen, tailors, and dresswalas for what Ganti terms "gentrification" is as easy to find as disparagement by contemporary designers of their amateurish predecessors or of (in their minds) the dull-witted workers who resist bringing the industry into the twenty-first century.

A certain exhilaration at seat-of-the-pants filmmaking is palpable among those older film workers whose ability to improvise solutions to cascades of problems was critical to countless film endeavors. They are generally skeptical about the current trends in the industry, some believing that the industry's ability to reform itself is limited and others hesitating to disparage what has worked in the industry for decades. The most ardent proponents of reform, however, object to what they see as the essential unprofessionalism that demands such engagements as the old timers like to recount. The reformers appear to want to sweep both problems and solutions into one pile that they can, with no further ado, dispose of once and for all. The opposition between these two visions of making film (and of film costume)—one permeated with nostalgia, the other with brimming confidence, and both filled with the contempt that Ganti noted infused the discourse of filmmakers in her research—is exactly what we may expect to find in a field of cultural production (Bourdieu 1993).

## METHODS AND PROCEDURES

It was not initially my intention to focus on costume. My interest in the social lives of the people who are support personnel for films actually started, following a reading of Robert Faulkner's (2002) book on Hollywood studio musicians, with a question about who the violinists in the orchestra were, how they were recruited, and what their work was like. I set out for the first stage of my research having rearticulated the question as a general one about the various craft and technical workers on and off the set. Once I had settled in, however, my previous research into embroidery gave me a level of credibility with costume designers that led inexorably to my following up on issues to do with dress and look. The costume world provided a welcome opportunity to examine gender issues in the industry, and the long-established presence of women in hairdressing and costume helped obviate any difficulties inherent in trying to get an entrée into fields that are exclusively and affirmatively masculine.

While my choices made life easier, I cannot say that they made the work easy. To do anthropological research means hanging around, doggedly, in the places where the people one wants to know about spend most of their time (this clumsy circumlocution having to make do in place of the old, comfortable assumption that anthropological subjects mostly stay put in small, relatively contained settlements). For one thing, it may take weeks for the opportunity for participant observation to present itself, not just because trust needs to be built, or persistence rewarded, but because the pieces of the necessary social machinery have to fall into place. In my former, fieldwork on the embroidery industry in Lucknow, it took five months before I got a chance to learn how to make embroidery from a skilled embroiderer. My research trips to Mumbai were, in contrast, relatively short, four months at most, and one week at the very least, leading me to wonder what might have been achieved had I had more time in a single visit to inveigle myself into a form of participation I wanted. On the other hand, I did have repeated exposure to an industry and its city over the course of eight years, enough to see the most important themes and problems resolve themselves into some kind of pattern, or dissolve and take on new shapes as the years went by.

I began to accept, also, that the very resistance to the kind of participation I sought was the participation I got. Filmmaking is a business; its personnel do not want to waste time when there are so many other things to be done with it. A very few individuals consented to meet me for an interview more than once. Some have even become friends over the years. The vast majority came, spoke, and promptly absented themselves. Hopes to follow a film in the early stages of preparation foundered when the financing took longer than expected to secure. On other occasions, shooting-schedule changes stymied the chance to spend more time on sets. Requests to accompany costume designers or their assistants as they hunted for clothes around the city were received with enthusiasm, only for me to find, on follow up, that my calls were not answered or emails not returned. Reading about comparable false starts and abrupt endings in the work of Sherry Ortner (2009) on Hollywood film workers confirms that these are hardly unusual experiences. Instead, a mosaic of ethnographic encounters and interviews tended, in the end, to reinforce my perceptions of the film industry as a protean, energetic phenomenon, inhabiting many physical production spaces both within Mumbai and outside it, as well as reception spaces where a new set of cultural producers (the audience) commence a whole new set of transformations upon what they experience.

Success within Hindi film depends upon contacts and access. For the researcher too, access is critical, and one rapidly realizes that points of access, like so many pores, are numerous and close at hand. These points of access have included, for me, neophyte directors, established writers, one-time producers, veteran dress designers, and in one case, a contact that developed out of an introduction to an out-of-town guest of a friend at a Halloween party held in a moderately remote southwest Washington barn. A key source for reaching film workers was the *Film India* annual directory of film personnel. This publication includes listings, with addresses and phone numbers, for actors, directors, costume designers, dressmen, and other technicians. The directory itself is something of a curiosity. Some of the people my assistant and I reached through cold calling had not worked in the industry for years, or even decades; even worse, some people listed in the directory were dead. Apparently, payment of a small annual fee is sufficient to keep one's name in the directory, presumably in perpetuity (although it doesn't explain how a deceased film worker might master this feat). However, we needed to find only a few bona fide employees of film companies, actively engaged in film work, because once we met them, we could then use a snowball technique to reach other personnel. Through a combination of all these strategies, I was able to accumulate more than one hundred interviews.

For formal interviews, I met people in their workspace (if they were sufficiently senior to be able to receive guests on set and give time to me) or at home (if they lacked that degree of autonomy). Interviewees under the age of forty were often keen to meet in a public space, mostly in Juhu or Bandra, which are areas of the Western Suburbs of Mumbai that are well-populated with film professionals. Over the years, these sites included the J. W. Marriott coffee shop, the lounge of the adjacent Centaur Juhu (later the Tulip Star) hotel, Barista and Café Coffee Day coffeehouses from Bandra to Lokhandwala, and the Prithvi Theatre open-air café in Juhu. At other times, I would converse with a film contact on the phone (usually our mobiles), by email, or on Skype, demonstrating to me that anthropological discourse in the digital age as reverting once again to the verbal and textual, all alternative experiential modalities emphasized since the 1980s notwithstanding. At the same time, these occasions fall solidly in line with the lingering predilection of Mumbai film production for conducting business through verbal and aural means (narrating stories, singing songs, relaying information and requests on the telephone). Although I cannot even claim to have talked to a representative sample of the industry, the accumulation of discussions with people of the same kind of rank, occupation, and background began to yield convergences of evidence that made me feel secure that I had managed to identify something in some sense real.

Like Ganti, I found that more influential film figures were more willing to meet me once I convinced them I was engaged in academic and not journalistic work (Ganti 2012, 31). In fact, this was a point they liked to emphasize, conveying the message in no uncertain terms that their time was valuable and not to be frittered away on talking to people whose interest was superficial. I am not sure to what extent this was a rhetorical gambit, since it is not as though one never sees the same individuals interviewed periodically in newspapers and magazines. For designers, my background in studying textiles, plus the fact that I knew what *chikan* and *zardozi* (forms of Indian embroidery) and handlooms were, made a distinct impression on some, more often the older designers than the younger ones.[4] As a white scholar, who is British yet based in the United States, I know I enjoyed some advantages in getting access to the higher ranking film personnel, certainly in the early years of my fieldwork. In 2002, film research was still a novelty, and my queries about film costume made me a curiosity. The vaunted business card, as essential to verifying credentials in 2002 as it had been in my dissertation fieldwork in 1989, smoothed the way once I was able to wrangle an appointment out of an interviewee (and not a few appointments were made and canceled innumerable times). As time has gone on, however, access has become both easier and harder: easier because I have made the contacts that help oil the wheels of communication and access; harder because the greater gentrification of the industry, as Ganti terms it, has introduced a more formal demeanor to a previously freewheeling industry. Getting onto sets is not a simple matter of bluffing one's way in, and neither my foreignness nor my whiteness has allowed me to bend or break the rules.

My age and gender were additional factors governing what I could and could not do. My age barred me (with one important exception) from being a candidate to appear in films (Wilkinson-Weber 2011). On the other hand, it lent a gravity to my interests and elicited many gestures of respect. My gender may have given me a slim advantage in approaching the female designers and hairdressers who have been the only consistent groups of women in filmmaking (aside from female actors) until very recently. Every single interviewee was unfailingly considerate, kind, and extremely patient with my questions, whether the interviewee was male or female, senior or junior, famous and powerful or obscure and (from an industry standpoint) insignificant.[5]

Mediating my interactions on many occasions was Monalisa Dand, who was kind enough and patient enough to collaborate with me on tracking down and interviewing a large number of film personnel. A fluent speaker of Gujarati and Marathi, as well as Hindi and English, the holder of a graduate degree in philosophy, and an astute commentator on the people we met and the things we saw, Mona was simply indispensable for navigating an industry with so much linguistic and social diversity. True, Hindi is the lingua franca of the set as a whole, even as English is becoming firmly established as the language of choice among the more powerful members of the film fraternity. Nevertheless, many dressmen, dresswalas, makeup artists, and so on were more at ease with Marathi or Gujarati. We used Hindi as much as possible, but interviews might shift periodically to Gujarati or Marathi, with periodic glosses in Hindi or English as the situation demanded. Interviews conducted in Gujarati or Marathi were transcribed and translated directly into English, whereas Hindi interviews were transcribed into Devanagari first and translated later. Translation was done cooperatively with Mona and with two other assistants, one in India and one in the United States.

Sandwiched between film and media studies, anthropology, and fashion studies, my research allows me to make use of more than ethnography and in-depth interviews, however much they remain the touchstones of whatever it is that makes this particular book unique. Thus, I have spent hours upon hours watching films and taking notes on costume, or reading glossy magazines devoted to the lives, loves, and clothing of stars. Social science and humanities techniques are interwoven in this book, certain methods more critical in some chapters than in others, but all ultimately threaded together to produce a complex and multistranded interpretation of costume and what it means in contemporary Indian film.

I start, in the next chapter, with an account of the productive environment in which costume is put together, and the various specialists involved in its making. Here, the reader is introduced to the particularities of the Mumbai setting—where the costume work goes on, how articles move from hand to hand and then to the body of the actor, and how the various practitioners stand with respect to each other. The various lines of tension— between older and younger workers, men and women, and above all, creative and craft categories that are in essence reinventing themselves and their responsibilities—are highlighted.

In the following chapter, I inquire more deeply into what "dressing up" in a costume means as performance. Teasing apart the different statements that actors, dressmen, dresswalas, and designers make about what costume design involves, I discuss the ways in which costume effects transformations—of actors, of their characters—and why this is significant for the viewer. After this, I devote a chapter to exploring the way in which the costume modifies or is itself completed by the body, and then how costume, in its guise as fashion, is and has been a conflicted marker of modernity. I move on to historical costume and to crosscutting claims to knowledge concerning the authentic Indian of the past. Finally, I consider the passage of costumes and costume ideas into the public domain, and how the forces that combine to make film costume now turn themselves to the production of fashion as well.

# The People and Places of Costume Production

## THE WAY TO MAKE A COSTUME

Cultural fields are vulnerable to the effects of time in that no field can be expected to remain the same, even as its products and its rationale appear consistent. The essential framework of costume production in Mumbai has remained the same for nearly one hundred years, including its institutional figures (on-set costumers, or dressmen) and local economic contingencies (the vast number and versatility of tailors in the city). But any conversation with retired personnel brings to light the changes that have occurred, offered along with ample glosses upon what caused these changes and what they mean. The impact of consumer capitalism since the 1990s on costume and on the nature of film work was clear to all by 2002. This impact could be seen both in the kinds of costumes that were being made and in the kinds of people who were taking the lead in designing them.

As striking as these recent social and cultural realignments in the film world are, other moments of change in costume design and production conventions are just as important. For example, there was the rise of the very same designers, from the 1960s onward, who now see themselves marginalized by the designers at the forefront of the industry today. In turn, the pointed (and sometimes public) generational and class antagonisms between designers can very easily obscure the adjustments and adaptations taking place in other parts of the costume field occupied by such figures as costume supply shops, tailors, and so forth. In this chapter, I introduce the principal characters whose practices and interests reverberate throughout the field. In reviewing the most significant changes in how costume is conceived of and produced, as well as the key points of contention between the chief costume "actors," I hope to lay the groundwork for explorations of more detailed costume matters in chapters to follow.

But before going further, I want to pose the question of whether it is possible or even desirable that any aspect of film production (here, costume design) should take the same form over geographical space. In formal interviews, I would ask everybody (tailors, dressmen, designers, and so on) to describe how they did their work, as a way to open up an exchange about the many components and considerations of making costume for Hindi films. As a starting point for a concrete, detailed narrative about the elemental activities of costume design, the question could not be more straightforward; yet, designers, assistant directors for costume, and costume assistants (and no one else) almost all equivocated to some degree with statements about the idiosyncrasy of costume production in Mumbai, taking care to draw attention to its difference from American (or even perceived global) norms. Take, for example, this explanation provided for me by *Amina*, who has designed for many of the top male stars in the industry:

> First of all, in India, I mean since you've met so many costume designers, the system is not like Hollywood, where a particular designer does everyone. Here the star system exists, like Salman has his own costume designer, Shah Rukh has his own costume designer. Like I work for five stars exclusively. I am their designer whenever and whichever film they work on. It's a completely different system from Hollywood, where one designer does the entire film, whether it's Russell Crowe, Nicole Kidman, anyone. Here it's completely different, so the star will tell [the producer], in the beginning, and since I've been working for so many years, everyone knows, this one is his costume designer. So the producer and the director approach, the director tells you what the subject is, what he sees the star in, then he'll give you inputs, and that's the way it is.[1]

In other instances, quibbles came later, as the narrative of "how I do my work" touched further upon the relative power of the star versus the designer in determining a star's costume. This comment was offered by *Ravi*, a menswear proprietor making costume for a major superstar for more than twenty years:

> It is very different from the Hollywood way. I feel, from what I've heard and what I've seen, if a costume designer [in Hollywood] is in charge, then that person is in charge, that person has to decide everything. This is what you have to wear. The person coordinates with the director also. That is what I've heard.

As a last example, Lovleen Bains, a designer who has worked on prestige projects for Merchant Ivory Productions, as well as both art films and commercial projects, reflected upon her preference for working solo on one film at a time before noting:

> Over here it's more between the star and the designer, and they do their own thing, and they land on the set and everyone does their own thing, and so there is no sort of coordination. But I guess maybe it's not required also.

I generally assumed that it was my status as a white foreigner that prompted these equivocations; clearly my interviewees thought I knew all about how costume got made in the American, European, Chinese, or indeed any other film industry. In fact, at the time I did not, since I had made a point of approaching the study of costume in Mumbai with as few preconceptions as possible, precisely so I would not be tempted to measure it against a putative Western (or Hollywood) norm. That I encountered these norms just the same did not simply remind me of my own ethnographic status; these moments were occasions for my interviewees to exercise "self-othering," or offering a distanced reflection upon practices that they otherwise took for granted.

The fact is, while costume design everywhere draws on the coordinated labors of the people conceiving, drawing, stitching, embroidering, finishing, pressing, storing, and so on, there is no invariant occupational structure that costume production in different locations demands. The arrangements one finds in any given setting arise out of the peculiar historical and social circumstances that prevail there, and any change responds to the same principles. The fact that there are a number of different organizational and conventional routes to creating costume, however, does not mean that we simply dismiss the comments of designers that allude to the Hollywood way of doing things. To claim that there is a single correct way to do things that current practice flouts is a reminder that the relationships and assemblages that bring costumes into being are suffused with conflict and anxiety, no matter that in one way or another they seem to work. Equally as significant is not making such claims at all, for as much as not doing so implies ignorance of alternative conventions, it may also signify fluency with materials and persons in the costume production network that contrasts markedly with designer expressions of frustration.

I shall return in later chapters to the question of why designers and their peers in the film hierarchy worry so much about the right way to do things, whereas tailors or dressmen do not. For now, I will refer to the American and European practice less as a yardstick than as a springboard to understand the historical and social factors that explain the industries' divergence. In the sections to follow, I situate costume in its geographical context and then begin to chart the main shifts in the creation of the present-day costume art world via an examination of the flow of responsibilities and relationships between its various members. These are, in turn, tailors and designers; designers and dresswalas; and dressmen and assistant directors for costume/assistant costume designers. Additionally, I describe other creators of film "looks," such as hairdressers and makeup artists (who, along with dressmen, belong to the same labor association), as well as production designers and directors, whose activities have a bearing on costume either directly or indirectly.

## THE GEOGRAPHY OF COSTUME

During the shoot, costumes are worn and re-worn; duplicates are made, broken down to convey age or injury, and otherwise used up. Their initial use value is exhausted, and they move to the next phase of their existence—as part of a dresswala's stock, as a costume in a trunk destined for reuse by a junior artist (extra), or (at the other extreme) as the personal property of a star or as a celebrity collectible. From start to finish, costumes traverse a wide range of productive and commercial spaces and move, hand to hand, body to body, among just as wide a set of workers and producers.

Costume producers can be found in distinct work and residential spaces in Mumbai. The workspaces include, obviously, film studios dotted about the suburbs (such as Filmalaya in Andheri, Filmistan in Goregaon, and Mehboob Studios in Bandra), as well as Film City to the northeast of the city, whose sheer size allows for the construction of multiple massive outdoor sets. Costume personnel must also adapt to conveying costumes to and from the many sites of location shooting, ranging from the ever-popular landmarks of the city, such as Marine Drive or the Gateway of India in South Mumbai or Juhu Beach in the Western Suburbs, to private bungalows rented out for movie shoots, to—as I have witnessed—apartment blocks under construction, juvenile prisons, vacant hotels, and many more. Increasingly, the suburbs of Dadar or Khar northward contain all that costume producers need to get their jobs done: dresswala and tailoring shops, embroidery workshops, boutiques and department stores, street markets, malls, storage units, and commercial office space. There is a laundry storefront in Vile Parle, with its washing operations located near Lokhandwala. There are godowns (warehouses) in Oshiwara for storing costumes after a film has wrapped, and hair salons all over Bandra, Versova, and Seven Bungalows. The offices of media companies fill new complexes in Goregaon and Malad.

Actors, directors, and other people in the creative ranks have been migrating for several decades from the environs of Malabar Hill, Worli, and other areas to Bandra and northward. Several generations of film people have now called Bandra home, and a drive around its winding roads takes one past house after house that once belonged to a deceased superstar. The Western Railway tracks mark a boundary of sorts between the residences of actors, producers, directors, and creative personnel on the west side, closer to the sea, and the homes of technicians and craft workers on the east side. As the northward movement of production personnel and facilities has gathered pace, ties to the craft industries of South Mumbai have been loosened. The unmatched textiles resources of Crawford Market, the diverse treasures of Chor Bazaar, and even the cheap and plentiful ready-mades of the Heera Panna shopping center in Mahalaxmi continue to lure designers and art directors. But designers active from the 1950s to 1980s sought out shoemakers, launderers, haberdashers, and cloth merchants in "town" to a far greater extent than do designers today.

A few actors, writers and even costume designers (notably film costume Oscar winner Bhanu Athaiya) doggedly remain in South Mumbai, but there are fewer of them as the years go by. For the sake of proximity and efficiency, the industry's promotional events, such as book launches, awards shows, and fashion shows can be held in large, suburban luxury hotels, including the J. W. Marriott in Juhu, the ITC Grand Maratha Sheraton in Sahar (along with others close to the international airport), and the Taj Land's End in Bandra. The city proper retains its cachet, of course, but reaching it becomes harder and takes longer as traffic increasingly clogs the main north–south routes. The spectacular Bandra–Worli sealink speeds drivers past the congestion of Mahim and Dadar, only to deposit them back into the traffic jams at either end. The effective remoteness of South Mumbai has benefited the suburbs, however, by compelling their residents to refocus their retail and productive energies in the areas around them. The mixed commercial and industrial landscapes of the rapidly developing areas north of Dadar have been invigorated, pulling the film industry as much as it is being pushed.

## THE INVENTION OF DESIGNERS

Prior to the mid-twentieth century, costume design was the prerogative of dressmen, dresswalas, and personal tailors, all of them men. Some historical and mythological films included special credits for persons who might be expected to have specialist knowledge to bring to the venture, but otherwise there was no costume designer as such directing the production of a film's look in the domain of clothes and accessories. The vast and complex studio costume units of Hollywood's golden age engendered a minute division of labor that lingers on in a broadly shared consensus on what jobs are, how they are done, and who can do them (Calhoun 2008; Nielsen 1990). In Bombay, on the other hand, costume production, even at the height of the studio system, was never contained wholly within the studio walls, and jobs and seniority were never broken down into fine levels of discrimination. Heroines and heroes routinely provided clothes from their own wardrobes, stitched by the same tailors they employed to make their personal wear.

The well-rooted custom of having one's clothes made by tailors has historically led to stars forming close attachments to their favorites, whether these were dressmakers who hired in-house tailors, menswear stores, or masters (the proprietors and head cutters) of independent shops. Before dress designers emerged as a distinct category in costume design, a tailor with several heroines as clients could command a certain degree of influence in the film industry. The same would have been true of the masters and proprietors of menswear stores with respect to heroes. Whereas female designers inserted themselves quite successfully into the relationship between heroine and master tailor, it took much longer for personal designers to be able to unbalance the conventional relationship of hero and menswear shop—in fact, the loyalties of heroes to their favored menswear stores, and the master cutters at those stores, remain unchallenged even today.

In Mumbai, many of the craft inputs to costume have always come from artisans removed from studio life, and we find no equivalent of an Adrian or Orry-Kelly or Edith Head presiding over in-house workshops for stitching, embroidering, or beading. On the contrary, according to *Mohan,* the oldest dressman I interviewed, who began work at the tail end of the studio era in 1947, the studio's tailoring staff was quite small: "Every company had tailor, 1940 to 1950 to 1960. [In] Raj Kapoor's time, they used to make clothes, two tailors, two machines, two assistants." Today, tailors and dresswalas are still to be found carrying on many of the same functions they had in the past. *Darzis* (tailors) are fundamental to the entire costume enterprise, since all costumes, except for draped or tied garments such as saris, turbans, and dhotis, need tailors to stitch them (and even saris, turbans, and dhotis may be sewn with drapes and folds in place to speed up costume changes). Given the lingering popularity among the middle classes of clothes stitched by tailors, one can find tailors almost anywhere around the city. In fact, the sheer ubiquity of tailors makes it easy for a film production, in a crisis, to get some kind of dress made on short notice, assuming quality is not an issue: several shops listed in the *Film India* annual directory admitted, when pressed, that they had done only one or two costumes for a film or television production in an entire career catering to local demand. Those tailors that work on a regular basis for film are typically clustered in suburbs so they are close to the studios, the designers, and the dressmen who carry costumes to and from the set. The tailor's job remains, in essence, a labor-intensive, humanly powered one. There is some hand stitching, but for the most part, tailors use treadle or hand-cranked machines; only rarely do they have electric ones. Cutting is done by hand, as is embroidery, which takes shape on rugged, wooden frames in workshops that are slotted inside slum districts or crammed into stuffy attics. Embroiderers work separately from tailors, although their labors have to be coordinated, since the tailor sends the marked-up fabric for embroidery before it is actually cut and stitched. Besides those tailors and *karigars* (artisans) with longstanding roots in the city, tailors and embroiderers also include seasonal migrants from other cities and permanent settlers coming from the countryside (for more on artisan migration, see Mohsini 2010).

Starting with Bhanu Athaiya, the category of "dress designer" (the term conventionally used in place of costume designer) took shape in the post-Independence era. She and other women who came after her, including Leena Daru, Shalini Shah, and Mani Rabadi, offered a new approach to the designing and making of costume (Wilkinson-Weber 2005). Designers have been among the most religiously diverse groups in the world of costume and include Parsis, Christians, Muslims, and Hindus. The older designers were coming of age at the moment of Independence, and all were educated to a high level in either visual or performing arts. They belong to what Rachel Dwyer terms the "old middle classes" (Dwyer 2000a; Dwyer 2006a, 274), immersed in the ideology and values of secular nationalism and committed to particular notions of Indian authenticity. Their gender, too, is significant, in that they disrupted the hitherto male-dominated profession of costume production. In Mumbai, the sexual division of labor in Hindi film costume production has generally favored men over women, unlike Hollywood, where women have always outnumbered men in costume design and production (Banks 2009). The appearance of well-educated, upper-middle-class female designers, each collecting a credit on the film, emphatically tipped the scales; however, their presence had no impact on the sexual division of labor in tailoring or embroidering.

The ability of women to assert their precedence with respect to tailors and dressmen who were often senior and more experienced derived primarily from differences in class. There is no mistaking the sense of distinction that the older designers share, their insistence that they had something to offer the business of design that could not be given by master tailors. Any attempt to lump them together with or identify them as tailors was and is even now vigorously repulsed. In 2010, Bhanu Athaiya publicly and strenuously objected to being (as she saw it) dismissed as a tailor, or someone who stitches rather than conceptualizes a dress, in reference to a court case in which fashion designer Tarun Tahiliani argued for tax-exempt status as a fashion designer (Dubey 2010). Athaiya, in particular, aligns herself philosophically and vocationally with the vision of costume design that is articulated by her peers in other major national industries. Her Oscar, won with John Mollo in 1983 for *Gandhi*, underwrites these claims and has served to set her apart from all other costume designers, old and new.

Designers establishing their credentials in the film business had to reconceive tailors as means to ends, as executors of visions that were firmly ensconced in the designer's, and not the tailor's, head (Wilkinson-Weber 2004a). The salience of the distinction emerged particularly clearly in one interview with *Maryam*, a retired designer whose career began with designing cutting-edge fashions for heroines in the 1960s and continued into the early 1990s:

> It's not tailoring only. It's not cutting only. Cutting I know. Tailoring I know. Everything. But you can't leave the workers to do it. Workers don't have a sense of proportion. . . . The designer is different from the master, from the cutters or from the tailors because they do not have that sense of proportion that we have of a figure. Each figure is a different figure; they are not the same. It is not a stamp that you can produce, cut, cut, cut like that.

This splitting of mental labor from manual labor is fundamental to the continued elevation of designers over tailors, and its persuasiveness depends upon a parallel separation of their social lives and professional discourses.

Dress designers historically have secured tailoring labor in a variety of arrangements. Some hired tailors to work for them in their homes (often in no more than a converted living room or bedroom); others took their work to independent tailors with their own operations. Tailoring is characterized by a certain fluidity, in which tailors are subject to different working arrangements throughout their working lives. A tailor who is employed by a dresswala may go on to work for a designer, then go back to working for the dresswala. Or a newcomer working for an independent master tailor may attempt to launch his own workshop. At each stage along the way, the tailor gains crucial knowledge and skills that can be parlayed into a new position with a new client or employer.

The dress designers who emerged in the 1960s never aspired to a position as head of a costume department, with a team of tailors, dressmen, and assistants working under their direction. Rather they worked for a succession of major film stars, so that any film with several stars might have two, three, or more designers attached to it. Heroes, meanwhile, typically expected their preferred menswear firm to make their costumes. Even Athaiya, who had more opportunities than most to design costumes for all the characters in a film, was often asked to design for just one heroine, so that the rule (rather than the exception) was for designers to work on their stars' looks in parallel, communicating sparsely, if at all. Films with major stars and larger budgets routinely listed several names as responsible for costume, and heroes and heroines began to look upon bringing a personal designer to the film (along with a personal makeup artist and—for heroines—a personal hairdresser) as a statutory condition of their employment.

Tailors work closely with embroiderers for those costumes that require elaborate decoration. Tailors include both Hindus and Muslims, but Muslims predominate in embroidery production. Muslim tailors are stereotypically regarded as the most adept at achieving a superlative fit. But given the vast number of tailors who have had some connection to the film industry— whether films are the heart of their business, or they are called upon very irregularly to make an occasional dress for some media production—it is

**Figure 1**   The master cutter, pictured here in his shop in the Western Suburbs in 2002, directs the operations of the other tailors and is responsible for the most important stage of making the costume—cutting the fabric and, in essence, establishing the architecture of the finished dress. (Image courtesy of Clare Wilkinson-Weber.)

**Figure 2**   Electric irons and sewing machines are used, even in 2012, alongside hand- and treadle-powered machines that can be extremely efficient when used by a skilled practitioner. (Image courtesy of Clare Wilkinson-Weber.)

hard to be precise about the regional and communal mix that film attracts. In 2002 and 2012, I met a number of Hindu Gujarati masters who were working independently on film work received from designers, as well as taking some private contracts for women's tailoring. The tailors in their workshops included both Muslims and Hindus. Their own estimates (which could not be confirmed) were that there were six or seven independent masters like themselves taking work from three to six designers at a time (as well as private clients, when it suited them) (Wilkinson-Weber 2004a). The oldest business had been producing film costumes since the late 1960s, when the popularity of personal designers began to increase. With years of experience in the unique demands of film costume, and a willingness to work all hours of the night, the independent tailoring shops are able to charge good prices for their services. As a result, when they are asked to do work for private clients, the prices they charge are significantly higher than the norm for the same kind of work.

Throughout my various visits to Mumbai, I did not meet a single tailor who was fluent in English. A few had several years of schooling and even had prospects of white-collar jobs, but they turned to tailoring mainly because of the monetary and creative rewards of film work. For example, a successful master cutter whose independent shop was still going strong a decade after I first met him, related to me that he had intended to go into civil engineering but decided instead to take a course in cutting and then to come to Mumbai to join his *mausa* (mother's sister's husband) in a tailoring business. Subsequently, he began his own business after several years of learning the intricacies of film tailoring. A brief email correspondence with the son of another of these independent tailors indicated that he had access to and familiarity with computer technology, as well as some knowledge of the English language, both the outcomes of enhanced educational opportunities. In 2002, phone usage was already widespread among tailors (and other technical personnel); by 2012, email had also become a preferred method for disseminating messages and photographs. Whether successful film-industry tailors prefer to educate their children so they can get more prestigious occupations is hard to say, given that the rewards of independent tailoring remain substantial.

In 2002, the low number of independent masters represented a constriction in the supply of costumes as demand from the advertising, television, and film industries was inexorably increasing. This was puzzling, since *filmi* tailors were well paid for their work, charging up to four times as much for a garment destined for a film as for the mundane equivalent prepared for an ordinary client. The reasons given then were that most tailors would not be interested in working the grueling hours that *filmi* tailors were used to; secondarily, not all tailors knew how to cut fabric and stitch finished costumes the way that *filmi* tailors did. One theory mooted by a designer who found herself depending upon these shops was that they simply refused to train young apprentices to the level where they could set up shop by themselves. However, by 2010, there were indications that the explosion of demand engendered by advertising, media events, and reality shows, as well as films, seemed at last to have been matched by a jump in the number of suitably trained tailors.

The contemporary picture for embroiderers is more mixed. Embroidery for film costume overlaps considerably with embroidery for private clients and the fashion market, and its specialists share the same social attributes. Several independent workshops are located in known slum areas of the city, where artisanal industry flourishes owing to the concentration of urban craftspeople and the availability of affordable space. The proprietor of a shop in Juhu selling heavily embroidered special occasion wear remarked that, while the skill set for embroiderers working for films or for fashion was the same, they occupied distinct workshops. On the other hand, two embroidery workshops I visited in the Western Suburbs (one also in Juhu, the other in Santa Cruz West) took work from both film costume designers and private clients.

One of these workshops had downscaled between 2002 and 2012, when I last visited. The reasons given were a fall in the amount of film work and difficulty in finding and retaining skilled workers. Absent further information on film embroiderers, it is difficult to speculate as to the broader significance of this observation.

The tremendous growth of the advertising and fashion industries from the 1990s onward propelled a new contingent of designers into film circles. They share several characteristics of their social class with their designer predecessors, for example, fluency in English, university education, and marked confidence in their own good taste. They differ in their overt affiliation with what are called, a little confusingly, the "classes" in India, in other words, upper-middle and upper-class people set apart by their refined tastes and cosmopolitan lifestyles, unlike the relatively undiscriminating "masses." The new middle classes are generally trained in business and commerce or in fashion, and they take a keen interest in film as an adjunct to a career designing couture and prêt-à-porter lines, accessories, and "lifestyle" commodities (Dwyer 2000a; Dwyer 2006a, 274). They are as determined to set themselves apart from *darzis* as the designers who preceded them; the difference is that they are just as eager to distance themselves from a film costume

**Figure 3**   Tailors and embroiderers take on work for private clients as well as film work. Film embroidery work is often more ostentatious, mainly so that it makes a more gripping visual impact, while work for private clients can often be very subtle and delicate. (Image courtesy of Clare Wilkinson-Weber.)

**Figure 4**   In the workshop owned by the master in Figure 3, two pieces of work are in prog-
ress. In the foreground, two embroiderers work on a dress collar for a television drama; in the
background, a frame is being prepared for a piece of embroidery for a film. (Image courtesy of
Clare Wilkinson-Weber.)

past (and by extension its designers) that they dismiss as gaudy, ostentatious, unsophisticated, and unprofessional (Wilkinson-Weber 2005). Between
2002 and 2012, several of these new designers with film and fashion credentials transitioned from using independent tailors and embroiderers to forming
their own, in-house craft shops, in effect subsuming craft labor and its distinct skills and knowledge into the designer's own brand.

It was at this point, however, that an even newer variety of designer came
on the scene: that is, a costume designer focused on film costume to the ex-
clusion of almost all other activities. These designers share many of the attributes of the new middle classes with their immediate predecessors, but they
also have a wide range of backgrounds and experiences. Some come from
theater; others come from university training that had little or no connection
to fashion, art, or textiles; still others have worked as assistant designers
with costume responsibilities. They, too, employ the language of distinction,
this time ranged against the fashion-conscious designers of the postliberalization years, and they draw explicitly upon a claim to be striving for greater
screen realism.

## THE BUSINESS OF COSTUME:
## DRESSWALAS AND DESIGNERS

As the second of the costume pillars upon which the film industry has conventionally relied, dresswalas embody the longest continuous connection of any costume-making institution to the film industry. Dresswalas exist in towns and cities all over India to supply local theater troupes and amateur-festival organizers with costumes for pageants, plays, and dress competitions. In Mumbai, several prominent dresswala businesses are run by members of Gujarati merchant castes. There are also shops run by Muslims, as well as Hindus of Maharashtrian origin. The core of a dresswala operation is renting costumes to the public; large operations have shops dotted all over Mumbai, with only one branch dedicated to supplying media companies. Maganlal Dresswala, among the oldest and biggest in the city, has several outlets, one dedicated to selling saris and another to manufacturing and stocking embroidered clothing for export to the Middle East. Dresswalas may also be approached to supply costumes for festival celebrations being held by Indians living abroad (commonly referred to as NRIs, or nonresident Indians).

The oldest dresswala businesses I visited, Maganlal Dresswala and Sureshbhai Dresswala, both got their start in the 1920s. Their founders were *pagdiwalas* (literally turbanmen, or experts in the tying of turbans) for

**Figure 5**   The inside of any dresswala's shop is immediately identifiable by its shelves of brightly colored costumes and a tailor with his sewing machine nearby. (Image courtesy of Clare Wilkinson-Weber.)

theatrical and festival productions. From there, specializing in making a complete costume to go with the *pagdis* was a very short step. The film industry, which was strongly influenced by Gujarati language and culture in its early years (Dwyer 2006b, 49–50), soon beckoned, giving dresswalas orders for all manner of historical and mythological costumes, with the costuming of junior artists and crowd scenes especially in mind. The rise of television gave dresswalas an outlet for their work in making costumes for historical and religious TV series, as well as novelty costumes for television commercials. At least two of the other shops I visited were founded in the TV era, and Maganlal and another long-established business, Chhotubhai Dresswala, enjoyed renewed fame with their costumes for the 1980s TV serializations of the Hindu epics the *Ramayana* and the *Mahabharata*.

The dresswala has several important attributes and abilities. First, a dresswala business draws on a vast stock and a staff that can be expanded and contracted as the workload demands. Dresswalas can also subcontract work to other kinds of craft specialists, such as shoemakers and jewelers, that a film production might require. Second, the dresswala is the supplier par excellence of costumes for films in which villagers or townspeople appear dressed in any way traditionally—meaning in *pagdis,* dhotis, kurtas, and so on. Other demands that dresswalas are particularly well suited to satisfy are for uniforms (police, army, and others) and dance costumes that need to be made for a large troupe. Arrangements between a production unit and dresswala vary depending upon the costume requirement and the scope of the film. If the film is a large one with substantial costume demands, then the arrangement will be for the production house to buy the clothes. Rental becomes expensive the longer costumes are needed, and besides, not all costumes can readily be re-rented to ordinary customers.

Because of their long service in the industry, the dresswalas are effectively the oldest sources of visual film costume conventions for historical or regional films. Yet, dresswalas today have no hesitation explaining that they supply costumes to order per the designer's requirements. In fact, the owner of Maganlal Dresswala drew a deliberate parallel between his business and major costume shops elsewhere in the world, such as Angels of London or Western Costume in Los Angeles, positioning the dresswala as a service specialist as opposed to a designer as such. There is certainly an affinity of sorts between a dresswala and a European or American costume shop, in that dresswalas actually keep costume stock, including accessories, on hand, though one does not hear of designers "pulling" (choosing costumes for a show) costumes from the stock in a dresswala shop as one does with American and European productions.

Dresswalas' understanding of the regional styles of India in headgear, dress, footwear, and so forth—"different culture, different language, different costume"—is a topic to which several returned in interviews, emphasizing the breadth and authority of what they know compared to what they regarded as the scanty cultural knowledge of designer parvenus. At the same time, the dresswala is the target of condescending mockery both inside and outside the industry from critics who point to the endless shelves of bright satin or the tinseled dresses and shirts that make up the collections in their showrooms. In these discourses, the dresswala is denounced as the author of everything kitschy or over-the-top in film costume. What is visible in the shop is not, though, what goes to a film set; rather, the glittery costumes in the showroom are costumes sought for pageants, religious festivals, weddings, and other such occasions by a local clientele (outfits range from gorilla suits to hussar or clown costumes to, in 2002 at least, Osama bin Laden costumes). And of course, industry people know very well this is the case. Quietly, the dresswala gets professional recognition via the repeated necessity of film productions to call in dresswala services for any number of purposes as the film is shot. Tangible evidence of this embeddedness in filmmaking comes from the numerous plastic bags of clothing bearing a dresswala's name that fill the trunks and dressing-room areas of the present-day set.

## THE MASTERY OF PROCEDURE: DRESSMEN AND COSTUME ASSISTANTS

The last of the three enduring figures of the costume field are the dressmen, or on-set costumers who take care of costume once filming begins. As though to confirm their place among this trio of costume specialists, it is they, rather than designers or indeed anyone else, who mediate between the film set and the tailors and dresswalas from whom work is obtained. Dressmen belong to an occupational specialization that has no clear equivalent in so-called traditional society. It is, in essence, an open occupation that requires no traditional knowledge or inherited caste status. Several dressmen that I interviewed had a tailoring background; however, the life histories of several dressmen traced several other tracks into the job. These included working up from a position as a canteen boy or production boy; a stint as a junior artist; working as a club bouncer and being befriended by a patron from the film industry; or stumbling upon the profession after visiting a set with friends (in this case, the dressman was a factory worker but had failed to find work). Approximately one-third of the dressmen interviewed had fathers or uncles who

**Figure 6**   On location, a small film sets up its dressmen with the lead actors' trailers nearby. Costumes and accessories are stored in the trunks. A larger production, or a larger location space, might have costumes put out on rails. (Image courtesy of Clare Wilkinson-Weber.)

were dressmen before them; others were the sons of *chowkidars* (watchmen) or mill workers.

Dressmen today come from a range of caste and regional backgrounds, some having shifted to Mumbai from other regional industries. For the most part, though, dressmen are recruited closer to home, and Maharashtrians and Gujaratis tended to predominate among my interviewees. Dressmen include both Hindus and Muslims and are members of the lower-middle classes, with gradations of status depending upon whether they have risen to a position of authority over other dressmen and whether they have found work with production houses that pay well—and on time. With skills and good contacts, a dressman can hope to rise to the level of head dressman, overseeing the work of several assistants. Head dressmen are well compensated for film work in comparison to the other jobs for which their background and training qualifies them. Job opportunities in television have mushroomed since the 1980s, although the pay has remained consistently less than for film, and the long hours and intensive schedule make TV work less attractive.

The functions of a dressman were probably imported from the theatrical model of the dresser, who assists an actor with his or her costume (Hansen 2003; Rajadhyaksha 1996a, 398). Dressmen are responsible for getting costumes laundered, mending them if they get damaged, pressing and steaming them to make them presentable for the actor to wear, and keeping them safely stowed in trunks until they are needed again for a later shoot. Dressmen are usually given the job of aging and distressing costumes that need to look old or bedraggled. They are also responsible for fetching costumes and accessories from the dresswalas, jewelers, designers, and tailors. Sometimes, dressmen are required to buy items in the marketplace or get costume duplicates at the last minute.

Dressmen have no formal relationship with the costume or dress designer; a head dressman is appointed not by the designer but by the direction and production team. He brings with him, typically, two assistants, who may be either newcomers to the business or more seasoned professionals. Extra dressmen are hired on a daily basis if there is to be a crowd or dance scene. Training consists of little more than what Jean Lave and Etienne Wenger (1991) have called "situated learning." I asked several dressmen how they got to know their job and was offered in response little in terms of concrete details. As assistants, they began by simply following the instructions of the head dressman, keeping a close eye on what is done and how best to do it. Mastering the art of networking is as crucial as learning the duties of a dressman. In at least two accounts of making the transition to head dressman (accounts, moreover, of events that were at least fifteen years apart), the dressman telling the story attributed his success to being able to forge a more congenial relationship with a production team than the head dressman under whom he had trained. Other dressmen made the leap by taking over from a head dressman who fell ill. A golden opportunity like this might allow a dressman to vault into a position of authority in a matter of months. Most though reported working for about two years as assistants before being able to move up to being a head dressman. Other dressmen linger as assistants almost all of their professional lives.

Before the advent of the designer, dressmen took on the major responsibility for organizing costume production. Small productions of "social" films (the films of the highly respected director Bimal Roy in the 1950s and 1960s, for example) would work from a brief developed by the art director, transmitted to the dressman and a team of tailors. Alternatively, instructions came straight from the director or producer. Stars, if they wished, would have their own costume stitched by their preferred tailors, but depending upon the kind of film and the costume, they might be quite content to leave the details to the dressman. *Gaurav*, a veteran dressman who had worked since the 1950s on many major film projects explained: "We used to have meetings with the director, and they used to tell us about the script. In our times, producers like Manoj Kumar used to give us the responsibility and trust our creativity."

From the beginning of my research in 2002 until 2012, I noticed that dressmens' grievances accumulated with ever more intensity and bitterness. This was in response, I believe, to the diminishment of the dressman's job as a direct result of new conventions in the industry. The dressmen seemed to weather the first arrival of designers well, mostly because designers largely stayed away from the set and saw the handover of the costumes to the dressmen as the end of their involvement in the filmmaking project. By the 1990s, however, assistant directors were being appointed to take care of costume, and a short time after that, costume assistants to the designer were beginning to act as the designer's representatives on the set. Interference in the domains of practice and influence dressmen had assumed were theirs was inevitable.

Costume assistants and assistant directors (ADs) in charge of costume are typically female, solidly middle class, college educated, and young (usually under 35 years of age). Female ADs remain a minority among ADs as a whole, though some, like Lakshmipriya Devi, who has worked as second unit director and first assistant director on films including *Rang De Basanti* (2006) and *Talaash* (2012)—have built up impressive reputations. ADs for costume are typically among the lower ranks of the direction team but costume is an area in which the male bastion of the set has been significantly breached. Like designers, ADs come from Mumbai's new middle classes and are supporters of the new business and entrepreneurial environments that have expanded since the early 1990s. They are among the beneficiaries of the new economic environment in India, not simply in the sense of finding work within it, but also as consumers of the plethora of commodities now available and affordable for the affluent, urban middle classes.

Assistant directors are in many ways some of the most dedicated standard-bearers of efficient filmmaking practice, ready at a moment's notice to articulate the case for streamlining and formalizing industry practices so as to fall in with global standards. Criticizing the failings of the commercial industry is hardly unusual. However, assistant directors do not merely carp at the old-fashioned ways of doing things; they can talk in detail about the initiatives they have taken, either alone or in a team, to rationalize certain processes. The authority of ADs to manage costume was not itself based on any formal authorization—a training course or extensive experience, for example. In fact, the sources of their systems were never clear and rarely consistent, as each AD did a fair amount of improvising, as well as applying systems learned elsewhere; the latter often amounted to little more than glancing at a book maintained by another AD or costume assistant on another film.

The principle difference between the AD for costume and the costume assistant is that the latter serves as the designer's representative on the set akin to "set supervisors" or "prep costumers" in American parlance. The costume assistant often has some fashion training and does much of the sourcing of local costume, including buying accessories and arranging for short-term rentals from boutiques. Costume assistants may go to the same shops that they patronize in their personal lives, using their own consumer acumen to serve their work goals (Wilkinson-Weber 2010a). As a kind of apprenticeship for becoming a dress designer, this role has much to recommend it. But it seems to me it is also the one most likely to lead to a position as wardrobe supervisor or as coordinator and budget manager of the costume department, under the overall leadership of the designer.

With the entry of ADs for costume and costume assistants, the dressman's executive responsibilities have diminished. Dressmen are still considered capable of fulfilling simple costume requirements, doing basic costume aging and distressing, and functioning as go-betweens for the dresswalas, tailors, embroiderers, launderers, and so on. But continuity is now monitored by the AD, using handheld and computer tools the dressman is unlikely to have encountered. ADs described carrying out activities that sounded very much like some of the same jobs that dressmen say were theirs—for example, finding costumes to reuse from a storage locker or warehouse. Dressmen conceded that ADs were the ones who came to them with directions as to the scene and costume required, but the dressmen stressed that, in this situation, the ADs were merely helping *them*, not that they were helping (read: "serving") the ADs. At least one dressman said that he left all the continuity calls to the ADs, given that "it's their job." I was unsure whether to interpret this as the equivalent of the dressman shrugging his shoulders, letting the AD do continuity, and watching the (anticipated) mess that would ensue with a certain schadenfreude: dressmen were not typically willing to concede much to ADs or costume assistants in terms of their competence. Alternatively, tasks that dressman had never approached in a particularly coherent way were readily handed over to the ADs.

The costume assistant and assistant director for costume's advantage over the dressmen comes from the kinds of educational and cultural capital they possess by virtue of their class. They can all, for example, speak fluent English, a skill that places them among the actors, directors, writers, and the like and apart from the technicians who could speak only their regional language (say, Marathi) plus Hindi (to varying degrees of fluency). As a counterbalance, dressmen, along with makeup artists and hairdressers, are extended some protections in the industry by the Cine Costume, Make-Up Artistes and Hair Dressers Association, which has many of the functions of a union. The association was established in 1955, registered under the Trade Union Act, and belongs, with 22 other associations, to the Federation of Western India Cine Employees (FWICE). In 2009, the total number of members, including all three areas of specialty, was 3,388, made up mostly of makeup artists (1,448), followed by dressmen (1,051), with only 889 hairdressers in comparison. The association establishes yearly minimum rates of pay for workers, although the negotiation is done in practice by the FWICE. Given that film occupations, like those in the informal sector, carry few guarantees, protections, or benefits, the association also offers its members assistance with pensions and health care.

In theory, membership of the association (secured with an entrance fee and, after eighteen months, with yearly subscription fees) is required in order for workers to get a job on a set. It is well known, however, that this is not what happens, and workers who are prepared to work at lower than negotiated wages are employed all the time (Wilkinson-Weber 2012). In fact, the dressmen that I spoke to painted a distinct picture from the association's in terms of how many dressmen were credentialed and eligible to work, and how easy it was to circumvent the rules of the association. In 2002, a former officer in the Cine Costume, Make-Up Artistes and Hair Dressers Association related that hundreds of new members had been enrolled very recently in response to new opportunities in television, resulting in an enlarged pool of labor. A clear majority of dressmen that I interviewed agreed that there were more dressmen every year, competing for the same jobs. In 2002 and again in 2005, a figure of 3,000 card-carrying dressmen was repeated several times, but why so many dressmen managed to be of the same mind on that particular number was hard to tell when the dressmen themselves weren't sure where it came from. There is a perception among dressmen that there is considerable pressure on jobs from bona fide association members who are nevertheless prepared to work for less money than the association minimum. Large budgets have also driven an absolute increase in the number of costume changes, so that the dressman's work is commensurately increased. A head dressman whose career had spanned three decades remarked: "In songs, for several people there are up to 90 dress changes. It didn't used to be that way; in songs, there were [only] two to three dresses." What the dressman was alluding to was a level of indulgence facilitated by the current, commodity-rich environment that didn't just create the visual effect of limitless bounty but strained long-standing work patterns to their limit.

The discontent I heard expressed in 2002 seemed to have been ameliorated in 2005, only to become acute again a few years later, when a crisis over pay and conditions arose. The association's protections notwithstanding, dressmen have always worked on several projects to shield themselves against inevitable delays in or even nonpayment of their anticipated wages. Having to wait for pay is a complaint heard even in today's supposedly more rational film-financing climate. By 2008, association attempts to hold the line against incrementally longer work days and chronic delays in payment to their members foundered, and frustration spilled over into a noncooperation movement (Wilkinson-Weber 2012). All members of the FWICE joined the action, but negotiations brought a quick end to the dispute. Inquiries that I made just a few weeks after the action was ended suggested that there was short-term improvement in the speed and reliability of payments and fewer demands for long work shifts. Yet, considerable skepticism remained that these steps would lead to long-lasting reform and an easing of work conditions.

With respect to the pressure on the occupational categories of dressman, makeup artist, and hairdresser from newcomers in the fashion world, the association response has involved little more than asserting the customary sexual division of labor by which only men can be dressmen or makeup artists and only women can be hairdressers. The effect of such intransigence is that, where men cannot get an association card to do a heroine's hairstyling, while women cannot get an association card to do makeup on either men or women (Wilkinson-Weber 2012). In actual practice, producers will hire female makeup artists, but they have to be very circumspect about how they deploy these workers on the set, in case association inspectors decide to make an impromptu visit. There are no comparable pressures on dressmen, since there are no women competing to be dressmen as such. Instead, the upper-middle-class women who are moving in on the dressman's domain do so from positions that operate in parallel with or in authority over dressmen, so that the question of whether these women can become members of the association is not relevant.

What a large number of the dressmen I talked to wanted was to reclaim a place at the table with the creative personnel who had taken so many of the costume decisions they felt used to be theirs, a challenge the association was not in a good position to meet. For years, designers rarely set foot on the set, thinking their job was done once the garment was stitched and the fittings complete. Accustomed to this way of doing things, dressmen chafe at the presence of designers, via their assistants, poking their nose into the dressman's business. The dressman is left alone to store things, take them out, or iron and mend them, but his ability to direct costume decisions has been severely curtailed. Head dressmen, whose authority is most compromised by the costume assistant, are predictably the unhappiest about this development. One head dressman remarked to me in an interview in 2006 that "now we only iron their clothes, and that's the only job left for dressmen." Another, in the same year, charged that the dress designer "sidles up to the director and says to him, 'Why have you kept a dressman, he'll only do the ironing, right?' and then inserts one of his own people instead."

## COMPLETING THE LOOK

My primary focus in this book is on the making and meaning of costumes. Makeup and hair are, however, indispensable parts of a character's look. Here, as with dressmen, there is a resilient sexual division of labor. Makeup artists are conventionally male, and hairdressers, who entered the industry to work with female stars in the 1950s and 1960s, are all women. Strict rules also apply to whom practitioners work on. Hairdressers work only on women, while makeup artists do both hair and makeup for men and makeup only for women. Makeup artists and hairdressers today include Muslims and Hindus, but in the past, there was a distinct skew among hairdressers toward Christians, primarily because their long-standing embrace of Western styles meant they were the most familiar with fashionable hairdos. The majority of the present-day practitioners interviewed were Maharashtrian-speaking locals, and family traditions among makeup artists seem to be more common than is the case with either dressmen or hairdressers; many makeup artists reported fathers, grandfathers, and brothers all in the same occupation.

Makeup artists emerged from the theatrical antecedents of film and were sometimes actors themselves. Just as personal costume designers emerged to take care of stars in the mid-twentieth century, so makeup artists as a group began to split into those who did company work and those who were employed as personal makeup artists. The same pattern became true of hairdressers, with a company hairdresser attending to the lesser cast and personal hairdressers looking after their own stars. Although base rates are set by the association, it is well known and widely accepted that personal makeup artists and hairdressers command much higher rates—and are far more likely to get paid on time. As with costume designers, a popular hairdresser or makeup artist may work for more than one star at any given time. A well-established makeup artist, *Ramesh*, from a family of makeup artists, described the routine his father followed when he was working for several heroines in the 1960s:

> [H]e used to handle four artists. He used to start his work at 5 o'clock. He used to reach Juhu, Asha Parekh's place, say 6 o'clock. He used to do her makeup. He used to go to Mala Sinha at Bandra. He used to finish her makeup. He used to go to Saira Banu in Pali Hill. He used to do her make up there, and he used to come back to the studio at 9 o'clock to do other artists.

I was assured that this kind of arrangement would be impossible today, whether because artists would flatly refuse to get up so early or because traveling around the Western Suburbs with their heavy traffic would make for a daylong venture. And in fact, there is a perceptible shift toward the biggest stars of the present engaging one makeup artist who goes with that star, and that star only, from films to commercials to stage shows and so on. Amitabh Bachchan has had the same makeup artist (Deepak Sawant) for many years; so, too, has Shah Rukh Khan (Ravi Indulkar).

The recent expansion of salons and spas in Mumbai and elsewhere since the 1990s has produced its own cohort of superstars—for example, makeup artist Mickey Contractor and hairstylist Adhuna Akhtar of b:blunt salon (wife of director and actor Farhan Akhtar). It has also yielded a formidable crop of young men and women trained equally in hair and makeup. The maturation of a substantial professional hair and makeup scene poses a challenge to the conventional Bollywood arrangements, among them the rigid sexual division of labor that forbids women from doing makeup and men from doing women's hair. Since no effort has been made to change the rules by which makeup artists and hairdressers get formally accredited in the industry, the result is a deflection of what are differences of generation, and importantly, class onto gender, with established makeup artists and hairdressers expressing skepticism and resentment about men and women taking over jobs that "belong" to the other sex.

## DISCIPLINING THE COSTUME ART WORLD

In an effort to capture the distinctiveness of Mumbai filmmaking practice, Madhav Prasad (1998, 32) has argued that it falls under what he calls (borrowing from Marx 1976, 461–3) the heterogeneous mode of production, as compared with Hollywood's homogeneous mode. While American films are made with each and every component of the film systematically developed in concert with the others, in the Mumbai industry, parallel yet largely autonomous domains of practice (such as music composition and recording, dialog writing, and set design) are put together at the point of shooting, with very little planned in advance or in conversation with other domains. Prasad's model works quite well to explain costume production as a relatively independent set of activities; even more striking is the extent to which the traits of the heterogeneous mode have penetrated *inside* the costume domain since the rise of the personal designer. When heroes and heroines (and sometimes character actors) are free to choose their own designers, costume production is fragmented to the extent that designers make clothes in almost total ignorance of what other designers are doing for the same film. This is indeed one legacy of the star system that replaced the studios after Independence: the rise of a star entourage—designer, makeup artist, hairdresser (for heroines), and so on—reinforced or perhaps even created tendencies toward heterogeneous practice via the separation of tasks rendered as personal services to stars.

Splintering costume production for any one film among several different agents allowed for personal designers to work with several stars on several films at once. In no small respect a response to the unreliability of film financing, this was a way to spread risk for both the actor and the members of the actor's entourage. Without consistent and reliable funds to bring a film to a speedy conclusion, shooting instead might start, stop, and restart innumerable times. Stars would take on two, three, or even more films at once as a response to these recurrent interruptions, to the point that getting a film finished came to rely not just on sufficient money but on finding dates on which the star could work. It was therefore to the benefit of star designers, tailors, makeup artists, and other personal staff that their own heroes or heroines would make several films at once. In this way, the risk of not being paid or being paid late was spread. At any one moment, a personal designer might work for several stars and by extension several films, for which the designer would surely be paid at least something.

With the long awaited recognition of filmmaking as an industry in 1998, financing for film projects has become far less unreliable and mercurial, meaning that some (if not all) of the justifications for taking on several films at once have become moot (Govil 1998, 204). Foreign corporate investment has enabled greater investment in mandatory preproduction activity (Ganti 2012, 6), and budgetary management has become, at least in principal, core to filmmaking operations. Productions are motivated to engage production designers to help steer the film's visual characteristics on several fronts, including costume. In fact, preference for multiple personal designers over a single costume designer has been targeted as one among many archaisms the film industry ought to dispose of.

Far from being a view endorsed only by enthusiasts of the "new" Bollywood, a preference for a single designer was articulated to me, from the earliest days of my research to the most recent, by all kinds of designers, both old and young and even including personal designers to stars. We ought not to forget that Hindi filmmaking has always been quite diverse and includes productions big and small, with great variability in how they are made. Films with a small budget have always, for reasons of economy, had to hire a single designer or, at most, just one for a lead actor in addition to a designer for the company. Art films led the way in this regard, especially since they emerged from a filmmaking ethos in which multiple designers had no particular place. In other words, the principle of a single costume designer for a film was neither unknown nor unprecedented. In 2002, however, even after nearly a decade of consolidation of neo-liberal economic policies, stabilization of film financing, and the growth of advertising and public relations industries concerned with "look," the possibility of a single designer taking the reins in a major film with even one star in it was, in the minds of the designers I interviewed, remote in the extreme.

By 2012, much had changed. The growth of multiplex cinemas screening both big and small films for the benefit of (necessarily fairly affluent) urban audiences has offered a viewing environment for urban elites that includes *hatke*, or offbeat, projects as well as big budget films. No longer is "parallel cinema," with its art films, as ideologically or pragmatically distinct from the mainstream. Hatke films are far more likely to hire a single designer, and any stars who turn up in these films seem willing to trade the privilege of their own designer for the prestige that goes along with being in a high quality film. Some directors, such as Vishal Bhardwaj, then carry practices established in their early films into subsequent, larger-budget ones. Costume designer Dolly Ahluwalia has collected single credits in *Omkara* (2006) and *Kaminey* (2009) for Bhardwaj (earlier, she took sole credit for costume in 1994's *Bandit Queen*). In another example, Arjun Bhasin has been the single designer credited in films directed by Farhan Akhtar or his sister Zoya Akhtar, including *Dil Chahta Hai* (2001), *Lakshya* (2004), and *Luck by Chance* (2009). Bhasin has also taken designer credits under Mira Nair, whose work falls outside the Mumbai industry's parameters. Single credits also tend to crop up more often with historical pictures, although it is by no means a requirement for them: Lovleen Bains got sole credit on *Mangal Pandey: The Rising* (2005), Neeta Lulla on *Jodhaa-Akbar* (2007), and Anna Singh on *Taj Mahal* (2005).[2] Even as the preference for a single designer is becoming more pronounced, stars may still insist on involving their preferred designer. More than ever before, though, that designer must comply with the larger design principles of the film and with a more developed notion of a script around which production revolves. The stage is set, therefore, for the dissolution of the heterogeneous mode of production, at least as far as costume is concerned.

Might then the idealized ways of making film costume in the United States come to prevail in Mumbai filmmaking? Few designers go as far as to claim that an equivalent system can be installed in the Indian context. The older

**Figure 7**  The exterior of a multiplex cinema located at Infiniti Mall in suburban Mumbai. Multiple screens carry both Hollywood and Hindi offerings (the Hindi releases at the time were *Shanghai* [2012] and *Rowdy Rathore* [2012] pictured on the bottom right). (Image courtesy of Clare Wilkinson-Weber.)

designers tend to settle for calling for more organization in planning and executing the making of a film, while younger ones argue that they are almost there already. For myself, I think it unlikely that we shall see an ushering in of homogeneous production, but not because I share the recurrent pessimism of some designers and filmmakers that professionalism will remain elusive. Rather I believe that capturing the differences dualistically in the contrast of heterogeneity and homogeneity oversimplifies the matter: Hollywood is not as homogeneous and Bollywood not as heterogeneous as we are led to believe. Moreover, any tendencies toward homogeneity Prasad describes are thwarted by factors he does not fully consider.

Prasad's argument hinges on the existence versus the absence of the script as an organizing factor of production in the American and Mumbai industries, respectively. There is no doubt that the work of costume production is dramatically altered by whether one works to the specifications of a script or not, but the division of labor and material conditions of production seem at least as, if not more, significant. The tightly coordinated procedures of American filmmaking (in the homogeneous mode) depend in no small part on a compartmentalization of roles and responsibilities that are specified not just through conventional practice but also in law. Job titles are zealously protected, and guild and union membership is designed to reinforce solidary bonds within and differentiation from without. As we have seen, though, the picture is very different in Mumbai. A dressman is just that: a dressman. There is no distinction drawn between a set supervisor, a costumer, or even various kinds of costumers—prep, truck, and so on.[3] Assuredly, one can credit a certain pragmatic thriftiness for this. Just as the studios of the pre-war era did not see fit to have any more than a handful of tailors, so nobody in post-Independence times has ever thought it necessary to define and delineate the duties of a dressman to a minute degree when anyone with minimal competence can do whatever is needed to be done at a moment's notice.

But the price of this flexibility has been uncertainty as to what the limits of any given job might be. This uncertainty leaves some occupations vulnerable to infringement by other ones, or new ones—in essence what took place when designers entered the industry and assumed some of the tasks previously done by tailors, or costume assistants came in and co-opted the territory of the dressman under the banner of professionalization. Bollywood unions and associations share some of the attributes of Hollywood unions and guilds, but the circumspect worker is well aware that stability and security derive not from union solidarity but from cultivating powerful patrons and family connections. These relationships insulate workers against unemployment and total marginalization; they do not, however, prevent the realignment of responsibilities and entitlements within the field of costume production. As long as job categories are minimally defined and costume production proceeds informally without a departmental structure to guide it, it is far easier for new entrants to the costume business to establish themselves within the industry and possibly infringe upon the roles of the practitioners already there. The contrast in commercial North American and commercial Hindi film systems—one of which tightly defines job titles and the responsibilities and duties that go with them, while the other leaves these roles and responsibilities exceedingly broadly defined and indifferently monitored, is at least as meaningful, if not more so than a difference that depends upon the existence or not of a script.

## COSTUME AS FIELD AND ART-WORLD

The introduction of professionalism in the industry is related, rhetorically at least, to the implementation of filmmaking strategies more akin to those that are perceived to exist in the United States and Europe—and as far removed as possible from what has existed in the past (Ganti 2012). Each generation, meanwhile, must press against what came before as fractiously as its predecessors did; thus, the very system that personal designers put in place to reform tailoring and designing in the 1950s and 1960s later became an oddity that a new cohort of designers and producers in the 1990s felt compelled to dispatch—and, in turn, a fresh set of faces in the 2000s saw fit to do the same. The device of consigning all previous efforts to India's supposed "deferred modernity" is as apparent in film discourse as it is in politics and in the philosophy of work and labor in post-Independence India (Deshpande 2003). In every instance, it is a fraction of the upper middle classes that typically offers itself as the bridge to a final realization of India's potential.

Thinking about costume as an "art world" in Becker's sense alerts us to its fluctuations of personnel and conventions. Bourdieu's notion of "cultural field" forces us to pay more attention to the flow of power and the structural implications of change. So far there is no evidence of a change in the direction of the flow of power from the creative categories (directors, actors, producers) to everyone else in the field. No matter how designers change their attitudes and activities, they still manage, practically and rhetorically, to differentiate themselves from costumers, tailors, dresswalas, and so forth. If anything, the autonomy of these latter categories is being eroded over time, rather than enhanced.

And yet, the three pillars of the costume side of the industry—tailors, dresswalas, and dressmen—retain a measure of integrity and a distinct identity. In the chapters that follow, I change course to address costume questions and dilemmas more directly, and as I do so, the play of relationships among these costume figures as they defend, transgress, or try to dissolve the boundaries of their various specialties will come into clearer focus.

# Costume and Character:
# Wearing and Being

My clothes may express the dressmaker, but they don't express me.

Isabel Archer to Madame Merle

Henry James, *Portrait of a Lady*

Costume realizes many intertwined objectives, both implicit and explicit, of personnel involved in filmmaking. Outwardly, however, there is consensus that costume is instrumental in crystallizing character. In fact, the whole point of a costume is to take what is relatively indeterminate—the actor's flexibility, no matter how circumscribed, to take on different roles—and make it determinate (the character that is assumed). Costume is also intrinsic to a character's transformation, within a film, from one kind of person into another. Among the best-known (and joked about) kinds of transformation is that of a young, carefree, unmarried heroine (first seen in a variety of fashionable, even risqué outfits) into a demure, marriageable woman wrapped in a sari. Even the play of characters and roles in masquerade depends heavily, sometimes completely, upon costume and is one of the great, enduring sources of enjoyment and beguilement in Hindi film, speaking fundamentally to the challenges and limitations of attempting to refashion the self.

Assuming that putting on a costume is indispensable to becoming a character—becoming in some sense "other"—I turn my attention in this chapter to the constraints upon how a character is to be imagined. How do the conditions of filmmaking impinge upon characterization via costume? What about the interests of the star actor, for whom a film is not simply an exploration of character but an occasion for consolidating his or her star persona? How indeed is character to be defined in Hindi film, given the kinds of imaginative spaces that are created in scenes that are alternately dramatic, comedic, or musical (the song sequences)?

Most scholarship on performance and characterization—what it is, how it is done—focuses on the actor (Barber 2003; Hastrup 1998; Schechner 1985; Turner 1982). Here, I draw particular attention to the practitioners around the actor—the designer first and foremost—to show how they are indispensable to shaping performance. Constructing a character is a participatory affair, in which the costumes, as material entities, "assert their presence as simultaneously material force and symbol" (Miller 1997, 105). The quote that opens this chapter, from Henry James's *Portrait of a Lady*, both captures the paradox of clothing—that it is simultaneously personal and social—and raises the question of whose agency dress enacts. Delving into what designers have to say about the process of designing exposes the extent to which their intent is impressed within the dress, as well as the limitations that press upon them. Do film costumes express the designer? the tailor? the actor? What costume does and how it does it are bundled up inside discourse and in the actions that together create character.

## FINDING AND DEFINING CHARACTERS

Whenever I asked a designer in India to describe his or her work, every single one said that costume is made according to character. In Mumbai, designers of all ages articulate a vision of costume design that is strikingly repetitive, no matter the differences in costumes, films, and production conventions between the pre- and postliberalization eras. Thus, a designer for important heroines from the 1960s to the beginning of the 1990s, said much the same kinds of things about making costumes as one whose career began in the early 1990s. First, here is what *Meena*, the older designer, had to say:

> So when they [the director and/or producers] come to me to narrate the entire story, first I have to hear the story, then you know I come to know it is a social story, so the director wants to show the character, that they are in Bombay only, and the story, the total story is moving along in Bombay itself. So I have to design accordingly. Then, I listen that the girl is a young girl, going to college, and then, while studying in college, she falls in love, and then she completes her study, they both decided to get married, they go abroad for further studies, and you know how the story moves. Accordingly, we have to decide how the colors and styles then balance. They show that the girl is from a rich family, the boy is not from a rich family, so those kind of outfits.

Then, here is the account of Anna Singh:

> You work according to the character. You work according to where the character is situated, what environment the character lives in, what kind of background the character is coming from, what kind of financial status the character is in, as in what does he do, where is he coming from. Then, you look at perhaps what his mental makeup is. That's got a lot to do with what one wears. You know, the kind

of person you are . . . normally reflects in the clothes—the casual person, or what exactly the body language of the character is.

How the embodiment of character differs from designer to designer, and era to era, is less important here than the fact that these statements (and others I collected) show that costume designers all agree, in principle, to be doing the same thing—paying attention to character, thinking about all the social factors that influence how a character appears, and mulling over the events that overtake the character in the film. Yet, in actual fact, even according to their own qualifying comments, no designer designs solely according to character. All kinds of other factors—pragmatic, aesthetic, and strategic—enter into their calculations. Among these factors are consideration for the demands of stardom and the imperative to work within the unavoidable constraints of the system. In order to tease apart the implications of this apparent paradox, we need to understand more about character, stardom, and how the production system tends to favor certain approaches to design over others.

## Melodramatic Entailments

A melodramatic style of presentation has prevailed in the majority of Hindi films, a heritage of the Parsi theater, whose many attractions (comedy, song, romance, spectacle) and manner of storytelling had a heavy influence on Hindi filmmaking (Dwyer and Patel 2002, 14; Hansen 2002). Writing about melodrama in the Western dramatic tradition, Christine Gledhill notes that "melodrama sets out to demonstrate within the transactions of every life the continuing operation of a Manichean battle between good and evil which infuses human actions with ethical consequences and therefore with significance" (Gledhill 1991, 209). It is a description that fits the Hindi film situation as well. Characters in performative traditions like these are rarely plumbed for psychological depth; instead, they make up a repetitive set of figures who together stake out positions in the film's moral universe (Vasudevan 1989, 30). Acting involves "embody[ing] ethical forces" so that "moral forces are expressions of personality, externalized in a character's physical being, in gesture, dress and above all in action" (Gledhill 1991, 210).

Complaints that Indian films are unrealistic miss the point that melodrama can work only if the action unfolds in a setting that at least appears to be true to life. Twists of fate, startling revelations, and irrevocable mistakes feature prominently in melodramatic narratives, but these "excessive" elements make sense only within a diegetic universe in which ordinary life is otherwise the order of the day. Dress is critically important as a reliable guide to the position of the character within the moral landscape of the film, as well as a means to connect the story to the real world. In practice, this means the costume must be both maximally expressive of emotional states and meaningful as a style of garment that exists, or can be imagined to exist, in the world.

The repositioning of characters as the film unfolds is marked by costume changes. Analyzing costume changes in the 1989 film *Hum Dil De Chuke Sanam*, Emmanuel Grimaud emphasizes the importance of costume change to the intensification of emotions throughout the film (Grimaud 2003, 272). He suggests that a sequence of new costumes worn by a character within the span of a single day (as given by the diegesis) is a visual clue to the emerging love between the protagonists, with the synchronization of their changes confirming their compatibility and unification. Consider, he writes, how many times we change our clothes throughout the course of a week or over a period of months or years. By packing as many changes into the compressed time frame of the film, an equivalent emotional and transformational sweep is introduced into the narrative.[1]

These effects are magnified in song sequences, in which the use of costume changes is notorious for materializing excess; however, excess here works to encompass a surfeit of feeling that only a song can convey. Song sequences take many forms, but one evident pattern is for them to condense personal and social passages in vivid visual and aural terms; the fantasy of cast-off and put-on costumes invites several ways of projecting a relationship into an imagined realm. A change in costume can be read in several ways—as a marker of passing time, as a clue to inner states, or as an indicator that the characters are enjoying the imaginary pleasures of embodying different kinds of people, with all the implications that may have for the relationship that is the focus of the song. Here, costume changes are apprehended on a conscious level, making actual and graspable the many identities a character can take. They give a material form to the unspoken desires of young lovers. They give assent to the view that identity can be known and fixed through the medium of clothes. At the same time, they show, time and again, that identity is far more mutable and complex than conventional wisdom admits. Sangita Gopal and Sujata Moorti (2008, 5) add that song sequences have the distinct responsibility of locking films in time and place (or places) via the choice of music and lyrics, as well as the settings against which the song unfolds. Costume, I would argue, contributes centrally to this heady fusion of the "realist and the utopic" (Gopal and Moorti 2008, 5). The demonstrative cosmopolitanism of song and dance doesn't simply invite the use of a wide range of costumes; it derives, in good measure, from these costumes.

## Stardom

There is another characteristic of melodrama that must be borne in mind: the affinity between melodramatic performance and the production of film stars (Gledhill 1991, 211). In melodrama, "moral forces are expressions of personality" and are made manifest in external signs such as dress, gesture, and action (Gledhill 1991, 212). The intensity and allure of film stars issue from cultivated personas that include both the characters they have embodied and the offscreen life the public is invited to witness (via film magazines, newspaper reports, and online film blogs and websites). Several scholars have argued, in fact, that the production process of film favors a form of characterization that hovers close to iconicity (King 1985). Unlike the stage, where performances unfold linearly with the narrative, film acting requires that the actor give discontinuous performances. For example, scenes are not shot in sequence, but may be repeated several times until the director is satisfied with the result, and the final product is brought to completion only in postproduction. Stability in the appearance of the star from film to film mitigates this fragmentation, reassuring the viewer of the star's authenticity (Dyer 2003, 10).

The mode of performance that film stardom and melodrama share is widely referred to as personification, or the overvaluing of persona relative to character, and it is distinguished from impersonation, or the careful delineation of character associated with "good" acting. In actual practice, screen acting makes use of both modes, for while personification may be an adaptive response by film stars to secure their position when performance is liable to fragmentation, impersonation serves the construction of the star as an accomplished actor (King 1985; Naremore 1988). In Hindi film, however, the predominance of melodrama impels stars toward personification as the preferred and often the exclusive performance mode (Dwyer and Patel 2002, 29). The continuity between character and actor, and the extent to which it is signposted by filmmakers and acknowledged by audiences, is developed far beyond what is assumed to be the case when American screen audiences draw connections between characters and the stars who play them: Indian filmgoers are experts in apprehending the "actor as parallel text" (Chakravarty 1993, 201; Mishra, Jeffery, and Shoesmith 1989, 52). This continuity is facilitated by the frequent and very deliberate overlaying of character with well-known facets of the star's offscreen life, as well as by the repetition of dramatic scenarios and even character names to underscore the resilience of stardom across several films.[2] One of the most complicated star "texts" belonged to Nargis, whose persona drew its power from the entwining of her iconic roles with a compelling personal story of love and disappointment

(Thomas 1989). Indeed, Neepa Majumdar (2009: 147) contends that the widely circulating stories about Nargis's personal life were "acknowledged, fixed, and contained in the screen roles that replicated the gossip, with a resulting tendency to conflate star persona and film role."

In other words, what designers, directors, and the actors themselves know, before a costume scheme is discussed at all for a given film, is that persona is an intrinsic part of the character. In a very real sense then, they are designing for the star, or at least with the star's persona very much in mind. I do not argue that this invalidates the claim by designers to be making costume with character uppermost in the imagination; rather, designing for character invariably means an assessment of what befits the star that is brought into alignment with what a character is thought to need. Given the considerable significance of outward signs—mise-en-scène, gestures, and so on—to the function of melodrama, one can hardly argue that this alignment is inappropriate (Gledhill 1991, 211). To demonstrate how this works out in practice, I reproduce below an extended description of a consultation between a star, a designer, and later a director, followed by an analysis that teases out the various considerations that the designer must pay attention to do a successful job of making costume.

## WORKING OUT THE LOOK

The episode I am about to relate, which took place in 2002, began in the apartment of a designer with whom I was doing an interview. This particular designer, whom I shall call *Anita*, had been trained in a formal arts program but had shifted into fashion design fairly quickly. As with many film practitioners, her entrance into the industry came about as a result of a fortuitous introduction via a friend. Thereafter, she had interspersed film work with fashion ventures. Interviewing young designers currently working in the industry invariably meant having to stop while they took texts (known as SMS messages in India) and phone calls on their mobile phones. During this interview, one call turned out to be particularly momentous because it was part of a wily arrangement between the designer and the star to figure out a costume scheme before the director could deliver his input. The moment the star knew that the director was on his way to the star to talk about the character and his look, the designer was to come to the meeting place immediately so that the designer and actor would have a chance to discuss details that they could then present as a *fait accompli*. I tagged along with the designer as we went to the meeting, which was held in an unremarkable, ferociously air-conditioned suburban hotel room:

The star and his designer start their discussion with a review of some magazine photographs that capture the look the designer has in mind. The designer points out where changes and adjustments would be made in the star's version of the shirt and vest and brings up possible color combinations. The star and designer also list off accessories, down to the kind of watch the character might wear, props such as a mobile phone, and even the haircut the character might have. The designer suggests a cut that the star wore in another of his films. "One hundred and twenty films, I can't remember how I looked," he jokes.

At this point, the director arrives, very surprised to find not just the designer there, but me as well. He proceeds to give a detailed narration of the character he has in mind for the actor to play, while the actor retreats into a contented and inscrutable silence. The director spells out the visual impression he wants the character's accessories and props to have: "chunky, solid, a gold chain." "Could I kill someone with it? Could it be a weapon?" asks the actor, momentarily alert. As designer and director banter back and forth, several possibilities are ruled out on grounds that the actor has worn something like that before, and so the look can't be repeated. The director thumbs through the magazine pictures, liking some and dismissing others: "This is too Marlon Brando." Finally, having worked out almost all of the look, the actor, director, and designer get to the matter of footwear. "This guy," states the actor, "he wants to be fast, he needs to get out of there, move fast." The designer has been rapidly writing notes but asks the director to annotate the pre-prepared list of clothes. The director then goes into a narration of the scene in which the character first appears, describing the entire room, down to the furniture and the lighting he wants to use. This prompts another round of suggestions regarding the colors the actor might wear, again ruling out anything the actor has worn recently but alluding to the relationship of the character to others in the film. "The other two characters are in white. Why not contrast him? He is a go-between figure. Why not emphasize his character in a different visual way?" asks the designer. The debate goes on for several minutes until the actor calls a halt, directing the designer to make two sets of possibilities, and they will decide when they shoot.

The director then adds that he wants the actor to be in different clothes in each scene. He needs different-colored glasses in each scene, and new costumes as well—"a complete change every time. He wears Western wear for seven days, then chucks it out." After the director has finally departed, the actor and designer continue their discussion, fleshing out not just the way the character will dress, but the cigarettes he smokes, the music he listens to, and so on. "So you're not just designing a costume?" I ask the designer. "No," comes the answer, "it's a lifestyle."

The interaction of actor and designer just described is not necessarily typical—the same designer had discussed a film that very morning with a client who was content to contribute very little input. Nor should one assume that, with one conversation, all future questions about the film and the costume were settled. But I have reproduced this exchange in detail to illustrate how the designer and actor together manage to accommodate the star's preferences and persona within discussions about costume and character. Before going into these considerations in detail, I want to draw attention to the fact that this meeting was not based on a script, and no reference was made to a script. Whatever scene preceded or followed the one in which the actor's character was introduced was not discussed. Yet, clearly, the designer and actor were laying down some ground rules concerning his appearance in this and other scenes to come.

## Color

Fairly quickly, the issue of color and color combinations came up. The phrase "color combinations" was one commonly used by designers, old and new, to talk about the essential elements of their work. Coming up with the right kinds of colors, and putting those colors together, is one of most important visual decisions designers have to make. A designer known for developing good color combinations can stand out from others. Talk of a color palette comes up in connection with the making of art films or independent films, where it refers to a far more elaborate visual pre-planning for the film that extends to sets and locations, as well as costumes. In mainstream film, color works, and is described as working, in a contrastive and declarative manner: a color may be chosen for the simple pleasure of its appearance; at the same time, colors form a system signaling moods and shifting character positions.

Designers are acutely aware of the semiotics of color, and they must balance the visual appeal of a costume's color with the messages it will inevitably impart. These concerns were even said to affect the dressing of people in a crowd scene, where designers and dressmen must be careful to avoid certain colors and styles that could be taken (erroneously) as signs of public religious or communal distinctiveness. Film can, and has, moderated or challenged certain color codes, however—most famously in Yash Chopra's *Chandni* (1989), where Sridevi appeared in several white outfits courtesy of designer Leena Daru. White is a decidedly ambiguous color in Indian thought. It is associated with renunciation and widowhood, as well as with simplicity and purity. Dressing Sridevi in white saris, *ghaghara cholis*, and *salwar kameezes*, sometimes with some hints of color and sometimes not, was provocative but also incredibly influential. Almost instantly, the color white became not just acceptable for young and married women but highly desirable.

At their simplest, colors are a means to parallel narrative with shades and hues that tap directly into elemental forms of cultural literacy. A heroine wearing, for example, pastel pink is considered sweet and young, while a married woman generally eschews the eye-popping colors of a younger, unmarried woman. However, very somber, muted colors hint at a depressed and troubled state. The use of vibrant, saturated colors produces plenty of vivacity and visual excitement, particularly in song sequences. Decorative elements, such as embroidery, may be indispensable in scenes in which value is assertively proclaimed, whether the social and emotional value associated with marriage or the political and moral value of kingship and power. Dull, dark colors are indicative of either solemnity, or sadness, and even illness. Here, a designer, *Priya*, whose peak of activity was in the 1980s lays out the simple theory of color and mood, using as an example a film in which she designed for the heroine:

[T]he heroine was playing a bubbly character first, and then she becomes pregnant. I've given all dull colors, you know, to give her that character. [In the] first half, when she is very lively, I've given her all the bright colors, and again when she is in love, I've given all the bright colors.

Over and above the matching of color to mood and status, indulgence in bright, vivid color is one of the key characteristics of what is known as a *filmi* costume. *Filmi* costumes are those outfits that are intrinsically unsuitable for everyday life, whether because it would be socially inappropriate to wear them or, to put it as bluntly as a designer did in one interview, because "one would look stupid." *Filmi* can refer, at once, to what is associated with film in a general sense and also to the kinds of excess that have become synonymous with commercial film. Characters are to be distinguished by wearing different hues; inner states are materialized via color; and inapposite and frankly *filmi* use of color duly warns the viewer that all is not well. Villains in bright, even shocking colors are to be distinguished from virtuous, sensible men in the proper garb of mature adulthood, for example. Although "shininess" is also understood to be a component of *filmi* costume, color more than texture or iridescence was mentioned in my interviews as the touchstone of the design aesthetic.

Whether a costume designer gets any input about other colors in a scene—colors used in the sets or in the costumes worn by other characters—depends entirely on the director or other designers being willing to share information and decision making. There is no disagreement, in principle, that coordination of the colors in the sets and costumes is desirable, but in practice, the amount of information a designer gets about the other colors varies from film to film. Designers for different stars, if they know one another, may swap information about colors in a phone call, but most designers whose careers began in the mid-twentieth century said that, more often than not, they had no information at all about what other characters were wearing. The effect of these kinds of arrangements is to focus the designer even more intensely on the needs and demands of his or her particular star. Notice in the interaction above—"The other two characters are in white. Why not contrast him? He is a go-between figure. Why not emphasize his character in a different visual way?"—that while the suggestion of a costume color contrast shows the designer knows what color the other actors are wearing, it also shows a costume idea being mooted without the immediate input of the other actors' own designers.

## Lifestyles and Identities

Masquerade reifies identity via misrecognition and comedy. Most of the time, however, costume is chosen to coincide with the social position (and, by extension, the moral position) of the character. This is apparent from the discussion above about the various facets of the character's wardrobe. Without knowing very much about the film's plot or the actions of the character being discussed, it is not difficult to surmise that he is supposed to be a villain. Many of his costume attributes flow almost intuitively from this fact—the expensive (Western) clothes, the love of gadgetry, the emphasis on slick style are hallmarks of the villain identity that can be traced back to the 1960s. The requirement that the actor be in different clothes in each scene is indicative of an ironic sensibility, one that knows and chooses to exploit the convention that villains are prototypically given to dress (i.e. *filmi*) extremes.

Even more specific condensations of social diversity into carefully selected clothing signs are well known in Hindi cinema. There is the wearing of special headgear (turbans—known also as *dastaars*—for Sikhs; prayer caps for Muslims), sacred threads (upper-caste Hindus), or a *taw'iz* (an amulet pendant worn around the neck by Muslims). Muslim women wear burqas, whereas Christian women have been dressed either soberly in knee-length skirts and dresses or ostentatiously in outré fashions. The extreme fetishization of Christian dress (for both female and male characters) has diminished somewhat since the 1970s, when *Amar Akbar Anthony* (1977) featured Parveen Babi as Jenny being chased by *goondas* (thugs, gangsters) while wearing a dress slit to the thigh, along with Amitabh Bachchan as Anthony Gonsalves in a succession of jaunty caps, tight, flared trousers, leather jackets, and gaping shirts. In recent decades, however, the sartorial indicators of

**Figure 8**  A scene at the climax of *Amar Akbar Anthony* (1977, directed and produced by Man-mohan Desai) in which the brothers express and parody their religious identities (Akbar [Rishi Kapoor] masquerades as a Muslim tailor, Anthony [Amitabh Bachchan] as a Catholic priest). In the background, Akbar's love interest is appropriately dressed as a Muslim woman (Neetu Singh as Dr. Salma Ali). Offscreen, Rishi Kapoor and Neetu Singh are a married couple. (DVD distributors, Shemaroo Entertainment.)[3]

Muslim identity seem to have been sharpened, perhaps in response to as-sertive public sartorial affirmations of identity among Muslims with women wearing Gulf-style burqas and niqab (face covering) and men dressed in shin or floor length kurtas or *kameez*.

Designers take care to lock in the visible signs of a character's social iden-tity, whether that identity is a local fisherman, a middle-class college girl, a rich NRI boy, a typical Punjabi girl from Delhi, or a woman who has come from Kolkata. Plainly, there are designers who use systematic, quasi-ethnographic observation for the characters they have dressed: Leena Daru traveled to folk festivals to see the kinds of dress worn for ritual occasions and dances; Bhanu Athaiya spent time in a small village to prepare for costuming 1972's *Reshma aur Shera* (Athaiya 2010, 73–7). Most, though, tend to draw upon widely shared visual assumptions that are only occasionally verified in actual experience and, in fact, reflect salient distinctions of identity that owe more to what previous films have shown than what may actually be the case in reality. In a strange par-adox, film depictions bear great responsibility for shaping what passes for pub-lic knowledge about dress as an unambiguous marker of social origin, status, and identity—knowledge that then feeds back into designers' considerations when they feel bound to create readable characters. I shall have more to say about this problem in a later chapter about historical and regional costume.

## Innovation and Repetition

Two requirements for any star—that he or she remain recognizable while at the same time embodying new looks—can be tricky to manage. The warning that an item could not be used because the actor had worn it before came up at least three times in the costume-design meeting discussed above, and no one ever elaborated upon or challenged it. Other designers, too, mentioned this restriction as a perfectly normal and acceptable stipulation. Yet, stardom, as we have already seen, requires and develops out of consistency in the star actor's roles. Heroines are extremely reluctant to cut their hair short and thus alter their appearance, and heroes, if they begin their career with a mustache, tend to keep that mustache until they retire (for example, Jackie Shroff and Anil Kapoor). Why, then, should it be so important that costumes not be seen to repeat from one film to another?

To answer this question, we have to return again to the nature of stardom. For one thing, novelty is one of its privileges; stars can demand—and get— the newest and best of whatever is available. To repeat one's costumes would interfere with the star's reputation as the conduit of what is new and daring, as well as diminish the aura of glamour that surrounds the star. This is not arrogance on display so much as a canny appreciation of what makes up the real value of a star to both audience and filmmakers. And if "actors reach their audiences primarily through their bodies" (Gledhill 1991, 210) and dress is an extension of a star's body, then costume is not just an interface for the meeting of embodied character and audience, but it is also an interface for actor and character.

The related imperative that stars not repeat styles worn by other stars speaks to the importance of defining stars via costume specification. *Ravi*, a proprietor of a menswear store who had worked with several stars, and whom we met in the previous chapter, explained the precautions he took:

> I maintain a file of every film I do, because there are shootings happening today, [then] for six months there is a gap. Then, for the same artist, I'm doing six films. [Also] I have to be, constantly. . . aware of every trend, because I should not only see *ki* [that] what my hero or what my artist is wearing, I have to think about what other artists have done in other films that I'm not doing.

Keeping some kind of material archive of one's design work—for example, notes and files of fabric swatches, color schemes, accessories, and so on— is common, but it has never been required and is done at the discretion of the designer. Once a designer takes on more than one star as a client, all of them in different films, these kinds of records are important not just for the sake of keeping some kind of grip upon continuity, but also for ensuring that the styles and cuts for each star are distinct. Files such as these, if they are used, help prevent a character's costumes for a film splintering in a multitude of directions and visions, particularly as shooting schedules get stretched out over months or even years. This is not the same as doing an exhaustive costume breakdown scene by scene, but allows for some systemization of a star's look.

For Hindi film stars, the intensity, unconventionality, and allure of costumes reinforce the continuation of the star persona within the determinate character. Costumes may even, on occasion, undercut that determinacy and guide the audience in the direction of abandoning the very sartorial judgments that costume is supposed to suggest. In this way, films that turn on misrecognition and mistaken interpretations of social worth based in part on clothing can rely upon the leverage of the well-known star to push the point home. That a *tapori* (street tough) might have heroic potential would be unimaginable were it not that the man in the costume is a star such as Aamir Khan (in the films *Rangeela* [1995] and *Ghulam* [1998]). But the tapori, as a character, must be believable—must be presented credibly—within the scenario constructed for him for the effect to work. The singular capability of the star to enter into and amplify an endless series of characters is realized only if the costume can be different for each character and for each story. Proliferation, on the one hand, is necessary for stability, on the other.

The same principle is at work in masquerade, the taking on of alternate appearances that affirms the aptitude of the post-Independence hero to comfortably move in and out of an array of identities. In Sumita Chakravarty's insightful discussion of masquerade, a key point is that the cleverness of the hero is made manifest via the disguises he puts on, so that "the concept of 'Indianness' is naturalized through the mobile hero, an entitlement to a passport with the assurance of a return ticket" (Chakravarty 1993, 212). The pleasure of masquerade comes from the unequal knowledge the viewer possesses about the character's background, personality, and so on, which almost no other character knows. Masquerade always involves putting on another costume, one whose semiotic function concerning status and identity is stressed so as to fool other characters in the film. It is, in fact, a kind of performance that depends on the principle that dress tells truth to make costume an effective liar. Examples in Hindi cinema abound: in *Chupke Chupke* (1975), Sulekha (Sharmila Tagore) mistakes botany professor Parmal Tripathi (Dharmendra) for the porter at a hill station when she arrives with a troupe of schoolgirls for an educational field trip. All Dharmendra has done to merit this attribution is put on the warm shawl and hat of the real porter, so that he can cover for him while the porter makes an excursion to his home village. He is not even wearing a uniform, which would represent a more studied form of disguise; it is simply a collapsing of form and context (he is outside; he wears working-class clothes; Sulekha's peremptory demands give him no opportunity to speak) that permits the heroine to be misled. Later in the film, the same kind of trick is played, only this time the hero essays a chauffeur.

Disguising the star in a costume has the paradoxical effect of reinforcing the star's allure. The return to more appropriate dress and the reinforcement of the message that disguise is mere appearance, not the outward form of moral sensibilities, tend to authenticate the validity of the star. But a recent example flirts with the possibility that identities are always and forever conditional. Costume change and masquerade as confidence trick are elaborated in the 2005 film *Bunty aur Babli*, both in song and in the movie narrative. Two swindlers, the eponymous Bunty (Abhishek Bachchan) and Babli (Rani Mukherjee)—in reality the very provincial Rakesh and Vimmi—cut a swath across India posing as health inspectors (in a bad suit and a stiff sari), dishonest religious renouncers in ochre robes, and trendy capital investors to entice money and goods out of their various marks. Their prey is the petit bourgeoisie, those people dabbling in the world of goods who, as yet, are incapable of evaluating the people who lay a claim to them. Bunty and Babli embody the kinds of wish fulfillment of the middle classes described by Leela Fernandes (2000) as having been left behind by neo-liberalism. Where the pair get the costumes they need to effect their cons is never made clear. Rather Bunty and Babli act out their roles in a fantasy space not unlike the movie song, animated against a travelogue background of urban and rural India.

## CONTESTED INTENTIONS

It should be clear by now that the tendency to disparage the costumes of past film productions is not a practice restricted to the most recent entrants into the industry. Rather, it has lain at the base of all claims to greater distinction and acumen made by innovators in the industry for more than half a century. The raison d'être of the emergent personal designers of the 1960s was to outdo the tailor in their ability to sharpen and consolidate both characters and personas. Mediating between star and director, designers openly inserted their own tastes and acumen, and they assisted the star in constructing a sartorial identity that cohered over several performative arenas—including film, advertising, and public events. Ultimately, however, a designer's loyalty was first and foremost to the star—not to the director and not to the film. Among the various factors in the emergence of stars as the most powerful figures in Hindi film, retaining a personal designer has been significant as both a sign of star power and a means of materializing that power.

Designers since the 1990s, by comparison, continue to have close relationships with stars, but they articulate different goals with respect to what it is they can offer. Listening to complaints about the chaos and unprofessionalism of the industry from recently established or up-and-coming designers, it swiftly becomes clear that one of the core accusations is that costumes from earlier films have been thoughtlessly contrived and lacked realism. In part, this is a conflict in vision about how costumes should look (boiling down to discrepant opinions about fashion generally and about *filmi* fashion in particular); in part, it is a drive toward rethinking what character means in film. In turn, rethinking characters cannot be separated from reform of the way in which films are made, although the nature of the connection is not always articulated or perhaps fully realized. In the sections that follow, I draw out the implications of these critiques. I also examine the extent to which they presage tangible change in the construction of character via costume, rather than simply serving as means for designers to acquire a stronger position in the field of costume production.

## Star Privilege versus Professionalism

Design for a character is, as we have seen, inseparable from design for a star. In practice, however, designers must constantly struggle to finesse the management of character demands and star dictates. Overwhelmingly, older designers I interviewed stressed their ability to work well with stars, to design looks that were met with unqualified delight, and to be able to persuade stars to trust the designer when confronted with an innovative costume. In contrast, newer designers, while not universally condemnatory of star antics, were much more likely to fault stars for contributing to the poor state of film costuming until the present, sprinkling their comments with adjectives ranging from clueless to insecure to arrogant. There are several reasons for this divergence. One is the different conceptions that old and new designers have of their position vis-à-vis the film and fashion industries. Another is the nature of the claims the two groups need to make in relation to each other. With their livelihood and identity bound up entirely with designing for select stars, older designers might be expected to talk in glowing terms about the relationships they enjoyed with them. Contemporary film designers with strong fashion credentials are not beholden to stars in the same way, although the bluntness with which they itemized their frustrations with stars was frankly disarming given that they move in the same circles as stars and count stars among their friends. I came to realize, however, that present-day designers are heavily invested in staking out the parameters of their own professional practice during a period in which they are sure the industry is about to change for the better. As they see it, a key part of their mission, if one can call it that, is to drag recalcitrant, pampered stars toward a finer appreciation of fashion and a more subtle understanding of character.

Elevating star taste so that stars learn to reject *filmi* costumes in favor of more fashionable and sophisticated ones is one part of the new designer's mission. The other is to instill an enlightened view of character that they realize entails, in the short run, some effacement of the star persona. Among my interviewees, the second task was considered much harder than the first, either because of a level of fear and insecurity that the industry seems to instill in even its most glittering stars or because of the resilience of the bubble in which stars immure themselves as a response. Younger designers with fewer accomplishments to their name had the greatest difficulty. *Lisa*, a self-proclaimed stylist with two to three years experience in 2010, described her job as shopping for ready-mades to assemble into costumes, explained how the isolation of the star eliminates any thoughtful consideration of costume and character by rigidifying a sense of entitlement.

> The biggest problem is that actors get to decide whether they want to wear a particular costume or not. It's the biggest drawback because it limits creativity. They have a group of ten people around them, and they think they have a right to certain things. They get to decide what brands to wear, and they'll wear designer clothes even if they look bad in them.

The coterie around the actor has always included friends and relatives, as well as secretaries and assorted lackeys. In recent years, the entourage has expanded to include managers who organize all commercial engagements and give the star the necessary reassurance and coaching to deal with the range of responsibilities that the life of a celebrity now entails. Trying to persuade a star to embrace change means having to contend with both informal acolytes and businesspeople with a contractual responsibility to safeguard the star asset over all other considerations. Below, *Sunil*, a well-known fashion and film designer, who built a steady career in retail after his fashion training, talks about his efforts to get one of his stars to play with his look:

[H]e himself is not ready to experiment. You know he's very much into his image of what he is, as a star, [rather] than a character. So it's very difficult sometimes to convince him that this is the look that I want to do in this film. You're just going to be casual in this film. We're gonna do your hair gelled back, whatever, and sometimes it gets difficult because he is so much into his image of him being macho and this and that, and to get him out of that is very difficult. So it's always with every actor they have their own thing of their starry aura and things like that, which they refuse to let go of, even if they are playing a different character. Stars have this whole insecurity, which is the worst thing for them, and you do have to keep telling them, this is going to look good on you, this is gonna look good, and things like that.

These frustrations form the counterpoint to assurances that matters will improve as stars place more trust in the expert designer not just to craft their personal style, but to help them embody realistic characters. The designer quoted above went on to say of stars in the future that "they're going to be very character oriented in the film; I think all the actors are taking the characters very seriously." But without some changes in the organizational conventions of filmmaking, new forms of characterization may fail to take hold.

## Resolving Fragmentation

Notwithstanding that there are plenty of reasons, good and bad, for conflating character and star when it comes to designing costumes, the system of production—its hyper-fragmentation, the dispersal of the star among several films, the assignment of one designer to one actor—has tended to compound this effect. With personal designers becoming de rigueur from the 1960s onward, a proliferation of designers at the top has been the inevitable result, with a comparative dearth of designers for the lowliest character actors and junior artists. Personal designers take no interest whatsoever in the rest of the cast, and the narration they receive for a costume assignment revolves chiefly around the hero or heroine for whom they design, so that the costume that is produced relates less to the film as a whole than to the director or actor's instructions for that character in particular. Any "undressed" character has to be dealt with on the spot by the dressman, with or without input from the direction team. The realities of the stark power discrepancies on set are that stars always have more expensive and exclusive costumes than anyone else, irrespective of the character they are playing. Lovleen Bains, whose long association with independent filmmaking put her at odds with prevailing practice in commercial films, explained the difficulty of meeting the demands of the star over the demands of the film:

> [T]he heroine may be playing a girl from a lower-middle-class family, and you have another character, a secondary character, who's supposed to be a rich person. So the attitude of the producer is that the heroine's costumes can cost more. But this secondary character's costumes, how can they cost more—even though the actor's playing a very rich person who is supposed to be having rich clothes, and they're obviously going to be more expensive than this girl's. . . . Once I was told to prepare a budget, and they said how can it be that a character actor's clothes are more expensive than the heroine's?

The effect of all of this has been to draw attention away from costume as a design element among others in the synchronic and diachronic planning of the film, and toward a scene-wise parade of costumes that independently materialize several characters.

In another instance where characterization yields to the practical demands of filmmaking, there is the problem of having to make costumes at the very last minute. Very few designers, old or young, prestigious or obscure, have not had the experience of being asked to make and deliver costumes in a great rush just prior to a shoot (Ganti 2004, 71; Kabir 2001, 29). To attribute every instance of last-minute planning to the practically mythical disorganization of the Mumbai industry is unreasonable, for no matter how well organized a production may be, there is always the likelihood that a costume will need to be changed or altered at the last minute. However, what dressmen and designers alike insisted upon was that what ought to be only an occasional crisis too often was adopted as standard operating procedure on some productions. As a result, the threat of imminent chaos when a costume was not ready or missing, or was needed at top speed, invited the recital of what John Caldwell calls "war stories" and "against-the-odds stories" (Caldwell 2008, 39–47)—tales of success pulled from the jaws of disaster as a result of stupendous effort or ingenuity. Dressmen always had a good stock of such stories, of which some were plainly comical, like this one told by second-generation dressman *Madhu,* whose father had entered the line after leaving a cotton mill job:

> From Karjat [a locality to the east of Mumbai] we were shooting 10–12 kilometers into wilderness. There was a fight scene, and the trousers got torn. The director called me and told me to replace it. I told him to give me three hours. He got very angry and told me, "Should I stop my shooting? I have spent so much money." Now I am not God to produce clothes in the jungle. But as I say, God is also great.

In the crew, there was one boy whose trousers were stylish. I told him to lend me those trousers. He was the same size as that fighter. I gave the trousers to the director and told him it was Rs 600, and then gave the money to the man whose trousers they were.

Another story, this time related by a designer Xerxes Bhathena, illustrated the incongruities that last-minute costume production led to, but this narrative seemed redolent more of capitulation and sarcasm than of unexpected success. For the 1984 film *Sharaabi*, starring Jaya Prada and Amitabh Bachchan, Bhathena (a man whose heyday was in the 1980s and whose best-known clients included Parveen Babi and Sridevi) was called and told to provide a red-sequined dress for Jaya Prada for the following day's shoot. He did not have red sequins, only blue ones, and dyeing the sequins was out of the question. So he was given the go-ahead to make a blue-sequined dress. The song sequence plays out in the film with heroine Meena (Prada) singing and dancing as Vicky (Bachchan) watches on a television set. The designer continued to be puzzled over why the director had so urgently wanted red sequins but got the answer only when he finally saw the song in the finished film:

> I was there with the garment, jewelry, on the model form before the heroine came there on the set. . . and I was wondering why the red? Well it was because they'd already shot Amitabh's reaction to what she's doing, and he's getting a red reflection on his face. So she had to be in a red dress to get that reflection. But in the end they didn't care. It was the 1980s! No one cared!

It is not hard to see why fine points of characterization might be overlooked when a film has to be propelled along by periodic compromises such as these. Not that these continuity errors are apparent across all films at all time periods: smaller films, films with highly organized and authoritative directors, and films made by stable production units do not have these kinds of lapses. It is more that the likelihood of various visual mismatches and continuity glitches increases dramatically when there is a very dispersed system of production, in which stars might be committed to several films at once. As a contemporary designer *Shabana* with most of her experience in art films and independent filmmaking put it:

> With filming in one schedule, in eight or nine weeks, the actor gets completely under the skin of the character. Whereas on an Indian film, he's come at 2 o'clock, he's been dancing as a college boy somewhere, romancing his girl, and then suddenly has to come to another set and play a police inspector at 4 o'clock.

Another designer confirmed this observation:

> [S]o often, they are coming from one shoot to the next shoot. They don't even know which film they're going to half the time. I mean, they know literally which film they're going to, but, you know, in their minds they just [think] oh, we're doing another dance song, okay one two three four, what are the steps, wear the outfit, and that's it.

A reliable remedy of long standing is for the director to take unequivocal and complete control of the project. The director, referred to time and again as the "captain of the ship," is the only figure who can alter the dynamics of the filmmaking process toward greater or lesser predictability.[4] With a set of determinate characters that must be kept distinct, and a set of designers working independently of one another, the only way a color palette might be defined, or costume overlaps and clashes avoided, would be if the director (or art director) were to oversee the entire business. Contemporary directors such as Sanjay Leela Bhansali and Ashutosh Gowarikar, as well as the late Yash Chopra, have made films noted for their attention to visual detail and degree of "gloss" (Dwyer 2002, 130; Dwyer and Patel 2002, 24; Grimaud 2003). The only alternate solution is to shift away from the pattern of personal designers and designate one costume designer to manage costumes for the cast from top to bottom.

## REFORMING FILM: REMAKING CHARACTER

For designers accustomed to using the script as a springboard for a comprehensive design that is meshed with other elements of the mise-en-scène, the mainstream industry way of doing things is utterly baffling. One does not need to leave India, or even Mumbai, to find these designers, since they have been working for decades in films variously dubbed parallel, art or now *hatke* (offbeat). From 2002 to 2012, I encountered more and more designers who had become accustomed to thinking out costume schemes considerably in advance. In these contexts, it is typical for a single designer to take the lead, delegating where appropriate to personal designers (unless the star chooses to override the decision of the production team). Invariably, the template for the design was the script, plumbed for clues on what to design, how many copies to make, in what sizes, and in what condition. Shahnaz Vahanvaty, whose career was nurtured within Merchant Ivory Productions and later extended to include small-budget, independent Hindi films, described the process of developing costume via engagement with a script as one in which the act of reading itself, as well as other preproduction practices, imposes a temporal framework within which understanding and reflection can operate:

> So, you read the script. You start at the beginning. . . . You read it a couple of times to develop a feel of the characters, get the feel of locations, which later on they show to you once you're interested, and they've done a reccy [reconnoiter], and when you're shown pictures of actual locations, you begin to think of greenery, blue water, color sky, the kind of season, you know, what are the colors going to be. And then in your mind you start thinking of the color scheme, the color palette for your characters, which I must say, if you really sit and do a color palette, it doesn't work out. You know, it just kind of develops, but when you look at it developing, you are on the right track.

For Vahanvaty and others like her, forming an overall vision of how a set of characters develops and how characters interact over the course of the story is the foundation of proper costume design. Vahanvaty's process coincides fairly well with another account, this one from costume assistant (though now a designer in her own right) Priyanjali Lahiri, who had worked on the film *Dhoom* in 2004:

> The process is that first we read the script with [the costume designer, Anaita Shroff Adjania]. We all read the script. Then, we make a noteboard of the characters we are dressing, their color palette, the style differences, like for *Dhoom* there was a cop, there was bad guy, John Abraham who's very slick and in black. We keep a kind of color story with references of how different characters will dress— Dad, Mom, the sons. We do this with every character. Then, we sit with the director and producer, sometimes just the director, and they give us feedback on that.

The script at this stage is still open to modification, and parts may still be narrated rather than read. What is more important is that a script- or narrative-centric approach means that the story is systematically disassembled and the material and technical inputs isolated. A new order of operations emerges, dictated now by nonscript variables, such as the availability of the cast, access to locations, and economies and efficiencies to do with the reuse of sets, costumes, effects, and so on. As the shooting sequence becomes apparent, so regimes of costume supply and management for the film emerge. In fact, this is probably what Madhav Prasad has in mind when he argues for the centrality of the script to the production process in Hollywood (Prasad 1998).

The ad hoc accounts, in 2002, of trying to introduce more organization and preplanning into filmmaking had, by 2012, developed into confident recitals of just how a costume scheme might be created, constructed, and executed. With the prolongation of preproduction time and the greater familiarity of creative talent with script details, we see another dimension along which designers, costume assistants, and assistant directors are able to differentiate themselves from dressmen, none of whom are given a script or even a fragment of one. Not everyone working on a film needs to see the entire script: narrating the story for a scene and negotiating verbally over what is to be done for it, works well for many film technicians and craft talent all over the world. But to cut dressmen out of the script loop has a distinct effect on their ability to participate proactively in the business of costume supply and maintenance. I have asked designers and costume assistants whether they saw fit to include dressmen in their efforts to reform costume design. The usual response was that dressmen were not remotely interested in changing their habitual practices. If any dressmen were singled out by designers as being concerned to learn new skills, it was always the result of the dressman presenting himself as a potential aide rather than the dressman being approached by the designer to be a more active collaborator. Costume designers on small-budget art films did describe training dressmen to be more like costumers, familiarizing them with script breakdown, the importance of photographic records, the need to place costumes on rails if space allowed, and so on. Here, however, the dressmen benefited from a filmmaking milieu that was already wedded to different ways of working.

The management of time, materials, and space that is associated with reformed practices represents one stock of knowledge that designers can use to differentiate themselves from dressmen, in addition to matters of aesthetic distinction and narrative insight that the earlier personal designers used as their calling card. Designers and dressmen (and costume assistants) do not simply talk about what they know—they talk about what they do, what they have accomplished, and how they solve the problems that Hindi filmmaking is widely accepted as presenting. But it is just here, in the kinds of war stories used to assert craft mastery (Caldwell 2008, 38), that the dressman risks further alienating himself from good film practice, rather than asserting a value that those above him in the productive hierarchy are likely to acknowledge. Take, for example, this account by Gaurav, a dressman already introduced in the book whose long career in the industry began in the 1970s working under director Manoj Kumar. In this war story—which is similar to the earlier one I related—he describes how he adapted a wig for use when shooting on location in a remote part of Maharashtra:

[In] that place there was nothing, and we had to urgently give a black wig, so what I did, I applied shoe polish and poured a bottle of cologne on it. We told the actor that there will be a little smell but to my luck he agreed. I told the director what the problem was and also the actor. It was not possible to go to Mumbai and get the wig. Because even if the shooting is held for half an hour, there is lot of monetary loss to the team.

Regrettably for the dressman, the greater the ingenuity, and the more daring and desperate the solution, the more open it is to mockery by the latest generation of filmmakers; for young designers and stylists, all an example like this does is prove their point that films in which actors wear wigs covered in boot polish and perfume are just what they are seeking to replace. Whereas dressmen deal with the close-at-hand, scant materials of a commodity-poor India, designers and their cohort integrate into their work and relationships the sleek and fashionable components of an altered economic landscape—and through these components extend their influence and credibility, the essence of their professional personhood, into the world (Gell 1998).

So in the end, whom does the film costume express? The peculiar characteristics of stardom mean that it cannot but express the star, since to a large degree it *is* the star. The agencies of other people in the costume enterprise coalesce around the realization of the star, with only the designer as the other possible beneficiary of the costume's "work," and then only if the designer's name is attached to the appearances of the costume in its offscreen life—in stills, publicity shots, and so on. A film, though, is made up of more than its stars, and the purposes and practices that shape the costumes of the rest of the cast are considerably more variable. The character actor may be a star in his or her own right, with a designer in tow. If not, then very quickly the choices boil down to either an outfit of his or her own that is reconfigured from clothing to costume or a reused costume from stock. Who authors the look in the latter case is, as I have already noted, a matter upon which dressmen and assistant directors/costume assistants disagree, but still one that is of little concern or interest outside of the process of filmmaking. For now, any given designer's claim to authorship of all the costumes continues to be frustrated by production processes inherent to the industry, as well as by the stout loyalty of stars to their personal designers. This loyalty is, as I have shown, part and parcel of the star habitus—a response to the fragility of stardom and a means to stabilize it. In the next chapter, I turn to the next responsibility of the designer, this time in concert with the tailor—to remediate the star body.

# –3–

# Costume and the Body

The difference between a costume designer and fashion designer? The boutiques, they can just provide you with a *salwar kurta*, but not a good fit. For a film you require to be perfect. If you have a defect on the shoulders, if you have a defect on your arm, if you have a defect on your waist or hips, it is the costume designer who has to work on that and see how you are looking. Whatever defect is there in your body has to be removed.

*Maryam*, film costume designer (interview, March 2002)

Clothes are never simply hung upon a passive body, although wearing clothes is a cultural act so deeply engrained that we are rarely conscious of how fundamental it is to our perception of self and the world. Wearing means moving, interacting, and positioning oneself in relationship to the clothes to a degree that the body is mostly experienced as a dressed, rather than undressed one (Entwistle 2000; Entwistle 2001; Entwistle and Wilson 2001). But where does that leave film costume? Of course, actors wear costumes much as they wear clothes—with the important exception that they inhabit the costume as part of a performance that is not the same as everyday life. In a valuable analysis of theatrical actors and costuming, Aoife Monks comments on the difficulty viewers have pinpointing where costume and actor separate, and she notes that "when we speak of costume, we are often actually talking about actors; and when we talk of actors, we are often actually talking about costume" (Monks 2010, 11). In fact, this elision is apparent from the first quote above, in which a veteran designer talks about the almost symbiotic relationship of dress and body, in which each perfects the other.

Monks also points out that costume doesn't just impress itself upon audiences but is also an essential part of the embodied experience of acting. The actor does not simply "carry" the costume neutrally; rather, the actor draws energy from and imparts energy to the costume. In other words, "costume is the spectator's means to access the actor body, and is also a means for the actor to access the world of performance" (Monks 2010, 20). As the performance unfolds, actor and audience oscillate between different understandings of what costume means: semiotic, aesthetic, self-realizing, sensate, historical, and conventional (Monks 2010, 20–5). With film, the temporal dislocation between making it and viewing it means that actor and audience do not undertake these discoveries together, as they would in theater. And yet, the shifting frames of reference for the costumed actor are very much present in both the actor's work on the set and the response of the viewers in the movie theater.

To the experience of the actor, I shall add those of the designer, the tailor, and (in passing) the makeup artist and the hairdresser, all of them responsible for comanaging the body along with the actor. For the designer, his or her professional role depends upon a discriminating faculty, specifically an informed eye, in which observation, distance, and judgment are mostly privileged over engagement, immersion, and execution. For many of the most popular contemporary designers, there is also an emphasis upon the consuming, performing body, a distinction that distances them not just from the artisans and technicians of costume, but also from older designers whom they believe lacked taste. The intangible technology of a powerful language, English, is the common endowment of all designers, and allows for body discussions to be shared and monopolized within a linguistically select group.

For the tailor, professional status derives from the capacities of a working body that is inseparable from the tools of the trade. Where the designer imagines, the tailor effects, and in order for the dress as material artifact to match the actual body, the tailor's skills are indispensable, just as the necessary steps to perfect the face and hair require the makeup artist (and the hairdresser if the actor is female). Intention and desire cannot be realized without the practices of these film professionals, who effect the transformation of the mundane body into a set-worthy one, or in the case of a star, into a powerful and seductive body that is an indispensable part of the star's allure. This chapter is centrally concerned with these issues, with particular attention paid to the mediations and remediations of the star body in a number of settings—the set, the red carpet, and the advertising shoot, to cite a few.

## BODY HERITAGES

Intrinsic to the entire film-costume enterprise is an entire discourse about the "Indian body" that has been deeply influenced by colonial and postcolonial society. There was already a complex system of sartorial conventions and expectations when the British arrived, one that gave material form to differences and inequalities in social life, such as gender, caste, and class. On top of these, colonialism added a set of models of dress and deportment that were self-consciously distinct from what prevailed in the subcontinent. The dilemma for the colonized was whether to assent to these models, only to be regarded as inferior emulators of styles and behaviors that would never be their own, or to reject them as fundamentally alien to what might be termed the Indian habitus (Bourdieu 1977). The implications of these choices very much depended upon the social position of the potential wearer, with differences between the rich and the poor and between men and women being among the most striking. Anxieties to do with how to balance these discrepant dress injunctions, or what Emma Tarlo (1996) has termed "the problem of what to wear," have permeated film costuming, as actors and other personnel daily face what it means to embody Indianness.

European orientations to male Indian bodies and dress changed dramatically between the seventeenth and nineteenth centuries (Cohn 1989). European travelers, and then the first traders and factors of the British East India Company, brought to India an inventory of men's clothes that were viewed, at first, as unsuitable for wear both by Indians and by some of the British themselves. The heavy fabrics, confining silhouettes, and elaborate layering of garments were far from comfortable in the Indian climate, no matter who happened to be wearing them. For prospective Indian wearers, there was the additional disadvantage that British clothes failed to accommodate the bodily movements and key religio-moral requirements that Indian dress did (Bayly 1986; Bean 1989; Cohn 1989; Tarlo 1996). After some initial experiments by East India Company representatives living up-country to behave and dress like Indians, the colonial regime insisted on its representatives maintaining a separate identity to which British clothing was central (Cohn 1989, 310). Not surprisingly, this coincided with a steelier grip of imperial authority upon the subcontinent. No matter the discomforts and inconveniences entailed, clothing that was decidedly un-Indian was deemed the only acceptable dress for administrators, officers, and other Europeans who regarded themselves as superior to their colonial underlings.

The Indian male body came to be regarded by the British as either debauched (exemplified by undisciplined, effeminate finery among the elite) or weak (a condition made plain by most ordinary men being in a state of near nudity) (Tarlo 1996, 33–5). Both were a far cry from the British colonial ideal of robust, civilized masculinity, evoked by a stiff formal dress that made no concessions to the body in a tropical environment. There were some indigenous exemplars of masculinity that the British celebrated, one of which was the martial Sikh, turbaned, mustachioed, and fierce (Cohn 1989)—a characterization that continues in popular culture and in film to this day. The qualified approbation of some Indians almost always depended in part upon their retention of certain "authentic" features, while the effort to assume the dress and bearing of the colonialists was always open to critique as little more than aping. By such techniques did the colonial administration reinforce the racial divide that debarred Indians from higher office and political power, while at the same time appearing to preserve Indian cultural integrity (Cohn 1989, 336–8).

Women never did adopt Western styles on a major scale, and even now, the vast majority of women spend their adult lives dressed exclusively in garments that are unambiguously coded as Indian. British prudishness did assist in the normalization of the *choli* (blouse) for women irrespective of social status, and British influence provoked a loosening of rules regarding women's veiling among both Hindus and Muslims of the upper classes. But while Indian men were ambivalently invited to participate in the sartorial system of the British, Indian women were categorically distinguished from European women, sharing neither their clothes (and, one might add, their restricting underclothes) nor their public etiquette. Nineteenth-century European women were as scrupulously covered as their Indian counterparts (except for the face). As the twentieth century went on, Western women's clothing changed markedly toward a shortened dress or skirt hem, shorter sleeves, and even, on occasion, a version of male dress with shirt and pants. These items generally cover more than they reveal, but what they do reveal is inappropriate for most Indian women. True, working women habitually hitch up their saris to expose their lower legs and ankles, but among the middle and upper classes, a woman's legs are largely hidden, and scarves of various kinds or a *sari pallu* (the length of the sari that is draped over the shoulder) cover the chest or the head, as needed. In the West, a relatively modest skirt can show more of the legs and ankles than might be deemed suitable for a higher-status Indian woman, and the neck and head can be left uncovered, with the outline of the shoulders and chest perfectly evident. Trousers, meanwhile, when worn as most Americans and Europeans wear them, adhere to the contours of the buttocks and sometimes the legs as well. Adopting Western dress and its associated body hexis, or "the pattern of postures that is both individual and systemic, because linked to a whole system of techniques involving the body and tools, and charged with a host of social meanings and values" (Bourdieu 1977, 87; see also Craik 1994, 4), has always been more portentous for women than it has been for men—a state of affairs that is acknowledged in film, when it offers audiences the opportunity to see women in radically different kinds of clothes from what is typically the case in public life.

Hindi films have long been known for displaying fashion (the subject of the next chapter), but the "fashioned" body has changed markedly since the

1990s, with both men and women investing in various physical rigors (from exercise regimens to cosmetic surgery) to bring the body to a near-perfect form. For men, play with the body and dress in the past twenty years is part erotic, part ludic, but largely without disadvantages to the actor. The same is not true for heroines, who as both characters and professional women have had to negotiate a cautious path as they realize the benefits of a striking face and body while remaining respectful of the cultural chauvinism that labels women's bodies as provocative and shameful. The moral taint of exhibiting oneself on screen has diminished since the time when women were prevented from appearing in films altogether, but it has not disappeared. The challenge for the heroine has consistently been to decide when and how to assert her autonomy as a character and as a working professional. Control over the costume—what one will wear or not wear, or what one is forced to wear—goes to the very heart of these concerns.

## EXPOSURE AND PROTECTION

The actor's relation to his or her costume can be understood in terms of the contrary imperatives of revelation (it is necessary to be seen) and concealment (the power to deflect intrusive scrutiny). In filmmaking, the actor dresses himself or herself with respect to two situations: the production floors or locations where they do their work and the imaginary situations in which their characters appear. The star prepares for this double performance in a dressing room or trailer, inaccessible to all but a select few (dressmen may not enter a female star's trailer and sometimes are stopped even at the threshold of a male star's trailer). On the sets that I have observed, female dancers and junior artists are given a modicum of privacy through being able to use a common dressing room or trailer that is off-limits to men. Male stunt actors and junior artists have few qualms about changing clothing in the open.

The ability to cordon oneself off from other actors and members of the crew is undoubtedly an index of power, just as, in public life, the well-off can achieve a level of seclusion that the poor cannot. The problem for stars is that they are subjected to the evaluative, even intrusive gaze of the camera and the crew once they start work to a degree that few others in the cast experience. That they may be required to effect what would otherwise be private displays in a semi-public setting makes for even more potential discomfort. The vain actor who demands to be photographed and dressed only in situations that allow face and body to be suitably flattered is as much a cliché in Hindi film as it is in other film industries. Given that the body is the most intimate and elemental of instruments of the actor, the concern is perhaps not surprising.

Consider what acting involves from the standpoint of self-embodiment: as the private is reenacted in a semi-public setting, exposed to the view of director, crew, camera operator, assistants of various kinds, dressmen, and so on, the conventions governing dress in everyday life are set in abeyance. At the same time as the actor must manage the social and psychological ramifications of such behavior, he or she must anticipate the assessment of an audience who will see the performance within its anticipated frame. At this point, the sense of being watched at moments of vulnerability—as defined by rules that dictate the appropriate dress for the appropriate space and setting—is considerably magnified (Entwistle 2000; Entwistle and Wilson 2001). Paradoxically, power and frailty may be subtly intertwined.

As we learned in the previous chapter, heroes and heroines have a core staff, including a manager, a makeup artist, a spot boy,[1] a scattering of close relatives, and (if a female star) a hairdresser—all of whom put up a loyal and virtually impregnable defense against outsiders. The very roles these figures enact—whether preparing the star for the shoot, fetching and carrying, or taking care of the weightiest, as well as the most trivial, demands—tend to demarcate and defend the private spaces in which, undressed and not made up, or wig removed, the actor is most vulnerable; these spaces include the fitting room, the dressing room, and the inner rooms of the home.

The male actor is certainly concerned with policing the space in which he prepares for work, and for both hero and heroine, the right to private space is indicative of their industry status. Makeup artists for male stars monitor their complexions, cover up spots, and administer various cover-ups (mostly wigs) for unavoidable hair loss. But female actors have the added concern that there may be gossip about possible impropriety, as well as criticisms of the body that men are rarely subject too. In the past (and even with some young stars today), having one's mother or grandmother close at hand on the set solved the first problem: it meant there was a close and trustworthy relative at one's side whose presence alone could deflect suspicions about the heroine's either instigating or agreeing to untoward sexual advances. Otherwise, the hairdresser, a woman who is neither exactly a friend nor a relative, can perform some of the same functions. Along with the makeup artist, she is the only film worker permitted into the heroine's dressing room (dressmen do not dress heroines; at most they bring the dress in and put it on a rail or hook, then depart). If she is older than the heroine, her age alone allows her to be protective toward the heroine without challenge.

Makeup artists are in a curious category since they can be in close contact with the heroine despite being male. Once again, differences of status and age offset any qualms, with many makeup artists being addressed as *dada*, a fictive kinship term that puts the addressee in the position of paternal grandfather towards the speaker. Favorite makeup artists (even more so than hairdressers) stay with a star for years or even decades. The loyalty and trust built up can translate into other kinds of associations, as with Amitabh Bachchan, who has supported his longtime makeup artist in his ventures producing Bhojpuri films. Makeup artists (and hairdressers, for heroines) attend to stars for all their other professional commitments: industry events, fashion shows, magazine shoots, and so on.

A sense of the dynamics of the dressing room, and the makeup artist and hairdresser's role in it, can be derived from the following ethnographic snippet. My assistant, Mona, and I were inside a dressing room at a film studio in the Mumbai suburbs to talk to a makeup artist and hairdresser while they waited for a star to turn up for her shoot. The wait was a long one, more than two hours, but the moment the star arrived (heralded by a production assistant's head popping around the door to announce her entrance), they shifted into high gear. She walked in, exchanged a few pleasantries, was effusively greeted by the director (who marched in a few moments later)—and then it was time to get to work. Without the slightest fumbling or hesitation, the makeup artist and hairdresser worked beside and around each other, as a never-ending stream of exchanges went on about how the heroine would be turned into the character. She reminded the makeup man that it was to be a morning scene, she described what she would be doing, and she also knew exactly what she needed to wear. It quickly became apparent that the costume she expected was not in the room. At once, the hairdresser, but not the makeup man, snapped into action, went to hail a dressman, and instructed him to check for the dress. Once it was confirmed that the dress was not even at the set (as they were informed by another oracular head poked around the door), the hairdresser picked up her cell phone and began calling the designer. With confusion mounting, and a slim likelihood of the right dress showing up on time, the actor prepared to change into a different costume, at which moment Mona and I, plus the makeup man, were shooed out of the room, leaving the star and her hairdresser alone as she began to undress.

We learn from this brief piece of business that the hairdresser is rarely only a hairdresser, but instead does a multitude of tasks for the star. She is neither an intimate nor a relative, but her right and obligation to do these things comes from the fact that she has some qualities of both. She mediates between star and dressman, star and designer, or indeed star and anyone else the heroine wants or needs to deal with by proxy.

Since there is no-one formally assigned to dress the lead female actors on a film, the hairdresser, as the only professional woman who has a reason to be in the dressing room or trailer alone with the heroine, is, in effect, the heroine's dresser. The hairdresser is also an important booster and confidant for the star, sometimes being entrusted with more complex secrets, such as carrying messages to and from actors in illicit relationships.

Changes in industry operations and organization have not altered the reliance on makeup artists and hairdressers as key intermediaries and confidantes. The prevailing pattern of dispersed responsibility for costumes meant that most designers I interviewed said they never went to the set, handing off all responsibility for costumes to the dressmen once the garments were collected or delivered. One or two among the younger designers said they were asked to be on the set on the first day a costume was to be worn, to make sure there were no problems with it; also, a star might implore a designer to hang around for the psychological boost the designer could offer. Only independent art productions or newer films committed to a model of costume design closer to the North American one expect the designer to be a more active presence during shooting, and in that case, the designer's responsibilities are less oriented toward accommodating star needs than toward professional responsibilities to the film. In the intimacy and immediacy of work on the set, the makeup artist and hairdresser retain their conventional, if formally unrecognized, significance as gatekeepers and go-betweens for the star.

## THE BODY IN THE COSTUME

Even before an actor has arrived on set, the actor has already put his or her body to work to have a costume made to fit. The body is what animates the costume, and in turn, the costume is modeled on the specificities of that body. For character actors, body type and facial features may propel them toward repetitive roles that represent, in essence, typecasting (this is particularly so for male actors who specialize in villainous roles or for plumper, older women that are destined to play mothers). The star, as we noted, manages to essay different looks from film to film without compromising his or her recognizability. The costume does much of the work that characterization demands, but it is so intimately interconnected with the star's actions and gestures that character cannot be said to exist outside of the moment-to-moment embodiment that the costumed actor provides. With respect to the body, the costume can be seen as a factor of production, restraining or revealing the actor's body and facilitating the actor's performance. As a two-dimensional image on screen, body and costume become one, although the visual treatment of the costume provides ample scope for viewers to imagine sensory details, such as texture, weight, or even the tactile contrast of costume and skin. The costume is also subject to certain minimal material demands, including comfort, cost, and replaceability (if there are to be duplicate costumes for the actors or their doubles).

To a certain extent, the costume can deviate from what might be considered normal clothing, whether this means a lack of internal finish or a certain roughness in external decoration that will be ameliorated, even perfected, in the process of lighting and shooting it. The costume simply has to last—and to "seem"—for as long as is needed, and then its task is essentially done. In fact, the relationship between body and costume in film is so close that we might say that bodies take on the adjustable, mutable qualities of costume, and costumes in turn become like bodies, reinscribing the shape of the wearer's unique body shape in their cut and finish (Monks 2010, 11).

All actors on screen have to look "right"; stars, though, have to look "good." In practice, this means that there is special attention paid to the fit of a star's costume. All bodies are different, meaning that the impact of clothes on one star will be very different from the same design on another one. The necessity of a good fit is widely recognized, and designers and tailors both refer to the "*filmi* cut," whereby even normatively modest clothes acquire a degree of sensuality from adhering so closely to the curves of the body. Ashley Rebello, who had designed for heroines for about ten years when I interviewed him in 2002, explained:

> The blouses have to be like second skin; even the Western clothes have to be like second skin. They do not believe in loosely fitted garments at all for Indian cinema, whatever it is, whether it is the jacket or whether it is the trousers, or whether it is anything, it has to be perfectly fitted.

Via the techniques of achieving the perfect fit, varied star bodies approach as close as possible to a visible ideal, the body and the costume speaking with apparently equal force. Men as well as women insist on a superlative fit, which nowadays means not simply tailoring new garments for a film, but also perfecting clothes bought from boutiques. Of a contemporary male star, his designer, *Sunil*, whom we first met in the previous chapter, commented:

> What happens is those [off-the-rack] clothes have to be reopened and made to his size, and cut and shaped and things like that. Because he's very finicky about

his fit—he's not finicky about what he's going to wear, what I'm giving he's wearing, but the fit has to be just perfect.

Costume always starts from a radical abstraction of the body into its measurements; the actor, in a sense, is summed up in a few numbers on a piece of paper. But once the costume has its rudimentary form, a process of fine-tuning begins, so that the actual actor body is brought into perfect harmony with the contours, the body one might say, of the costume. Here is where the costume's ability to showcase and extol the body must be balanced against its ability to conceal and mitigate flaws.

## The Fallible Body

A key task of anyone associated with creating looks is to erase the star's body "defects." Male bodies are as likely to be imperfect as female ones, but one hears far less about the continual need to critique and improve the hero's body as compared to the heroine's. For heroines, the rule seems to be that in order for the body to be coaxed into its most ideal form, one must first acknowledge that it cannot help but be imperfect. Whatever inherent beauty the heroine possesses is always open to improvement, and the female actor quickly learns to worry about flaws and weaknesses that continually threaten to fracture the illusion of her attractiveness. In effect, the heroine can become beautiful only after having acknowledged how unbeautiful she is. This inculcation of profound insecurity differs only by degree from the kinds of self-critiques that middle- and upper-class women in India are urged to undertake in order to meet proper standards of beauty. In film, though, there is a certain blunt practicality to the work of perfecting the body, and designers speak nonchalantly about the requirement of the costume to regularize what is aberrant. Designer *Maryam*, whose career began with introductions facilitated by her actor sister, worked for prominent heroines from the 1960s to the early 1990s. As she talked about perfecting the body through costume, she sketched an imaginary figure in the air with her hand:

Each is individual, and every figure has its good points and its bad points. There is no perfect figure as such. So we have to make it perfect. There were some heroines that were flat on the hip, so I had to see where she will be padded properly so she looks good. You understand? Same with the bust also. Everybody is not endowed by nature with such proportions.

Fear that the body might be deficient or fail is a fact of life for an actor, the more so for stars whose looks are fundamental to their appeal. An inescapable source of anxiety for both heroes and heroines is the unyielding fact of change, whether this is the long-term erosion of looks and body caused by aging or the fluctuation of a body that puts on or takes off weight, develops muscles, or acquires implants. The fact of change is a source of grief for the designer as well (the tailor's response we shall see shortly). There are a few paragons in the industry whose devotion to their profession is demonstrated by their keeping their body size and proportions relatively constant. Until the 1990s—and the introduction of additional pressures on stars, from advertising and fashion, to keep their looks constant—a large number were unsuccessful at keeping a well-controlled, stable body shape and size. Measurements had to be taken and retaken over and over again, and the longer a film took to complete, the more likely fluctuating actor measurements forced adjustments to or even replacement of the costumes.

The face too, is of great concern, since it is the key to the actor's identity and allure. Because of their purported expertise in skin care, makeup artists seem to hold a particular sway over heroines when it comes to advice about diet and exercise. Recipes and regimens to clear and lighten the skin are imparted at the same time as a particular film look is discussed or as makeup is applied. Ramesh, the personal makeup artist introduced earlier, with a family history in the profession and years of experience working with both male and female stars, recounted one of his successes in this vein in the course of an interview about the wide-ranging responsibilities of a makeup artist:

> [A heroine] had very bad skin, so this hairdresser had called me. So, I went on the first day. I saw the skin, which was in very bad condition. I asked what is your diet first. At that time, she used to have *sambhar*, curd and *acchar*, potato, beans. No proteins, no vitamins. So I suggested to her to go on a liquid diet for seven days. She tried juice, and on the seventh day, her skin started glowing, and I said stop that *acchar*. [On the] seventh or eighth day, full body filming [started], so I suggested to her, once a week, enema. So she started doing it, and her skin was so clear due to the liquids she was taking, and my problem was solved because 50 percent of the makeup is in the skin.

Whether a woman is playing a morally ambiguous character or a clear-cut heroine, the obligation to enhance and beautify the body is exactly the same. Costumes for song sequences must rise to an even higher standard than those used in other scenes, since they propel the star into imaginary domains in which idealization is to be expected. Here is where the audience will see the heroine in *ghaghara cholis* that are in essence tight carapaces bolstered with padding that mold and literally flesh out the body to a desirable hourglass shape. When one sees the pattern pieces outlined on fabric stretched on the embroiderer's frame for decoration, it is more than a little jarring to realize one is seeing, in its early form, the disjointed and parceled-out body that the tailor will "build" for the heroine.

## Remedying the Fallible Body: Master Cutter and Tailor

Before the rise of personal designers, and even during their ascent, the film tailor fulfilled a critical role in the process of making and remediating the star body. Although tailors collectively have fewer face-to-face interactions with actors, directors, and so on regarding the construction of a look, as subcontractors or employees of designers, they are still party to the intimate details of the body—its measurements, its proportions, its flaws, and its assets. Will the dress fall flatteringly? Will the heroine lose or gain weight in the course of filming, forcing a costume to be adjusted or, worst of all, made all over again? The designer appropriates for himself or herself the ability to predict what will look the best, but the tailor holds the key to how a costume and body will ultimately merge and, therefore, is crucial to the building of the costume and simultaneously the building of the star body.

Both heroes and heroines have had a long-standing interest in finding a good master cutter and tailor, someone who would do their film work and, quite possibly, their personal work as well. Some tailors' names still reverberate today, like Jaggi Tailor, who acquired an enviable reputation and had large client bases; tailors like Jaggi were the favored cutters and stitchers of heroine costumes prior to and just after Independence. When designers supplanted tailors as the interpreters of costume demands, they stressed their taste and ability to interpret the narrative and character demands of the film, whereas tailors were essentially confined to the day-to-day details of their practice—measuring, cutting, stitching. Even so, it is the master of the shop—the master cutter—whose operations upon the cloth anticipate the final form of the dress.

For tailors, the costume is not so much the automatic outcome of the designer's vision as it is the product of the interlocked aptitudes of both designer and tailor. "The designer's job is to draw, but the tailor's job is to cut," proclaimed *Suresh*, a tailor originally from Gujarat and one among several *filmi* women's tailors with their own premises, doing work on contract from dress designers. Tailor after tailor asserted the fundamental creativity and imaginative demands of their work, rejecting the idea that all they do is execute another person's vision (Wilkinson-Weber 2004a). Instead, the mental and manual labor involved in transforming a two-dimensional visual idea into a three-dimensional garment is, in their view, its own kind of design. The tailor is positioned at the most critical stage of producing the actor as dressed body, making a cut so precise and a fit so impeccable that the costume is like the "second skin" referred to by designer Ashley Rebello.

Whatever the inadequacies of individual bodies are deemed to be, the master's cut and attention to the mechanics of stitching the outfit "fix them" in the sense of inscribing both problem and solution in the garment itself.[2] The tailor is the keeper of actor secrets, for example, inserting a larger seam allowance for a heroine he knows experiences pronounced changes in size over the weeks or months of filming. Tailors are also tasked with finding ways to conceal or distract from parts of the body that fall away from the ideal but cannot be entirely covered up. *Ashok*, another tailor originally from Gujarat (and distantly related to *Suresh*) and also an independent women's tailor doing film work, explains some of the strategies that can be employed, talking quite bluntly about the physical faults that must be concealed:

> So if sometimes someone has big shoulders or big arms, so what do we do? So they think that if it's something sleeveless, then people with fat arms or thin arms will have trouble. So we make a transparent sleeve, or do something to cover it up. So the artist gets suggestions from the designer, and sometimes they ask by chance what can be done, so we say give tassels. Then they . . . go along with it. And if they have a big tummy, it won't look good; well—it's like a tire. So in front of the blouse we put net or choose tassels. You can see the tummy, but it's covered.

If a master and his tailors are consistently successful in conceiving costumes that enhance an actor's body, then the actor may insist on this person's doing the stitching work, no matter who the designer happens to be. Male stars' loyalty to menswear stores makes sense in that they offer design and stitching in one package.

Contemporary designers freely admit that some stars are slouches with respect to staying in shape, but on the whole, they assert that this kind of actor is becoming scarce—another "success" of the professionalization they espouse. Talking about the kinds of solutions described above meets with a certain disdain, given the reduced tolerance for a star who lets herself go than in the past. The attachment of tassels, net, fringes, and so forth, as effective as it may have been for concealing parts of the body deemed imperfect, unavoidably added to the impression of costume as a randomly assembled collection of fabric, trimmings, and knickknacks—precisely the kind of solution that the newest designers disparage. I contend, though, that there is a deeper level of difference at work here, essentially a difference in orientation to the "materials" in question—the star body and the body of the dress. Whereas designers have always been more likely, assuming they had the time and the inclination, to rethink a costume in its entirety if it did not look right, tailors were more likely to improvise a technical response to what they regarded as a technical problem. I have never met a designer who specifically endorsed these kinds of solutions, but it is noticeable that the more recent designers are more likely to call out the technical solution as inadequate to the mission of film costume design, in keeping with their indifference to the time and resource constraints that often dictated such responses in the past.

These disparate views of how one relates to the materials and the task at hand explain, in part, the gap between designers and tailors. More important, though, is the designers' professional self-definition that aligns them with those of a similar class and background in film production. Designers veer from praising the deftness and reliability of tailors to disparaging their disinclination to change their ways. Never do they allude to any kind of creativity in tailoring work. In fact, some designers said they had educated conservative, unenterprising tailors on the right kinds of cuts and stitching techniques to use. For their part, tailors (unlike dressmen) did not appear to begrudge designers their distinct position in the industry of coordinating with stars and directors and coming up with the looks they want translated into actual clothes. For tailors, the work remains plentiful and lucrative; they know that the job of making a star look good in clothes stitched for the film falls ultimately to them. Their own input might be considerable, particularly if the designer merely gave an impressionistic description of what he or she wanted, which the tailor was then required to flesh out. Designers often do not know how fabric behaves, how it is affected by being embroidered, or what kinds of operations can be done on certain kinds of material. Here is *Ashok* again:

> Nowadays, a lot of metal is on the dress [fabric with metal threads], and metallic fabric is such that when you hem it, you can't do it on a machine. So when they must use that kind of fabric, it takes a lot of time. Say there is a shooting in the morning, and they want that look, they don't understand that this is metal, or what it is, so we say, shift the shooting sequence, or we'll make something accordingly that'll look similar.

Designers with a stronger background in cutting and tailoring can speak the same language as the tailor, obviating the need to collaborate in person and instead transacting their business by telephone. As tailors argue, however, designers vary widely in their knowledge of the fundamentals of cutting and fabricating, meaning that the tailor has the ability to make many relatively autonomous decisions relating to the work.

In most (if not all) cases, designers have pushed ahead of tailors not so much because they have carved out for themselves a position of leadership (like a costume designer heading a department, as happens in other industries around the world). Rather, they have made a compelling case that their intervention between actor and tailor is both rational and beneficial. And they are, up to a point, quite right. The designer is an ally, possibly a confidant, and these days, may be on the equivalent social level, perhaps even friends with the star. Designers' greater knowledge of contemporary fashion, in which they are personally as well as professionally immersed, as well as their take on the connection of body, dress, and character, even among the first generation of designers, derive from their class position, which is more or less equal to the actor's while superior to the tailor's. But the trump card of personal designers is their ability to interact comfortably with producers and directors, sharing tastes and backgrounds, discussing nuances of fashion. I have yet to meet a tailor who could speak English, illustrating yet again how speaking ability in English is defining and walling off a community of practice for whom English is part and parcel of a generalized cultural distinction.

## TOWARD THE IDEAL BODY

As much responsibility as the costume and its makers have to sculpt and show off the body so that it appears at its best, so too does the actor bear a measure of responsibility for offering suitable raw material for the costume to work upon. This can mean anything from taking care of one's health to scrupulously maintaining those parts of the body that are habitually exposed (the face and the arms, for example). In the present day, some stars manage to actualize, if not perfection, then a very high standard of appearance. How is this done, and what does it entail? The arrival of beauty products and services hitherto unavailable in India has led to actors becoming more proactive in the pursuit of the idealized body (Wilkinson-Weber 2012). Contemporary designers are more likely to refer to heroes and heroines who "take care of their bodies" and strive not just for thinness but for health. The most professional actors in this regard pay scrupulous attention to diet and health regimens, and they probably employ a personal trainer to coach them through a rigorous fitness schedule. In a crowded marketplace of beauty services and products, heroines are expected to submit to the physical rigors of gym routines on top of spa treatments, cleanses, and—if necessary—cosmetic surgery, resituating some of the discipline of the structured, padded, and sculpted bodice on to the body itself. Even male bodies are becoming more and more circumscribed by aesthetic ideals that demand discipline, effort, and money. Male stars who were faulted for not having very good bodies when I began my work in 2002 were sporting rippling muscles by the end of the decade.

## From Style to Power: The Hero Body

For the most part, heroes until very recently were not remarkable from a physical standpoint (Dwyer 2000b). Bodies were enclosed in and enacted via clothing, and the robust, imposing body epitomized by the wrestler-actor Dara Singh in the 1950s and 1960s was the exception rather than the rule. By the 1970s, the increasing popularity of action scenes required the hero's body and persona to appear credible in hand-to-hand fighting. From the actor Dharmendra's first films in the 1960s to his peak in the 1970s, his career mirrored this genre shift; he transformed himself from sensitive romantic lead to robust action hero, a transformation in which physical strength and an overpowering body were emphasized (Kesavan 2008). Dharmendra's contemporary Amitabh Bachchan also relied on a demonstrative physicality in his characterizations, but this was the product of his height and long legs (Dwyer 2000b; Dwyer and Patel 2002, 34).

By the 1980s and 1990s, however, the strong, muscular body had become a more common and, ultimately, a normative dimension of the hero's persona. It is no accident that Bollywood heroes of the 1980s and 1990s cite Sylvester Stallone as a major inspiration. Dharmendra's son Sonny Deol continued in his father's footsteps, with a career based largely upon roles in action films. Among the first stars to use bodybuilding to craft a precisely muscled body was Sanjay Dutt, son of Nargis and Sunil Dutt. Shortly after, Salman Khan installed the prevailing standard for the contemporary hero in the 1990s, with an astute blend of a fashion sensibility and a conscious, even narcissistic pleasure in his body. Khan has made the removal of his shirt an expected, even clichéd element in his performances, to the extent that the moment of disrobing is now itself a kind of special effect (see, for example, his films *Dabangg* [2010] and *Bodyguard* [2011]). The originator of these scenes is the action director, who then works with the costume designer to come up with the style of shirt that is to be removed at a critical moment. Some postproduction special effects are inserted, and the end result is ever-more-ingenious ways to separate Salman's shirt from Salman's torso. As explanation, an industry insider suggested to me that "Salman Khan's films are tailored to suit a certain class of the masses, hence these type of sequences have become a kind of necessity."

Between them, Khan and Sanjay Dutt have set a standard of male body discipline that persists, and indeed has expanded (like so many chests), today. Surveying the parade of magnificently muscled creatures who auditioned for the part of Jamal in 2008's *Slumdog Millionaire*, director Danny Boyle lamented that he couldn't find a single young Indian actor with a body that could convey the vulnerability he wanted for the character (Farndale 2009). He had to turn to Dev Patel, an actor from Britain, where the superlatively toned body is not yet the gold standard of masculinity. Decades after British colonists derided the nakedness of Indians as inconsistent with their own notions of a mature, authoritative masculinity, there is a fairly rich irony here.

The carefully toned and cultivated body can be as singular an attribute of the star as the face, a phenomenon put to striking use in Ashutosh Gowarikar's *Jodhaa Akbar*. Starring as Akbar is Hrithik Roshan, an actor whose physicality is communicated via his command of dance and his finely toned, muscular body. In a scene that takes place shortly after Akbar and Jodhaa's politically strategic marriage, Jodhaa surreptitiously watches Akbar, stripped to the waist, as he goes through the routine of sword practice on the terrace outside her living quarters. The scene (which, following an earlier episode in which Akbar tames a wild elephant, adds to the impression of Akbar as a physically adventurous man) allows for the audience (and, of course, Jodhaa, in a striking reversal of the usual direction of the covetous gaze) to admire his grace and his physique. With the focus on the anachronistically hypertoned body of Hrithik Roshan, the sexual allusions of the scene are obvious, predicating the growth of Jodhaa's love on a good measure of physical desire. Roshan evokes none of the images of the Mughal emperors so much as he resembles himself, a star whose persona is rooted in an idealized male body. In setting the semiclothed Roshan body next to the meticulously recreated, and clothed, Mughal emperor, one gets the impression that the character Akbar is not bounded by the clothes (as bodies are in Mughal portraiture) but is barely contained by them.

And yet the ambiguous entailments of cultivating a desirable body and showing it off—offering oneself up for appraisal as vamps and heroines typically do—are not lost on either male stars or their designers and directors. The terms and process of exposure are carefully plotted. Clothes must set off but not obscure the musculature, the tension between fabric and flesh becoming as charged as it has historically been on the woman's body. The casting of the male star in a prototypically female role was brought out explicitly in Shah Rukh Khan's performance of the song "Dard e Disco" in *Om Shanti Om* (2007), in which he appears shirtless with an oiled torso, wearing nothing more than carpenter jeans and hardhat. He and director Farah Khan only half-jokingly remarked on the resemblance of the song to the "item number" common to many Hindi films, with its provocatively dressed "item girl" (Shiekh 2008, 134–5). Mapping the visual conventions of this song-and-dance number featuring a woman onto one with an undisputed male box-office superstar spoke to shifting notions of the appropriating gaze. The film's director was a woman, Farah Khan, and in addition to Shah Rukh Khan's many female fans, the audience is now understood to constitute a cross section of desires and orientations. In fact, the studied body display of muscular heroes is a key element in the appeal of Hindi film to gay audiences at home and in the diaspora (Dudrah 2008; Kavi 2000; Rao 2000).

With the rise of the toned or frankly massive muscular body has also come a preference for removing body hair. Anthropological thinking on hair has mostly focused on the structural implications of hairiness versus hairlessness for social identity or on the psychoanalytic implications of the same with regard to sexual (or displaced sexual) power (Hallpike 1969; Obeyesekere 1984). The meanings of hair are subject to local patterning, but analytic and ethnographic studies have strongly gravitated towards positing a close connection between hair, gender, power, and control, so that the "physical body is used either to consolidate or to challenge the social body in terms of sex roles and ideology" (Synnott 1987, 406). The uninhibited display of the hairy body (the chest specifically) in films from the 1960s until relatively recently was an affirmative sign of masculine power and virility. Body hair distinguishes the male body from the female one, not simply because women do not have hair in the same places or in such quantities, but because women (in India particularly) are taught to remove body hair as part of a regimen of body maintenance. In a scheme such as this one, the hairless male body is associated with weakness and immaturity.

The swing toward creating and maintaining a hairless body has overtaken male stars both new and established. Among the older stars, one can tell which have gone in for depilation and which have no need to, because for the first set there are photographic and cinematic records of before and after that confirm the actors aren't naturally hairless. The proximate cause of this trend

**Figure 9**    Shah Rukh Khan's muscular torso in the film *Om Shanti Om* (2007) was the subject of much comment (and admiration). Here, a promotional poster has found its way onto the side of office machinery. (Image courtesy of Clare Wilkinson-Weber.)

is bodybuilding practice, in which removing all chest hair (and even underarm hair) is mandatory in order to exhibit muscle definition. The hypertrophy of the male body as a result of bodybuilding effectively redefines hairlessness as synonymous with supermasculinity (Synnott 1987, 406). There are other factors at work, however, specifically the contrast of hirsuteness and hairlessness that enacts contrast at another level between the animal body and the cultured one. Disposing of body hair elevates the lumpen male to the status of civilized, self-controlled citizen.

Facing off against the hero, the villain has tended to push to extremes what are merely tendencies in the hero body. Thus, in films of the 1960s to 1990s, the villain's ostentatious indulgence in clothes and accoutrements impressed the viewer with its excess, a crass materialism that subordinated feeling and humanity. The villains I am most interested in here—ranging from the ever-popular *dacoit* (bandit), to the Naxalite (Maoist insurgent), to assorted thugs and gangsters—are by contrast closer to nature, resembling in essence beasts. This kind of villain has often been hairier than the hero—for example, with a mustache, a beard perhaps, a messy head of hair, and noticeable chest hair: a figure of disruptive political and sexual power.

The foundational narrative model for the beast-like villain and the civilized hero is the story of Rama and Sita, and Hindi film's prolific intertextuality has allowed many films to be read as versions of the *Ramayana*, in full or in part (Booth 1995; Thomas 1995, 166). One example is Subhash Ghai's 1993 *Khalnayak* (The Antihero), named not for Jackie Shroff's upstanding character Ram, but for Sanjay Dutt's knavish protagonist, Ballu. Ballu is the muscle for a criminal mastermind, while harboring his own deep (and not wholly unjustified) grudge against "civilized" society. Appropriately enough, he is inattentive to his appearance; he wears a stubbly beard, his hair hangs over his eyes in greasy hanks; his hairy arms and chest are often exposed. He becomes Ravana (the villain of the *Ramayana*) in the context of the film after he spirits away Ganga (Madhuri Dixit) in his flight from the law. While complete reform and redemption are too much to expect with a precedent like the *Ramayana* to contend with, nevertheless it is important to note that Ganga touches a nerve in Ballu and influences him for the better. This is made evident in a makeover that Ballu undertakes to impress Ganga, which includes a haircut, a new suit, and a well-pressed shirt. These do not replace the body so much as overlay it with what is recognizable as another facet of Dutt's own star persona. The transformation is essentially incomplete, mirroring perhaps Dutt's own ambivalent positioning within films—and in life—as alternately hero and villain. The character of Ganga, meanwhile, underscores some of the problems that heroines face in the display of the body, to which I now turn.

## Between Sex and Shame

### *Some Ambiguities of Tradition*

The heroine's beauty is a necessary condition for her very existence—a beauty that emanates from her face, but also from her body; in turn, she has always had to handle the paradox that her body is both the instrument of her fame and the fragile container of her reputation. The body's beauty is heightened and projected through costumes and jewelry. Costumes both reveal and conceal the body, defining its margins with respect to the environment and with respect to the meeting of cloth and skin. Beauty is inseparable from physical allure, the core of the heroine's claim to relevance, as well as an ever-present source of moral suspicion.

There is a stubborn association of Western clothes with vulgarity and exposure, as we have already seen, but to go along with the easy opposition of Indian and Western misses the critical point that Indian costumes may themselves be decidedly ambiguous markers of proper Indian womanhood. The athletic, sensuous dance number often features a heroine in a tight-fitting *ghaghara choli*; the *choli* may even be backless. For an example, I return to *Khalnayak*, already discussed above. The film includes the now-notorious song "Choli Ke Peeche Kya Hai" (What's beneath my blouse?), in which Madhuri Dixit plays the vamp to Sanjay Dutt's villain. Removed from its narrative context, the song, with its provocative title, plays like a cabaret routine in which a prostitute sings seductively to a sexually overstimulated villain. The costume, uniquely perhaps in film history, grabs attention both for its form (a curvaceous, highly decorated, and low-cut *choli*), and for its hinted-at absence (to invite speculation as to what lies beneath an item of clothing is in effect to convey nudity without ever having to show it). This is, however, a case of "false transformation," in which an altered exterior is at odds with the character's true nature (McDonald 2010, 75). The performer is not in fact a professional dancer or a prostitute, but instead a policewoman (albeit one who is surprisingly talented in the song and dance department). Ganga (Dixit) throws herself into the role without reservation; she calls herself a *veshya* (prostitute), and of course, the song sequence is staged with the élan and enthusiasm one would expect from what is, in effect, a showstopper.

Ganga's performance successfully entices and bewitches Ballu, but her plan backfires once she comes to develop some sympathy for her quarry, and she helps him escape certain death in a police encounter. Ganga is now fully assimilated to her mythic equivalent, Sita, and her virtue and probity are in serious doubt until Ballu turns himself in and vouches for her at the film's conclusion. The reassurances offered in advance that Ganga is a moral woman are important no doubt for her final vindication to make sense. But for the song to be successful, both inside the film frame and outside it, Ganga must display such a degree of commitment to her wanton character that the suspicions that fall on her later appear to have some justification.[3]

Even the sari, the otherwise thoroughly respectable dress of the adult, married woman, is as readily associated with emotion and intimacy as it is with status and power; its erotic potential emerges from its essential character as a sinuous wrapping of the body that continuously hints at unwrapping (Dwyer 2000b). The sari's animation makes it seem as though it has a life of its own, moving and shifting according to the physical logic of its draping, as well as with the body of the wearer (Banerjee and Miller 2003, 28).

Hindi film has taken full advantage these possibilities and has even invented some of its own, including the *filmi* sari, in which the *choli* reveals a substantial amount of cleavage while maximizing the breasts via strategic padding, the sari pleats are made low on the hips, and the *pallu* makes only a token pass across the torso, allowing more of the back and stomach to be seen (Banerjee and Miller 2003). Dress designers also have the scope to modify saris in other ways that ordinary wearers do not necessarily adopt—for example, stitching the pleats in place to make the garment adhere closer to the body's curves. The opportunity to redrape and readjust between takes also assists in elevating the sari's (or indeed any costume's) appearance far above the standard that clothes in the real world can achieve. From one shift to another, dressmen press and starch clothes, so that there are few moments in the film in which the sari is creased or rumpled. The sleek fit and impeccable finish of the glamorous saris in a film such as *Silsila* owe themselves not simply to the choice of fabric and expert stitching (of the blouse) but to the kinds of draping, fastening, detailing, and maintenance that a film crew provides.

Perhaps the last word in eroticism has been the drenching of the sari-wearing heroine in a rain shower or waterfall, imprinting the body's surface features into the clinging folds and effectively making the body emerge into

**Figure 10**   Pictured side by side are the two women of *Silsila* (1981, directed and produced by Yash Chopra), Chandni (Rekha) and Shobha (Jaya Bhaduri), who are fighting over the same man. The costumes in this Yash Chopra classic are without exception gorgeous and beautifully fitted, providing a counterpoint to the narrative of adultery and betrayal. (DVD distributor, Yash Raj Films.)

the cloth. Some of the most memorable of these scenes came from two films made by Raj Kapoor in the latter part of his career: the first featuring Zeenat Aman (*Satyam, Shivam, Sundaram* [1978]) and the second, Mandakini (*Ram Tera Ganga Maili* [1985]). Scenes such as these are often dismissed as cynical attempts to appeal to prurient (in other words, lower-class male) tastes while claiming that there can be no offense because, strictly speaking, there is no nudity. Whether filmmakers are so mercenary or the tastes of some audience members are so debauched, Dwyer (2000c) points out that Indian audiences across class and gender boundaries effortlessly understand the cultural link between rain and fertility that wet-sari scenes evoke.

If the sari can variously embody chastity, eroticism, restraint, and sensuality, then plainly it is a garment that "lives" not only on the boundary of the heroine's body, but also on the boundary between the good and evil character or the judicious and reckless actor. In other words, the proper clothing of women can be as suffused with ambiguity and tension as the less-approved form. What films have done is make the most of the fact that the sari is not merely a kind of wrapping that demarcates and identifies the body within, but acts as a flexible boundary that enables meaning and motivates action across layers of readable surface. Simply because the sari's symbolic and material qualities are known so well by audiences, filmmakers are able to construct out of them multiple layers of meaning and feeling. Assuredly, the reluctance until recently to clothe unruly or sexually assertive female characters in saris could be attributed to the sari's status as an exemplary garment, a recognition, in effect, that the collaborative potential of body and garment in wear can become realized only through the body and sari both being beyond reproach. Nevertheless, there are examples where a sari's moral weight can be used to broadcast counter-discourses with respect to characters whose social standing is ambiguous or in some way compromised. A good example can be found by going back to *Silsila*, Yash Chopra's film about a love triangle in which Rekha and Amitabh Bachchan play adulterers, Chandni and Amit, and Jaya Bachchan plays Amit's wronged wife, Shobha. As it happens, all three have something to be ashamed of: Shobha became pregnant before marriage by her late fiancé, before marrying Amit to save her reputation. Not only are both women decked out in saris throughout the film, but the contrast between them is drawn in part via the different kinds of saris each prefers. Shobha's incline toward rich colors and patterns, while Chandni's are plain. Chandni's saris, though, are unfailingly flatteringly draped, beautifully colored, and luxuriously shot. Here the seductive beauty of the clothes on film star bodies is used to complicate what might otherwise be presented as a straightforward morality play.

### *Vamps and After*

The contemporary heroine is extended much more freedom over her clothing choices and body dispositions compared to heroines of the past. Yet, the specter of the vamp—incorrigible, alluring, disreputable, and (unlike the ingenue heroine) fully aware of the effect her exposed body, or the suggested body beneath her clothing, has on men—still hovers over the heroine as an alternative version of adult femininity, one that is distinguished by a lack of inhibition, an enjoyment of fashion and novelty, and the boldness to break social taboos. Most film professionals still know exactly what is meant by the contrast of heroine and vamp, even if the boundary between the two is practically defunct in terms of characterization, and costumes aim in all cases to magnify the female actor's bodily attractions. It is as though both have always and will always exist, proof of the remarkable effectiveness of clothing at establishing apparently timeless categories.

Ranjani Mazumdar (2007) links an increasingly prurient interest in night-clubs and cabarets as sinful spaces of urban modernity to the high-water mark of the notorious singing and dancing Hindi film vamp of the 1960s and early 1970s. Cabaret scenes often take place within hotels that also had a reputation for harboring dissipation and sexual license (Pinto 2006, 54). The alluring but scandalous vamp epitomizes dangerous modernity in full flight, and she happily indulges in clothes that showcase her body in hitherto unprecedented ways. The cabaret dancer's costumes opened up to the gaze the midriff (back and front), the arms and legs, and the cleavage (although flesh-tone bodysuits and net sleeves and stockings acted as a kind of moral insulation against accusations of nudity). The most outrageous vamp costumes were there simply to offer a spectacle to the audience; few of the costumes could be regarded as wearable or desirable for consumers.

The actor and dancer Helen Richardson (known in films by her first name only) remains the exemplary cabaret vamp. Throughout her career, Helen was known mostly for her spectacular dance numbers, most of them staged for the pleasure of nightclub patrons within the film's frame. In addition, she had several significant acting roles in films such as *Jewel Thief* (1967) and *Teesri Manzil* (1966), in which she perfected the role of the "brazen hussy . . . a cigarette in one hand, a glass of whisky in the other" (Helen, quoted in Kabir 2001, 98). The fantastic, almost hallucinatory otherness of her roles is accentuated by her dramatic costumes—leotards, flamenco outfits, body-hugging sheaths, feather boas, leggings under diaphanous skirts, and so on. The Helen brand of vamp recalls Caroline Evans's observation in her analysis of avant-garde fashion that the showgirl, the burlesque dancer, or the cabaret artist effectively "drag up" to enact hyper-feminine versions of more complexly gendered selves (Evans 2003, 124).

The difference between the prototypical showgirl and Helen is that the cabaret costumes of a Helen do not refer to any sartorial model of femininity that would be widely recognizable in India. (As Helen's frequent personal designer Mani Rabadi explained, when talking of making her first cabaret costumes: "I'd never seen a cabaret in my life—I used to produce out of imagination.") Instead, the otherness of the flamenco gown (designed by Bhanu Athaiya for *Teesri Manzil*), the leotard (*Jewel Thief*), or the slit-to-the-thigh dress with hip level cutouts (*Don* [1978]) is startling on its own terms. Like the spectacular iconoclastic fashion garment, it speaks as loudly for itself as does the woman's body on which it appears (Evans 2003, 113). The viewer is presented with the tantalizing challenge of what to look at: the exposed and eroticized areas of the woman's frame or the compelling colors, light, and brilliance contained in the costume. The heady surfeit of beads, sparkles, frills, and whatnot that prevails in the vamp costume recalls Stephen Pattison's comment (2011, 133) that decorative detail induces an "unfinished fascination with objects . . . . making objects 'sticky' for the human gaze."

The beginnings of the vamp's eclipse are typically located in the 1970s, just as glamorous heroines such as Zeenat Aman and Parveen Babi began to dominate the screen (Kabir 2001; Mazumdar 2007; Wilkinson-Weber 2005). It is possible to argue that the door that the Helen variety of vamp opened, and that the Aman and Babi heroines stepped through, led to a new conceptualization of the female body—putting it into motion and making awareness of one's body a source of pleasure. Both Aman and Babi had modeling backgrounds, and they brought to film a level of self-confidence concerning bodily display that was unprecedented. Aman, in particular, took an approach to her body that combined pragmatism with pleasure. When Gina Lollobrigida was given the honor of holding the clapperboard at the *mahurat* (the ceremonial start of shooting) for the international film *Shalimar* (1978), with its star-filled cast, Aman was determined to outdo Lollobrigida in voluptuousness, in an episode Bunny Reuben dubbed "The Battle of the Boobs" (Reuben 1979).

The consumerist, neo-liberal environment of contemporary India has granted heroines some of the unapologetic liberties of the vamp while diminishing the risks. Stylish but essentially conservative, modest costumes in one film are replaced with daring and provocative outfits in the next (see, for example, Kareena Kapoor's dress in *Bodyguard* [2011] next to her show-stopping *mujra* [a kind of dance performed by courtesans in the Mughal period and after, and the dress associated with it] scene in a cutaway, cleavage-baring kurta and *salwar* in *Agent Vinod* [2012]). Even the item number, a high-octane dance scene in a movie conventionally performed by specialists, is now becoming the moment for a cameo by a mainstream actor (famous recent examples include Aishwarya Rai in *Bunty aur Babli* [2005], and Katrina Kaif in *Agneepath* [2012]). But a level of propriety is still important to maintain. For example, it is important that the heroine must be seen to work—in award shows, in advertising campaigns—in taking care of her face and body as extensions of a professional identity, not simply as pleasures in themselves. The kind of indulgence for male stars pursuing personal pleasures such as drinking and carousing is not extended to women.

### Trust and Power

Heroines place the utmost trust in tailors, and more recently designers, to work for rather than against their need to balance decorum with beauty and novelty. If a heroine has indicated her willingness to wear glamorous outfits—glamour being defined in a little aphorism by a designer as "ha[ving] two facets: one is sequined dress, the other is body showing. Both? Better"—then the designer is entrusted to do his or her utmost to make sure she looks her best. The more frantic the production conditions, the narrower the focus of the designer becomes with respect to his or her obligations: The gamble is that a costume that is sufficiently striking and well fitted will compensate for any anxieties about its impropriety. Not many designers were prepared to state it openly, but the frank declaration of the same designer who opined on sequins and exposed bodies that "I take nobody's dictates but my customer and her body" speaks to the bedrock obligation of the personal designer to protect and support the star.

This, though, is the case only once a heroine, having used her body to attain a level of success in the industry, has worked up to a position of sufficient power that she can exercise some control over how her body as asset is used in future. Thus, fully aware as they are of the body as simultaneously instrument and commodity, stars are able to lock down a position from which they can direct the uses of that body, whereas junior artists and neophytes are subject entirely to others' uses of them. The junior artist or dancer cannot expect to improve her position, and her body is determinative of what she can and cannot do. They are the lowliest performers, simply anonymous bodies or ambulatory costumes, as demonstrated in an anecdote from Mushtaq Shiekh's book on the making of 2007's *Om Shanti Om*, in which extras are referred to as "hey white shirt, hey red pants" (Shiekh 2008, 46). As for the heroine, her first films are when she is most vulnerable to criticism about her body and subject to pressure to use it in ways that may be distasteful to her. The newcomer heroine, the starlet, receives more attention than the junior artist, but that attention is fraught with risk. She is completely at the disposal of directors and designers who craft her look. Designers mince no words about this: "[I]f it is an ordinary girl, a new girl, she has no say. Only her body has say, because we have to see what kind of body does she have."

The female actor's hand is strengthened, first, if she is a member of a powerful film family, in which case her name and associations can help her gain leverage, and second, if she can secure the services of a trusted designer who understands her body and how to enhance it. Even as the heroine's star rises, the body remains the starting point for all negotiations, but once she is at the top of the heap, she gains the unambiguous right to be able to pick and choose what she wears (most powerfully demonstrated by rejecting a costume rather than accepting it). I encountered a few designers, mostly ones whose careers peaked in the 1970s and 1980s, who noted that they had to try to persuade their heroines to wear more revealing or sexy clothes than the actors preferred; equally, however, they might shrug their shoulders and say that if a heroine vetoed a costume, that was that. Costume calculations are an integral part of testing the social capital an actor has amassed, a means of gauging their leverage vis-à-vis other film professionals and peers.

As the female actor gains the right to dictate her costume choices, she can better police her own boundaries in terms of what she is willing, or unwilling, to wear, what she prefers to conceal as opposed to what she wants to reveal. If she is up against a star director, then other tactics are required. Consider, for example, this story, told to me by a designer, *Varun*, about how he and his client conspired to frustrate the wishes of a director in a matter of costume for a "sleazy girl singing this dance number":

> Now, this star, the girl that she is, her image, she says, I will not wear the low neck, I will not wear sleeveless, I will not show my waist. I want the *ghaghara* right up to here (above the navel). The director tells me—I want the *ghaghara* up to here (well below the navel), you're to show her waist, I want it sleeveless—exactly the opposite of what the heroine has told me. I told her that the director has told me this. She told me, you take the advance from him, and just make what I have told you. And come straight over with the outfit on the set on the day of the shoot. But give me a trial before. So I go to give her a trial before, and I reach the set with the outfit, and the director freaks out. What have you given her? He says, I can't see her. . . . I can't see any portion of her body. So what is the point of the song? The heroine says I don't care what he thinks.

This story illustrates how the heroine can rely on the unquestioned loyalty of the designer not just to respond to her demands, but also to collude with her in outwitting others on the set. The designer is given sanction to do this by virtue of his or her professional relationship to the star, as well as by the privilege of being of a comparable class to directors, producers, and so on.

The terms of a heroine's refusal of a costume may vary. However, disallowing a costume because it is overly revealing or sexy does not merely allow the heroine to stake out her domain on the set; it can be converted into public pronouncements about modesty and self-respect that continue to reap a measure of cultural capital. Between 2008 and 2012, stories still surfaced in Indian media about heroines refusing point-blank to wear bikinis, including Ayesha Takia (BBC IndiaFM 2008), Asin Thottumkal (Bhutia 2011) and Sonakshi Sinha (Indo-Asian News Service 2012). In offering commentary on her scruples, each woman, in effect, directed a barb at colleagues who did not share them. Sonakshi Sinha stated, for example, that she wouldn't wear a bikini because "I am not that kind of a person. I have been bought up in a certain way." Ayesha Takia added an appeal to the authority of Indian tradition; as BBC IndiaFM reported: "semi-nudity, in her opinion, is not something for family viewing. [She] likes Indian women to be respected for their elegance and dignity" and believes that "levels of decency have to be maintained especially in our country, we live in a city and a very hip society but that's not our country."

The BBC IndiaFM and Indo-Asian News Service articles reported on Takia and Sinha's contractual no-bikini clauses straightforwardly. The *Times of India* article by Peden Doma Bhutia depicted heroines as, in essence, falling into two categories: those who astutely insist on no-bikini clauses and those who, because of passivity or haplessness, do not do so and, thus, have to provide the glamour for the film. There is a third category, however: that of heroines who embrace a sexy image and make few, if any, efforts at amelioration off-screen. Actors in this third category are also expected to be free of the limitation of the Indian body that made such sartorial adventures misguided in other heroines. The full consequences of this shift were not seen until the 1990s, when a wider variety of clothing demanding an equally diverse repertoire of body dispositions became available. Whereas most female actors trod carefully, stars such as Bipasha Basu and Mallika Sherawat chose films that played up their sex appeal and that demanded more moments of body exposure. This is a risky strategy to adopt, but it is one that is more viable since the fashion industry turned modeling into a recurrent, rather than periodic, source of new stars, a phenomenon I examine more closely in the next chapter.

## INHABITING OTHER BODIES

Before moving on to think about fashion and film, I want to return to the issues raised by Madhuri Dixit's performance of "Choli Ke Peeche Kya Hai," in which she is an actor, dressed as a character, who is herself in disguise. Masquerade is a common device of melodrama, depending for its effectiveness on the audience's possessing knowledge that is not shared by all the characters. But what is going on at the level of costume and the kind of body work that the actor is required to do? In Dixit's performance, the masquerade is the very point at which her star persona asserts itself most vigorously: Ganga is dismissed not just by the masquerade but by the bravura dance performance that Dixit stages. Her costume is meticulously made and precisely fitted, so that she can do this to the best of her ability. But in other instances, the disguise, while never erasing the star, nevertheless demands that he or she assume an appearance and demeanor that are alien to his or her standard persona. The rules that typically apply to star costume must then concede to other obligations.

Examples of cross-dressing are the most striking examples of this phenomenon—and the most illuminating about the assumptions about the body that continue to drive costume design. The absurdity of such disguise may be readily apparent (as in the song "Mere Angane Mein Tumhara Kya Kaam Hai" from *Laawaris* (1981), in which Amitabh Bachchan sings and dances in the guise of a series of parodic "females"—to the delight of an audience within the film); in other cases, the bizarre nature of the dress-up is known by the audience but is mysteriously and hilariously opaque to other characters in the film (for example, Aamir Khan as a police officer going undercover as a woman in 1995's *Baazi*). Women do not dress up as men as much as men dress up as women, most likely because, as aspirational clothing, menswear is something to be achieved, whereas women's clothing on men, as a kind of "dressing down while dressing up," brings with it only comedy or abuse.[4]

The performances of actors disguised in women's clothes run the gamut from broad caricature to more nuanced parody. The more complete the transformation of male to female (wig and makeup, as well as dress), the closer the voice, gestures, and behavior that are adopted approach actual impersonation. This said, all cross-dressing depends upon caricatures of female dress and deportment and, somewhat poignantly, assumptions about female vulnerability and compliance. Frequently, the cross-dressing character unexpectedly nets the attention of a hapless male character who simply refuses to leave "her" alone. Lost in these scenarios is the sinister point about women's vulnerability to sexual attention, as well as the casual assumption that dress and appearance are, in essence, advertisements of availability.

Cross-dressing is not so common that many designers have had any experience with it. On the one occasion when the subject did come up in my interviews (with respect to a costume for Govinda), the designer said the garment was made up by a women's tailor, just as if the costume were being made for a woman. What considerations go into making a woman's dress to fit a man's proportions, and to what extent any *filmi* elements are retained in the cut and fitting, I cannot say. Once again, I would predict that this would depend upon the degree of impersonation the actor is expected to effect. In fact, I would conclude that to be a woman in as total a fashion as possible, it is necessary always to pay attention to fit, since the dress and body are essentially coterminous for the purposes of film. Conversely, a heroine dressed as a man will relinquish the demand for a tight fit to the extent that her character is attempting to pass as a man. But for the benefit of the knowing audience, it is more likely that the men's clothes will be adjusted and fitted by a woman's tailor, so that they become more intrinsically female than their overt position within a fashion system would imply. Practically speaking, however, just as in Europe, North America, and other parts of the globe, affluent young Indian women have adopted elements of men's clothing as a sign and sanction of their greater social power. I do not mean here the corporate uniform of the suit or the ceremonial outfits that retain distinctly Indian features, but sportswear, T-shirts, and above all, jeans. So far, men have not co-opted any features of women's wardrobe. These are trends that unquestionably derive from the power and influence of a global fashion system, in which Bollywood has had a stake from its earliest years.

# –4–

# Fashion and Spectacle

Fashion is not something that exists in dresses only. Fashion is in the sky, in the street, fashion has to do with ideas, the way we live, what is happening.

Coco Chanel

## THE FASHION OF FILM

Over its long history, Hindi film has been singularly associated with fashion; in fact, it has been among India's most influential sources of fresh ways to dress and new things to dress up in. A summation of sorts of film history might be made from the long succession of its iconic costumes; to cite just a few: Raj Kapoor's tuxedo in *Shree 420* (1955), Sadhana's *churidar kameez* in *Waqt* (1965), Dev Anand's cravats in *Jewel Thief* (1967), Dimple Kapadia's halter top and skirt in *Bobby* (1973), Amitabh Bachchan's knotted shirt and jeans in *Deewaar* (1975), Madhuri's Dixit's purple *lehenga choli* in *Hum Aapke Hain Koun . . . !* (1994), Aamir Khan's leather jacket in *Dil Chahta Hai* (2001), and Preity Zinta's coat in *Kal Ho Naa Ho* (2003).

Cinema's role as educator and marketer—producing contexts in which to make sense of modernity and using the power of compelling visual images to spur consumerism—is by now well recognized in the case of Hollywood (Dyer 2003, 5; Sassatelli 2007, 168). Indian film is no different, and throughout the industry's history, its relationship with the apparel industry, as well as with the heady heights of exclusive fashion, has been both rich and complicated. Fashion both frames and explains the obvious interest that film has taken in urban life and urban activities (Calefato 2004, 100; Wilson 1987, 9), although the vast majority of Indian citizens continue to live and work in the countryside. The pleasures of urban life—technological, sumptuary, experiential—together comprise the escapism that the mundane film viewer is supposedly in search of when going to the cinema.

In spite of the close, some might argue even synergistic, relationships of film and fashion in many locations around the world, designers in both India and North America are unambiguous that film costume designing is never, and can never be, the same as fashion designing since its primary purpose is to construct a character. Deborah Nadoolman Landis's dictum (2006) that "[f]ashion and costume design have opposing goals: fashion = commerce, costume = character" would receive universal agreement among dress designers of all ages and experience in Mumbai. It is not that designers deny that there is a place in film for fashionable clothes or that film costume does not influence fashion. The important distinction to make is whether fashion follows character or precedes it. Everyone I talked to was adamant that it was always the former. However, close examination of the processes and procedures of obtaining costume suggested a more complex relationship to fashion than these statements implied. This, as well as the ways in which fashion is used rhetorically to stake out rival positions in the costume world, is the subject of this chapter.

There are two meanings of fashion that need to be borne in mind before I proceed. The first is the more comprehensive definition we find in scholarly literature, where fashion refers to dress both as a set of signifiers (Barthes 1990; Bernard 2002; Calefato 2004; Sahlins 2000) and as a means of self-realization through embodiment (Craik 1994; Entwistle 2000). Fashion, in this sense, can refer to the dress habitus (sensations, dispositions, and values) across and within a range of classes, ethnicities, castes, and so forth without necessarily having to affix itself to a view of fashion that considers only its production and consumption among a rarified elite—or for that matter, mass production for the benefit of middle-class consumers. In scholarly literature, fashion is replacing many previous uses of "costume," where costume was used to refer to so-called traditional attire. This is in part to emphasize the degree of change and adjustment in clothing in all parts of the globe as a result of colonial contact, the growth of postcolonial regimes, and the rapid transmission of new ideas and materials; in part also, it is to draw attention to the reach of consumer goods and manufactured garments that are co-opted into local sartorial systems (Hansen 2004, 372). The use of "fashion" is also intended to convey the realization that change and variation in clothing choices is a given (at least for the middle classes and upward) in almost all parts of the world, adding a degree of fluidity and uncertainty to clothing's communicative and phenomenological dimensions where, in the past, stability and conservatism were assumed. Fashion thus refers to all the ways in which human beings perceive meaning in clothing and in which choice, obligation, and transformation are materialized through its use.

Fashion in film, in this sense, is not a mirror of the world to which it refers, but instead something that might be variously described as a sample (in that it cannot contain all dress variants) or as a pastiche (in that it contains elements of imitation with oblique—or obvious—commentary). And just as film audiences may enjoy quoting films in their own sartorial choices, so film costume quotes the dress of other films, creating in effect a system of its own. Everyone in a film is presumed to be in costume, no matter that some individuals are extras wearing their own clothes and acting only in the most cursory sense. The costumes of a film's world (no matter how fragmented their assembly) then have to present themselves to the audience as real, based on what the viewers know of the dress conventions around them and what they have already seen on screen. As Patrizia Calefato (2004, 91–2) puts it: "[N]ot only is the clothed body on the screen credible, it is also socially 'true' and one can create from its image other like bodies, not only in film, but in reality, whether past or present." The film's world will forever revolve around its stars, but for completeness and credibility, it will include characters, both major and minor, in everything from police or military uniforms to work clothes to the dusty and bedraggled clothing of the urban and rural poor. Regional origins are broadcast via costume stereotypes, and older characters are typically outfitted in the garb of banal conservatism. There is fashion as a structured regime in such garments, but nothing of fashion as something perennially changeable and desirable, the object of choice that presents itself as a necessity.

It is in the latter sense that the term fashion is used among designers, dressmen, dresswalas, and so on, and the term pertains only to the costume of characters who have their own designers and menswear outfitters—in other words, heroes and heroines, with some of the most outré looks adopted by so-called negative characters, or villains (and, in the past, vamps). Recalling that the vast majority of designers have been (and continue to be) personally associated with a star rather than the film as a whole, it seems odd that they would disavow the role of fashion in an occupation that is dedicated to the burnishing of the star's onscreen image. The contradiction is solved, for the most part, by acknowledging that cinema's particular connection to modernity has meant that stars play characters who are intended to be fashionable—in other words, young, presumably affluent people—more often than just about any other kind of character.[1] And there are always the song sequences, which are wide open for bold fashion statements, since forays into imaginative worlds are fodder for costume spectacles that owe far less to realism than do a film's other scenes.

In spite of what designers say about the primacy of character, it is hard to overlook the alignment of the most fashionable figures with distinct personal designers. At the very least, this alignment suggests that the kinds of styles these characters require can be provided only by certain kinds of people and not others. The split between the providers of costume for the general cast (the dressmen, a designer hired by the production company, the dresswala) and the personal designer echoes the division between fashion as a general sartorial order and fashion as stylistic innovation. What the personal designer does, in conjunction with the star, director, and whoever else makes interjections in the costume process, is to give imaginative form to the effects that fashion as stylistic innovation provokes when it disrupts an existing system of dress and decorum.

This, I believe, explains why films have been able to explore and celebrate new looks and styles while at the same time appearing to endorse conservative proscriptions about improper clothing. Fashion betokened global consciousness, the positive values of modernization, sophistication, and self-possession; equally, the flipside of these qualities—a paucity of Indian authenticity, indifference to tradition, arrogance, and narcissism—were harmful to social order. From the standpoint of dramatic effectiveness, infusing costume with fashionable elements added nuance and variety to the melodramas playing out onscreen. Moving the various figures around the dramatic chessboard (so to speak) could gain immeasurably from using new signifiers to refresh and complicate familiar narratives. Thus, new clothing, styles, fabrics, and so on would be placed on characters with the intention of either refocusing their place in the drama or having the dress propel them away from their anticipated positions. Having staged the collision, so to speak, of one notion of fashion with another, the film leaves the audience, ultimately, to decide how best to make sense of what has happened.

Since the advent of neo-liberalism and economic reform, designers, stars, and their colleagues are apt to point out that fashion has become regularized within film, swapping the edgy eccentricity of early styles for the more realistic ensembles that coincide with a more relaxed familiarity with Western clothing. In fact, for many persons in filmmaking and its related industries, the abstractly adversarial relationship of Western and Indian clothing has disappeared completely, and dress is more a personal choice than a political statement. Steve Derné (2005) has argued that while the upper middle classes and upper classes may have gone along with such a view of dress and morality, most Indians are relatively unmoved by the inducements of film and continue to adhere to standards of decorum that now seem old-fashioned. In the film world, it is the older designers and dressmen from all eras who are most in agreement with this more traditional view, illustrating the kind of philosophical and ethical gap that has opened up between generations and classes. These fashion skeptics belong also to those social categories, described by Leela Fernandes (2000), that covet but cannot always afford the material indulgences of the new economy and who, therefore, remain, wittingly or unwittingly, aloof from them. This differentiation—between a topmost category that is thoroughly at home with contemporary consumerism and lower groups that have limited experience of "shopping"—is very significant for the evolving occupation of costume designing, and it illustrates how a habitus cultivated to be at ease in contemporary metropolitan retail settings has come to supplant one that was adapted to cope with the stresses of material scarcity.

## THE SHOCK OF FASHION

In her analysis of the role of couturiers such as Coco Chanel, Hubert de Givenchy, and Giorgio Armani in film costume design, Stella Bruzzi (1997) argues that the spectacular aspects of the designer outfit confer upon it a degree of autonomy vis-à-vis the other film components, including the star script itself. Unlike the costumes made by the film's designated designer, the couturier garment does not seek to disappear into the narrative but rather seeks to push itself to the forefront of the scene. The scenarios Bruzzi describes do not coincide exactly with those in Bollywood, but the prevalence of personal designers and the historical *frisson* associated with Western clothes (both men's and women's) suggest to me that Bruzzi's argument about the demonstrative possibilities of costume have some applicability in the Indian context. The key here is the connection between fashion (in its limited sense) and modernity.

Film's association with all things modern found sartorial expression, in the industry's early years, in Western clothes for heroes and a wide array of dress possibilities for heroines, as innovations in Indian styles took their place next to other kinds of dress. While the overall flavor of dress was distinctly Gujarati, owing to the number of Gujaratis in the film industry at that time (Bhaumik 2005; Ramamurthy 2008), the leading female stars were arrayed in a variety of striking costumes. The superstar of the 1920s and 1930s Sulochana (the renamed Ruby Myers) wore a striking variety of costumes in roles that ranged from oriental vamp, to demure naïf, to working girl, to sophisticated woman in evening gowns (Bhaumik 2005, 92–4). Similar fashion hybridity was exhibited by Patience Cooper, Jahanara Kajjan and others, merging makeup and hairstyles from the United States with a host of adventurous sari styles (Ramamurthy 2008, 147).

As the 1930s wore on, however, the possibility of women as exemplars of modernity in the Indian context ran up against an emotive and antagonistic view of Indian womanhood nurtured by the Independence movement. An assemblage of images and associations developed around the figure of the true Indian woman: demure, pious, clad in a sari that was becoming increasingly conventional and normalized. In the 1930s, as India's independence struggle against its British occupiers became ever more intense, conventional and conservative versions of the sari began to replace the earlier eclecticism of dress in film, and virtuous women intended for marriage or already in a marriage were almost uniformly dressed in saris. The sari was solidified in the national imagination as an emotive symbol of national aspirations (Bhaumik 2005, 96; Ramamurthy 2008, 163). The value attached to the sari in life and in film gave it a certain aura that seems to transcend history and planted it, ever since, at one end of a scale along which women, and their clothing, have been positioned. In reifying the various forms of Indian dress, independence-minded Indians inevitably consigned certain kinds of clothing to the category of non-Indian, meaning that any intrusion into the realm of the Indian was, according to the logic so ably articulated by Mary Douglas (2002), polluting and dangerous.

In such a context, it was women's Western styles, embodying modernity in their very nature, that henceforth effortlessly earned the label of "fashion," while qualifiers such as "new," "on-trend," or "different" had to be added to Indian clothes to achieve the same effect. The lingering influence of this discrimination emerged clearly in my interviews with dressmen and older designers, in particular, where the word fashion was used not just to set apart the costumes of films of the 1990s and 2000s, but also to draw a line between skirts, trousers, and casual wear, on the one hand, and saris for women and formal suits for men, on the other. Fashion for women, therefore, found its gravitational center the moment one opted for elements of a Western wardrobe, while fashion for men occupied a more nuanced position within Western wear as a whole—a distinction that coincided well with the kinds of moral judgments about bodies and physicality that we saw in the previous chapter.

Dressed in Western clothes from the earliest years, heroes very rarely sought to impress male virtue through the use of Indian costume, even after Independence (Chakravarty 1993; Virdi 2003). In fact, the ubiquity and acceptability of Western clothing for men means there is no readily applicable code of Western versus Indian available to connect virtue to identity via sartorial choice, as there has conventionally been for heroines. Nationalists did include a call to men to discard their suits and trousers in favor of *khadi*, or homespun cotton cloth made up into kurtas, pajamas (Indian-style loose trousers), jackets, and so on of a distinctively Indian character (Bean 1989). Overall, however, efforts to keep Indian men dressed in traditional ways, whether initiated by the British or by anticolonial adherents of *swadeshi* (self-reliance), failed to enlist large numbers of adherents among the middle and upper classes. In sum, while women were prodded toward "signaling radical alterity" in Indian garments, men did the "mimetic labor" of wearing Western clothes (Taussig 1993). At most, a compromise was forged in which men would wear traditional clothes for various ritual occasions and swap the Western clothes they wore in the public domain with Indian styles for the home.

Because it has taken several decades for Western menswear styles to percolate through all of India's social layers, men's clothing communicates more readily about class (and possibly caste) than it does about any other kind of social or cultural characteristic. Films make much of this very point, emphasizing that success in life is sealed by the acquisition of Western-style trousers and shirts, while dhotis and kurtas relegate their wearers to backwardness and poverty. An early scene from Bimal Roy's classic 1953 film *Do Bigha Zamin* shows this power of dress to effect a dramatic change in social status. When the protagonist, Shambo, played by Balraj Sahni, asks his fellow villager about life in the city, the man responds by summing up the wonderful clothes that urbanites wear—"people dress differently [there]; they wear belts around their middle and shoes upon their feet!"

For the most part, the nationalist, noncommunal, and modern identity of the hero has meant that Western clothes, stripped of critical marks of subcultural affiliation, contribute significantly to his effectiveness, the key being the extent to which the hero can be seen to imbibe or exude the Indian values that clothes only treacherously convey. Sumita Chakravarty (1993) points in particular to the "signifiers of dress" alongside "accent and gesture" as the materials films have used to pose questions concerning male subjectivity, questions that, at this point in the book, we should not be surprised to discover are complicated by the knowledge about actors and their personas that film audiences possess. Viewers are thereby alerted to the possibility of making intertextual links between films that, as standalone projects, have no connection (they do not take place within the same diegetic universe, in other words). As a result, actors personalize the conflicts and struggles of life in contemporary India to a striking degree.

The ideas presented above are beautifully exemplified by Raj Kapoor's 1955 film *Shree 420*, named for the section of independent India's penal code that dealt with cheats and frauds. *Shree 420* is one of a number of films of the post-Independence period that articulates a dystopian vision of the city (Mazumdar 2007), and it uses clothing explicitly to give visual shape to the moral relationships it traces (Dwyer 2000b). The story follows the odyssey of everyman Raj (played by Raj Kapoor), whose trek from country to city deposits him amid the worst social parasites and leeches that urban life produces. Raj first appears dressed in a motley arrangement of clothes from countries all over the world, pulled together in a kind of bricolage that might be termed cosmopolitan were it not for the fact that the clothes are poorly fitted, worn out, and, presumably, secondhand. After some setbacks in the city, however, he begins to make good, and he replaces his old clothing accordingly.

Raj's fortunes turn upon his getting a job in, of all places, a laundry, where he is engaged in the repeated and thus unfinished task of removing stains from clothes that is just like the job of removing corruption from the people who wear them. Soon Raj takes advantage of his proximity to the seemingly limitless numbers of suits, shirts, and trousers of the well-off to "borrow" the items he likes and wear them himself. Raj, we are told in unambiguous terms, is trying on new personas via the purloined clothes—he is a nobody trying new ways of being a somebody. In one memorable scene, Raj stands inside the laundry and imagines he sees the suits and shirts flying in a dizzying parade, one after another. Raj Kapoor's narrative purposes, at this point, are served by clothes not just as symbols of an empty materialism to which the new nation is vulnerable, but also as the substantial form in which this materialism is made manifest.

The one beacon of integrity in Raj's life is a woman he meets shortly after his arrival, a self-conscious, slightly awkward heroine, Vidya (a name meaning knowledge), played by Nargis. Vidya is a dependent and dutiful daughter,

**Figure 11** From initial awkwardness at wearing the dress of a more sophisticated and richer man, Raj becomes more at ease, and in so doing, turns into Raj Kapoor (*Shree 420*, 1955, directed and produced by Raj Kapoor). (DVD distributor, Shemaroo Entertainment.)

and she is also every inch the hegemonic, anticolonial, pro-independence feminine ideal, appearing in one scene toward the end of the film wrapped in a sari, the *pallu* drawn over her head and modestly across the torso, like a figure out of a Raja Ravi Varma painting.[2] Positioned opposite her, across the line that demarcates the domain of fashion, is Maya (meaning illusion), played by Nadira. Maya is the manipulative, independent associate of the main villains. Of the costume she designed for the character of Maya, designer Bhanu Athaiya has written that her brief was to "break the norm" (Athaiya 2010), attiring her, for instance, in an asymmetric dress with one shoulder bared, tight bodice, and wide flowing skirt. Maya's norm-breaking continues throughout the film, as she displays her ostentatious jewelry, fiddles with a long cigarette holder, and reveals herself to be both a lover of fashion and a greedy reprobate. She is also extremely seductive to Raj, and her erotic appeal is showcased in two cabaret numbers, one of which sees her wearing a tight, shimmering mermaid dress that suggests all manner of psychoanalytic and symbolic possibilities.

The segregation of the women of the film largely follows expectations with respect to the style of clothes, the use of the body, and the preference for

**Figure 12**  Nadira as Maya wears her norm-breaking dress and smokes a cigarette to boot. Everything about Maya suggests her villainy, but her choice of dress is among the first warnings (*Shree 420*, 1955, directed and produced by Raj Kapoor). (DVD distributor, Shemaroo Entertainment.)

Indian versus Western appearances. As long as both kinds of woman (and both kinds of clothes) were present, pleasure and piety could be harnessed in a single narrative frame, satisfying aficionados of modernity and staunch traditionalists all at once. The transformation effected in Raj by his theft of clothes is, however, considerably more complex. Dressed in a black tuxedo and tie, Raj looks less like a small-time crook in a rich man's costume than he looks like Raj Kapoor himself (Kapoor took the character name Raj repeatedly throughout his career, an unsubtle invitation to read both Kapoor's own star text into each film and to imaginatively link character and star actor-director together). Raj betrays no discomfort in the dress of affluence; on the contrary, he looks as though he were born to it. The implications are many. The character's loss of self comes at the moment of the star's recognition, an intertextual interruption that depends upon audience collusion. Moreover, the emergence of a visually recognizable Raj Kapoor within the Raj character naturally blunts the disquiet concerning Raj's falling away from the path of virtue. How can any viewer believe that Raj Kapoor, the actor and director, is a willing participant in the bankrupt materialism the film seeks to critique? In fact, aside from the obvious villains of the film, one of the enemies of the people that Kapoor singles out is the politician who wears the uniform of nationalist virtue: a *khadi* ensemble of pajamas, kurta, Nehru jacket, and Gandhi cap. Even as the film equivocates on the meanings of Western clothes on men, authorizing them when they appear on the right kinds of people while castigating them as the source of immoral and excessive desires in others, no such critical reflection upon whether clothes are a legitimate externalization of true goodness is applied to women.

Of the female stars in *Shree 420*, Nadira spent much of her career playing negative roles, while Nargis overwhelmingly played heroines. Indeed, her last film, *Mother India* (1957), clinched her position in the national imagination as the ultimate embodiment of female sacrifice and self-abnegation. Early in her career, she appeared in Western-style dresses, including blouses and trousers, in films such as *Andaz* (1949) and *Anhonee* (1952) (playing a double role in the latter); these roles seemed to underscore the association of Western clothing with enabling narcissism and muddying moral boundaries. However, her appearance as the educated and enlightened Rita in *Awaara* (1951)—complete with Western clothes, including, in one daring scene, a swimsuit—inclines rather toward celebrating the commitment and energy of a thoroughly modern woman to both justice and love. This kind of ambiguity recurs throughout the history of Hindi film from mid-century onward, so that, while the normative connection of Westernization with fashion and with moral danger is never completely dissolved, there are still plenty of occasions in which heroines shift between

Indian and Western styles without necessarily being pitched into the realm of the vamp.

This can, in part, be attributed to the stars' (and other members of the privileged classes) own interest in following international consumerist trends, for which they evidently felt no particular embarrassment. In fact, to understand fashion in film means to step back and look more broadly at the media landscape in which fashion and stardom were so skillfully combined.

## MEDIA AND STYLE

For decades, films have been the most widely accessible means of introducing audiences to new styles, ideas, and behaviors. For the literate, there have also been periodicals and magazines, as well as newspapers in which news, commentary, and images facilitated "flows" across the growing global "mediascape" (Appadurai 1990). In the 1950s, editor and publisher Baburao Patel's wonderfully acerbic journal, *Film India*, featured photograph upon photograph of female actors in off-the-shoulder blouses, dirndl skirts, ankle-length slacks, and dressing gowns. Women's magazines in the 1950s printed drawings of dresses that could be copied, as well as film stills and photographs of stars in a variety of outfits. Before she ventured into costume design, Bhanu Athaiya wrote a column for the women's journal, *Femina*, including sketches of women's clothes that drew heavily upon styles featured in foreign (particularly American) films. Later, from the 1960s onward, color magazines such as *Filmfare* spotlighted film costumes in stills from the latest movies, and they began to incorporate articles that were in essence fashion photo shoots featuring prominent film stars. *Star and Style*'s fashion spreads and advertisements in the late 1960s and early 1970s showed stars wearing trouser suits, bell-bottoms, and tunics. As the 1970s transitioned to the 1980s, *Filmfare*'s earlier convention of dressing a major heroine in an elegant sari for a feature or fashion story switched toward outfitting heroines in the casual styles of jeans, blouses, and T-shirts that corresponded to an increasingly informal notion of leisure and private life. In short, at the same time as films continued to roll out the statutory cautions about the dangers of Western mores, for women in particular, *filmi* magazines were dressing up stars in Western garments ostensibly as sources of harmless entertainment.

The media notoriously proffer stories about the "daily life" of stars that are, in fact, meticulously staged. However, ample evidence exists to suggest that stars themselves have been extremely fashion conscious, and have actively sought out novel outfits, either at home or abroad. Athaiya's film career was launched after Kamini Kaushal and Nargis, who patronized her dressmaking business, requested that she make costumes for their film work. Athaiya's book includes photographs of both stars in her creations, and neither one of them is wearing the kind of demure Indian style that typified the modal film heroine (Athaiya 2010).

Male stars appeared in 1950s film magazines in various kinds of suits or trouser-and-jacket combinations. Stars such as Dev Anand acquired a particular reputation for style, with a look that evolved from wide-shouldered suits (reminiscent of American star Gregory Peck, who resembled Anand) in *C.I.D.* (1956), to flared trousers in *Guide* (1965), to cravats and patterned shirts in *Jewel Thief* (1967). Men and women alike used the opportunity of overseas travel to fill up their wardrobes with clothes and accessories that were far too difficult to acquire at home. These forays performed a double function: not only did they allow Indian film stars to claim equality with foreign stars from a sartorial standpoint, but they also ensured a flow of materials and one-off garments that could be integrated into film. Necessity was truly the mother of invention in these instances, and we are compelled to reflect upon the inherently spectacular status of such items, no matter their precise form (or color or texture or other visual and tactile characteristics)—simply because they were, in the Indian context, utterly unique.

## EXCESS AMID AUSTERITY

Inside the complex symbolic economy of fashionable clothing in the era before neo-liberalism, vamps or villains often had to be set apart by being dressed in the most spectacular and even shocking clothes that a film had to offer. The vamp was always an independent figure, assertive, active, and, as a species of femme fatale, a distillation of male fear of female sexuality (Doane 1991). The fact that she almost always failed in her schemes to seduce the hero diminished her power but did very little to alter her position within the moral landscape of the film (Pinto 2006). The love of excess is what united the cabaret-dancing, cigarette-smoking vamp with the other versions of the nefarious female whose plots might be hatched within the bosom of the family. An unashamed love of spectacular clothing and jewelry, the acquisition of such novel accessories as shoulder bags, fur stoles, and cigarette holders—all spoke of a selfish enjoyment of consumption that was openly distinguished from the more measured and tasteful desires of the good Indian woman (Mazumdar 2007, 87; Wilkinson-Weber 2005). At the same time, the rival attractions of the vamp in her fashionable, outrageous clothes and bodily display posed a challenge to the heroine's own embodiment of modernity. Heroine and vamp offered a counterpoint of sorts, but it was not one in which the heroine could merely stay put at the most conservative end of the dress spectrum. As much as the heroine's qualified embrace of fashion seemed to push the vamp to extremes to differentiate herself, so the vamp could also be seen as pulling the heroine toward more audacious expressions of youth, beauty, and joie de vivre.

Two heroines who emerged in the 1970s, Parveen Babi and Zeenat Aman, were among the first and most important performers to play sympathetic characters spanning the bright line separating the decent from the depraved; in time, instead of the negative character having to rise to more shocking extremes to allow the heroine to occupy the domain of fashion and style, the two positions began to draw closer together (Dwyer 2000b; Kabir 2001). Designers such as Mani Rabadi and Xerxes Bhathena (for Zeenat Aman and Parveen Babi, respectively) were being called on to design with an eye to glamour, and soon a new generation of heroines was popping up, both in film and in film and fashion magazines, in costumes that ranged from the eye-catching to the frankly bizarre. Making glamour normative meant that clothes at the farthest edges of fashion teetered into self-parody. This came dramatically to my attention at the National Film Archives in Pune in 2008, as I went through copy after copy of *Filmfare* from the early 1980s to the early 1990s. In no time, it became almost impossible for me to write dispassionately about the clothes in the film stills and fashion spreads on offer. Among the descriptions in my notes are the following: about a feature in the June 1988 issue: "Dimple in leopard-spotted, red skirt with Lycra leggings, boots and a funny hat, and tight black top and shades"; and about a feature in June 1993: "Sridevi in some crazy mess—bodice with yellow sleeves, satin, big headgear like a stuffed bird, fringe like a bordello curtain, harem-like *ghaghara*." This kind of freewheeling bricolage was, to some degree, emblematic of certain trends in 1980s costume that can be identified in other parts of the world. It was also, however, the paradoxical result of having to give material form to flamboyance and splendor in very difficult productive circumstances (a point I return to below).

A comparable attachment to the accoutrements of modernity typified villains. Like vamps, they tended to be sexually aggressive, but unlike them, no opprobrium attached to villains for this reason alone. In fact, it was far easier for a male villain to mislead the other characters as to his true nature, since he tended to favor expensive (or apparently expensive) Western clothing that was the sine qua non of achieved status. Typically played by mature, even middle-aged men, villains could take cynical advantage of signs of respectability—clothes included—in public, while displaying a lack of self-control in their proclivities for physical and sexual violence in private, indications of a fundamental immaturity. The villain's uneven identification with both youth and age is captured in striking ensembles that are well tailored, possibly brightly colored, and steeped in the visual language of power. Villains like to revel in the fabrics, colors, and styles of contemporary fashion, but their wealth and status mean that their style is more studied than the hero's: the suits are sharper, the accessories more expensive and ostentatious.

The villain's tastes may also stray into the bizarre or fantastic, as though the villain neither knows social convention nor cares about it: the costumes of Amrish Puri as Mogambo in 1987's *Mr India* are perhaps the best, but not the only, example of this phenomenon. The character actor Pran, when preparing for a villainous role, was wont to approach his designer and say, "*Itna fantastic getup dena*" (give me such a fantastic getup). Pran's comment here alerts us as well to the implications of the splendid outfitting of the villain from an extratextual standpoint. In the fairly strict division of acting labor by which actors specialize in positive or negative roles, the aging villain comes off somewhat better than the virtuous father figure, enjoying the expertly tailored suit or the splendid, scene-stealing outfit that effaces some, if not all, of the losses associated with an older face and body.

The pleasures to be had in making these kinds of costumes come not just from the creative opportunities involved but also from the skill needed to produce the illusion of luxury. Fortunately, as far as villains were concerned, menswear stores had sunk roots deep enough that they were quite familiar with how to work with and around the material stringencies of pre-1990s India. Madhav's Men's Modes is a menswear store in the suburb of Bandra that brands itself (not without some humor) as a designer for both movie villains and politicians. Madhav Agasti, the proprietor, began his association with film costume at Super Tailor, a well-known costume supplier to the film industry. He started his own business in the mid-1970s, and he began working for Madan Puri in 1976 and, after that, for Madan's brother Amrish Puri, as well as Gulshan Grover, Saeed Jaffery, and Om Puri (Patel and Dugar 2011). The public association of a store with screen villains seems, on the face of it, a detriment, but on reflection, it seems logical enough: since villains often dress very well, to clothe a villain is not just to connect oneself to a select category of Hindi film actors, but also to be able to advertise on a uniquely compelling stage. As I learned:

> [For a] hero, you can take jeans, T-shirts, but in a villain's costume, there is creation; there is a getup in the villain's dress and different types of dress only

villains use in movies. Villains are using bright colors; in public, they're [ordinary people] not using bright colors.

Agasti perceptively noted that the villain's look not only varies from film to film but also is the costume that is least affected by whatever anyone else is wearing. Admittedly, with several personal designers employed on a film, the degree of collaboration is always subject to chance (as I have already discussed). But Agasti's point is well taken, for the idiosyncrasy of the villain's costume could be regarded as itself an expression of the villain's egoism.

By implication, the menace of villainy stalks any and all dress innovation that appears in a film, a conundrum that filmmakers were all too aware of in the decades following Independence. Stars such as Dev Anand, Shammi Kapoor, and Raaj Kumar all appeared in roles in which an uncertain moral compass coincided with a choice of fashionable clothes. When jeans started being worn by stars (long before they became acceptable for most Indians to wear), they were, as in Hollywood, "endlessly adapted to the creation of new genders and sexualities" (Rabine and Kaiser 2006, 236). Even though, in public life, jeans wearers were generally among the affluent, in film, jeans were fitting signifiers for characters testing or even transgressing social norms (Wilkinson-Weber 2011, 53). These included Dharmendra in a denim ensemble as Veeru, the petty criminal turned hero in the 1975 film *Sholay*, as well as the new superstar of film, Amitabh Bachchan, in several movies that showcased his "angry young man" characterization. Viewed in light of the equivocal meaning of new styles, Bachchan's embodiment of the working-class antihero, dressed in jeans and wide-lapelled shirts (or the natty suits, bow ties, and flared trousers that went along with his character's rise in the criminal ranks), appears less singular. Stylish clothes had always carried with them the possible taint of corruption; emotion and action were ultimately what set the hero apart. When the pendulum swung back in favor of feudal melodramas and youthful romances in the 1990s, the new forms of dress added to the hero's repertoire in the 1970s and 1980s were not lost but were instead incorporated into an ever-wider range of dress possibilities.

For the heroine to co-opt the vamp, she needed to be elevated to a higher class of woman whose education and worldliness buffered the ill effects of "dangerous" clothing. The hero's trajectory was a little different. On some occasions, this might mean going in the opposite direction from the heroine to appropriate the street tough or gangster with a heart of gold by wearing leather vests and jackets, boots, string vests, and motorbike caps (Mazumdar 2007). On others, the hero (often an NRI or a person of Indian heritage who lives abroad) would occupy such rarefied environments of wealth and

**Figure 13** A scene from the huge hit film *Sholay* (1975, directed by Ramesh Sippy, produced by G.P. Sippy) shows both Amitabh Bachchan and Dharmendra, the stars, wearing denim clothes. They play a pair of small-time crooks who come to the rescue of a village preyed upon by a vicious bandit. (DVD distributor, Eros International.)

privilege that there was scarcely any light between him and the erstwhile fabulously rich and Westernized villain.

What is so surprising, given the overtly spectacular forms that were developed for negative female and male characters, is that almost all had to be done in circumstances of considerable financial and material stringency. Before the 1980s, high-quality ready-made clothes were hard to come by in India, and in consequence, the majority of costumes were handmade from scratch. Undergarments had to be made to order, and fabric had to be carefully hoarded since replacements would be hard to come by—in effect, the logic of material scarcity underscored the uniqueness of certain costumes for which no true duplicate could be made. The very substance of glamour had to be constructed from small bolts of material that might never be encountered again, from the imaginative reuse of accessories and jewelry from film to film, and from the collaboration of craft specialists in dyeing, stitching, and embroidering who were scattered all over the city. That glamour teetered on the top of a very fragile infrastructure, in which time and materials were always in short supply, makes it even more striking that such extraordinary and norm-breaking outfits were ever made at all. Ironically, it is only when off-the-rack outfits and a range of fabrics and dress ideas become more readily available that glamour begins to give way to forms of realism that categorically reject everything *filmi*.

Meanwhile, Indian film stars were not so thoroughly immersed in the endorsement and enjoyment of Westernized modernity that they lacked familiarity with and affinity for practices that were emphatically coded Indian. Coverage of weddings showed that they wore the customary dress for such occasions, and while formal wear for men was de rigueur at industry events, women almost always appeared in public in elegant saris. In fact, heroines were more likely to drive fashion trends via a degree of play with the silhouette, fabric, and decorative features of saris, *salwar kameezes, ghagharas*, and the like than they were through wearing striking, but for most Indian women unwearable, Western styles. The incorporation of these forms into a fashion sensibility is the topic I turn to next.

## FASHIONING TRADITION

One of the most interesting points of intersection between fashion as modern style and fashion as a larger system of meanings and embodiments comes in film's experimentation with forms of women's dress, such as the sari and the *salwar kameez*. Although film is not the only arena within which these kinds of ventures have been launched, its reach and influence make it the preeminent source of dress innovation as far as its viewers are concerned. Indeed, the normalization of the *salwar kameez* as a suitable garment for young and professional women can be attributed, in part, to film's co-option and development of the form. Initially thought of as the dress of Muslims, Punjabi Hindus, or Sikhs, the *salwar kameez* began to grow in popularity in the 1960s and 1970s with the emergence of the "college girl"—an overtly modern middle-class to upper-class heroine who had a university education. The *salwar kameez* is essentially composed of loose pants, a tunic (which may be of varying lengths), and a *dupatta*, or scarf. Variations include swapping the loose *salwar* for *churidar*, or tight, gathered pants, or more recently, adopting leggings under the *kameez*. Its modest character and ease of wear have caused the *salwar kameez* to gradually outstrip the sari as acceptable dress for both younger and older women, unmarried and married, in the middle classes in North India (Dwyer and Patel 2002, 88).

A *churidar* worn with a *kameez* was almost instantly popularized by the 1965 film *Waqt*, whose heroines (played by Sadhana and Sharmila Tagore) appeared in every scene in either a new sari or a new *salwar* or *churidar* suit, close-fitting around the upper torso and streamlined from the hip to the

**Figure 14**  The dresses worn by Sadhana (with her famous hairstyle) and Sharmila Tagore in *Waqt* (1965, directed by Yash Chopra, produced by B.R. Chopra) revolutionized the use of *salwars* and *churidars*, which thereafter became far more popular as respectable, neutral dress for unmarried women. Pictured with Sadhana here are Raaj Kumar and Sunil Dutt, both playing men with a distinct sense of style (in both clothing and American cars). (DVD distributor, Moserbaer Entertainment.)

knee. The film's strong visual aesthetic, with its almost fetishistic regard for cars, clothes, and the very latest word in household commodities (circular beds, trendy rotary phones, glossy magazines), helped reinforce the idea that Indian styles, skillfully adapted, could fit comfortably in a modern lifestyle. Subsequently, designers experimented further with the cut and color of the different parts of the suit, or with the interplay of the *dupatta* and other elements of the ensemble. Examples include Rekha's *churidar* and kurta outfits in *Silsila* (1981), Sridevi's white-accented *salwar kameez* in *Chandni* (1989), and Dimple Kapadia's "ethnic-chic" *churidar* kurtas and *salwar kameez* with *dupattas* in *Dil Chahta Hai* (2001).

With respect to the sari, variation came from using new fabrics, adopting unusual regional styles, or making dramatic modifications to the body of the sari fabric itself—such as cutting away existing borders and replacing them with new ones or dyeing the sari length a new color. Several older designers alluded to the unmatched capacity of chiffon to fall flatteringly and confer a lightness and linearity to the body; in the blunt terms of *Shila*, a woman who had happened upon costume design by chance and worked on a several films in the early 1990s:

**Figure 15**  Both Sharmila Tagore and Sadhana wear a different sari or salwar kameez in every scene in *Waqt* (1965, directed by Yash Chopra, produced by B.R. Chopra), a foreshadowing of continuous costume changing in later films from the 1970s and 1980s. (DVD distributor, Moserbaer Entertainment.)

I used to give the chiffon more to the ladies, because they always look fat, no? Everybody wants to look slim, so I won't give much cotton or silk; silk will make you fat, cotton will make you more fat. If you give chiffon, it will be very different. Chiffon, a nice border, border on neck or sleeve, it makes a different look.

Designers generally took on the task of designing clothes for both on-screen and offscreen appearances by their stars, in effect facilitating the fashionable images that stars were keen to cultivate.

Men's clothing presented far fewer difficulties, but the skewing of fashion toward more youthful, casual forms in the 1970s was not without its challenges for the Indian film costume supplier. By the mid-1970s, young urban male characters, no matter their class position, dressed in the casual clothing that came to the fore in the West with the various style upheavals of the 1960s. The urban, working-class antiheroes of the high-water mark of Amitabh Bachchan's career (in films such as *Sholay* [1975], *Deewaar* [1975], and *Coolie* [1983]) were dressed in slacks or jeans, a shirt, and a denim jacket, not in a dhoti or pajamas and a kurta. Denim—in jackets, but mostly in the form of jeans— was by far the foremost winner in the realignment of fashion after the 1960s, displacing other fabrics as the quintessential marker of contemporary style. Since India was then, and remains, a major manufacturer and global supplier of denim, there was no obvious obstacle to mainstreaming denim jeans for both film stars and film viewers. Conservatism in public life played a role in slowing the appropriation of jeans as fashion, as did opinions that elevated foreign brands over local ones. In fact, the studied fascination of recent years with well-established global brands originates with these early concerns, since jeans were almost never given out to a tailor to make from scratch but were bought ready-made (Wilkinson-Weber 2011).

## NEO-LIBERALISM AND AFTER

### Commodity Capitalism, Realism, and Altered Sartorial Forms

The arrival of foreign goods, including brand-label clothing, and media and advertising industries ready to show and promote them destabilized the system of film fashion (in its broader sense) more profoundly than any previous event or process. Contemporary designers, journalists, and other film professionals currently active were united in locating the beginnings of change in the 1980s with the diversification of the media environment—the availability of cable television, the growth in the advertising and publishing businesses. This diversification, they felt, gave middle-class and upper-class Indians an exposure to global trends in fashion and lifestyle that primed them to accept the new trends in dress and design that grew apace in the 1990s.

There is nothing new in Bollywood critics blaming films for their lack of realism, as though realism were the only standard by which cinematic quality ought to be measured. However, the particular spin on realism that the new crop of designers shares doesn't simply request that directors and actors put less stress on overacting or that films have fewer songs; instead, it attempts to plant characters inside worlds that are imaginable within postliberalization India, advocates greater attention to continuity, and seeks to create the impression of a film character as a person who does not wear a new dress every day but rewears, recombines, and revitalizes clothing items in each succeeding scene. This kind of realism demands, as a prerequisite, a more careful accounting of what costumes have been made, what has been worn, and when costumes will be needed again. Permeating all is a discourse of characterization and realism that justifies a rebalance of workloads and responsibilities as a sign of maturity in the industry, the long-awaited professionalization whose absence afflicted all films until the present.

Farhan Akhtar's 2001 film *Dil Chahta Hai* exemplifies the sort of realism that has now become an index of "quality" in the industry. The film came up repeatedly in my interviews with contemporary designers, ADs, costume assistants, and others as one in which the actors wore "real" clothes. Significantly, it was among the first of recent films aimed narrowly toward a metropolitan, upper-middle-class audience. *Dil Chahta Hai* is a ruminative, loosely structured film about three well-educated, affluent friends in Mumbai; the film does not draw on the connective threads of kin or community to either unite or divide them. The elements of stock Bollywood plotting are not entirely abandoned; Akash (Aamir Khan) and Shalini (Preity Zinta) overcome obstacles on the path to love, and tormented divorcée Tara Jaiswal (Dimple Kapadia), as the older lover of Siddharth (Akshaye Khanna), is doomed to die. The realism of *Dil Chahta Hai* relates less to certain narrative points than it does to the naturalistic style of acting, the thematic focus on the personal and psychological struggles of three upper-middle-class men, and above all, the determined attachment of all three men to the conventions of global fashion. Designer Arjun Bhasin, who has gone on to be the sole designer for many films, including those of Mira Nair, was reported to be determined "to get away from the big disaster of film styling till then—the matching look" (Gahlaut 2004, 60)—in other words, the singular combination of a set of garments into one outfit with jewelry and accessories. Keeping on top of continuity had meant previously that all the elements of a costume for a particular scene were stored together, with no piece being broken out to appear with another element, even though ordinary people regularly put certain accessories and ornaments with different combinations of clothing. However, "now, the same pair of trousers will be seen in different scenes, only put together with different elements" (Gahlaut 2004, 60).

Later in the 2000s, a shift back toward subaltern characters in at least some films allowed the experimentation with realism to develop further. Films depicting urban criminal gangs or political corruption in small towns and rural areas cracked open a space for costume design that directs itself to the minutely observed life of the ordinary person, rather than spectacular fantasy. This is costume realism in its sincerest form, and it returns heroines to *salwar kameezes* and saris (for example, Mahie Gill as Parminder in *Dev D* [2009] or Priyanka Chopra as Sweety in *Kaminey* [2009]), in recognition of the reality in India that the vast majority of women have not taken on the dress conventions of the well to do and very rich. The same stipulations of female beauty apply, but now actors can anticipate being asked to wear a wider variety of costumes over their careers than ever before. Vituperative comments about the poor state of film costuming from present-day designers are aimed squarely (if not consciously) at the outfits that were put on actors in the 1980s, the era that directly preceded neo-liberalism and that filmmakers today are most concerned with distancing themselves from. The general sentiment is summed up in this statement from designer *Laila*, and who has worked on prestigious projects for decades: "I find that there's too much escapism. I do understand that you need to have a certain element of glamour, but I sometimes find that over the top." It is only fair to repeat, however, that by present-day standards, costumes of the 1980s from almost any film industry look overstated and gaudy, and Bollywood costumes just pushed to an extreme trends that were very plain elsewhere.

Returning for a moment to *Dil Chahta Hai*, the impression of constant costume change borrowed from earlier films remains to some extent, in keeping with the effortlessly easy access to money and commodities the characters all share; in other respects, however, the clothes are generally understated and extremely casual, except for when Akash is shown wearing suits at his office. The result is that the self-consciously *filmi* costumes in the film's song sequences are even more striking than they would be otherwise. From this point onward, more and more instances of parody and irony crop up in the song sequences of other films, leavening the realism of the rest of the film with a distinct set of occasions in which fantasy and excess can be expressed. Spectacle, in other words, complete with disruptive and demonstrative costume, is increasingly diverted exclusively into the song sequences, where high-fashion outfits, fantasy costumes, and imagined spaces can be compiled. Self-reflective devices such as these have allowed designers in the 2000s to have their cake and eat it too, since they can indulge in *filmi* excess while investing it with a deep sense of irony and still have their realist costumes that function identically with costumes as professionally (and ideally) conceived in American and European cinema.

## Taming Western Clothing

As in the past, stars have been critical to mediating the new consumerism, through their own engagement with clothes, cars, interior decor, and so on. In particular, the connection between the film and fashion worlds has become tighter, as more entrants to the film industry emerge from modeling or beauty pageant backgrounds and, in turn, stars attach themselves to up-and-coming designers and take on high-value brand endorsements. For some, fashion was so significant a component of their professional activities that they were transforming from mere film stars into media celebrities. Nurturing a professional relationship with a film designer who has fashion training and experience, as well as ongoing projects in the apparel business, presented obvious advantages to a new generation of stars, particularly given the relaxation of standards for dress propriety in films. So important does the designer become as image consultant, adviser, beautifier, and moral supporter that actors may insist on the services of their favorite designer as forcefully as they have argued in the past for a particular tailor. Organizationally speaking, this is where conflict can arise between the drive toward realism via hiring a single costume designer and the personal and commercial interests of a star. When Karisma Kapoor returned to the screen in *Dangerous Ishhq* (2012), she insisted that Manish Malhotra, who had done her costumes for countless films and helped direct a makeover earlier in her career, would design her clothes for the film. Asked to explain this, the director Vikram Bhatt said that, "Nidhi Yasha [the film's designated dress designer] would now be researching Karisma's clothes. Manish would actually be designing them" (Jha 2011). This attempt at a diplomatic statement revealed that the solution was to break apart what are typically fused claims to knowledge based on research, on the one hand, and design based on aesthetic refinement, on the other. The expectation that a star's dress designer would do his or her clothes, whether or not the other actors have their own designer, has been so entrenched in the industry previously that it did not even seem worth noting. That a director would feel the need to speak out about it hints at a growing unease at prevailing custom in the industry, even though it by no means suggests that the practice is likely to go away soon.

Uncompromising commitment to fashion that passes muster on a global stage has gone hand in hand with marked change in the ways in which heroines are evaluated for wearing it. The mainstreaming of Western clothes that Aman and Babi initiated had, by the turn of the twenty-first century, led to a situation in which there was little the heroine could wear (or not wear, as the case may be) that compromised her position as a moral actor within the film—or jeopardized her right to wear the emblem of virtuous Indian womanhood, a sari. The increasingly matter-of-fact inclusion of jeans, T-shirts, blouses, and Western dresses in films since the 1990s differs substantially from earlier films. Shifts in the standards of what is considered appropriate dress among young upper-middle-class and upper-class women in India's metropolises are apparent to anyone who pays attention to such things, and altered conventions have both fed and feed upon the sartorial conventions that Bollywood seems now to identify with.

## Styling

Locating designer expertise in the fashion industry, specifically knowledge of brands and a sense of the pulse of global fashion, marks a departure from opting for an arts-educated personal designer and, for male stars, the menswear store. Sourcing overseas apparel has evolved from ad hoc trawling of boutiques and marketplaces as opportunity arose to well-planned and purposive shopping trips to the United States, Europe, Dubai, and Bangkok, where one can also easily pick up high street labels such as Zara and Topshop, as well as jeans and other casual clothes. Alongside the appearance of designers with active fashion and film careers has come increasing use of the term "styling." There are three distinct meanings of styling that I can identify. The first is a narrative and aesthetic sensibility that informs a character's look throughout the film. A second meaning, closely related to the first, is a sense of style, in that costumes associated with styling are fashionable as judged by the standards of the global industry. The final meaning of styling is that it involves buying off-the-rack clothes (whether brand-label or not) and combining them to make a series of outfits, as opposed to crafting a costume from scratch and having it stitched. Whichever definition one chooses, styling effectively connects film to larger global flows of fashion and commodity goods.

Designer Manish Malhotra says of styling that he brought it into play with the film *Rangeela* (1995) by working out a look for star Urmila Matondkar that was consistent with her character throughout the film, rather than designing ad hoc creations that spoke only (and sometimes bizarrely) to the scene in question (Team MissMalini 2013). Matondkar's appearance as Mili in *Rangeela*, a story of a young woman's dream to become a film star, transformed her career. Her character was shown juggling bohemian ensembles of hats, blouses, and pants with dramatic, off-the-shoulder dresses, leotards and leggings, and cleavage-baring bikinis tops and slit skirts. Opposite her, Aamir Khan played a *tapori* (a streetwise tough) character whose efforts to impress Mili—in, for instance, a loud and frankly *filmi* yellow suit—were played entirely for laughs.

It is not entirely clear that thinking about characters in terms of styling is as new as designers make it out to be, if we take styling to mean the assignment of visual and audible motifs to characters or the cultivation of a certain sustained appearance. But we can tell that the reason for stressing styling is that it implies a preproduction process and a degree of thinking through an entire film that seems far more organized and deliberative than common practices in films of old. And as for styling as the use of already finished items combined to make film costumes, this is by no means unusual from a comparative perspective. American and European productions regularly

**Figure 16**    Urmila Matondkar as Mili and Aamir Khan as Munna in *Rangeela* (1995, directed and produced by Ram Gopal Varma). Mili is a free spirit and wears a variety of offbeat clothes, including these pajamas. (DVD distributor, Pathfinder Home Entertainment.)

involve a "build" (the making of costume from scratch) alongside both shopping and "pulling" (the use of costumes from costume shops). The use of ready-made, off-the-rack items within styling is now a standard element in the design briefs of young designers and costume assistants, and it requires a knowledge of "how to shop" that calls especially upon the kinds of knowledge and expertise that young, upper-middle-class men and women are likely to have (Wilkinson-Weber 2010a).

The term styling has come into wide use alongside the rise of a figure specifically designated a stylist. Articles in the media sometimes use stylist and designer interchangeably (Screen Weekly 2007), but actual designers and stylists are fairly clear about how they differ. Unlike a stylist in Europe or North America, whose job it is to dress stars for various industry events, the Hindi film stylist is, in essence, a costume specialist who primarily makes up a film wardrobe from shopping rather than from conceiving a new set of clothes entirely. Some designers farm out styling jobs to their employees. Designer Krishna, whose fashion and film career began in the 1990s, explains:

> I'm not looking to chase the pants and the jeans and do that kind of a movie, like you notice there is this kind of requirement which is very basic, so my assistant is working on it, and he gets his commission. I just kind of sit here and supervise it: "No, this isn't correct, this is correct. Go." So he gets his commission, he's happy, he's learning work, and yet I'm putting in my little two bits to it. I won't even go for the meeting, I won't go for the shoot, but it's happening, it's happening under my name. Because there is nothing for me to do in it, *na*? What am I supposed to do when they want like two leather jackets, and two denim shirts,

and two straight jeans. All the boy has to do is fit them together. I just tell him what to wear with what.

That anyone would call this something other than designing (when it commonly is considered designing in other film industries) can reflect only the newness of such practices in India. I met several stylists toward the end of my fieldwork, when the role was beginning to become more common. They were very similar in background to costume assistants: English-speaking, middle class, but tending to have in mind a future in production rather than designing. *Lisa*, a stylist since 2005, explained that "I do accessories, go to a jewelry designer to get accessories, or get bags, scarves, but I do not create my own clothes." She also noted that "as stylists, we have an advantage over designers; we can shop, we can tailor, even designer items, we can do those," implying that conceding a degree of authorship over the design conferred upon stylists a flexibility that made them a better fit for certain films.

A certain skepticism prevailed among older designers about stylists, however; these designers felt there was nothing special about "people who just go and pick up a lot of stuff" or "go and pick up branded clothes all over the place, and they put the actors in them." Designers, their assistants, and stylists were adept at identifying and sorting through various labels, from luxury brands all the way to mass-market examples, whose significance evaded older designers and lower status costume specialists without the requisite consumer experience to know about these kinds of products. Film professionals everywhere are prone to feel abandoned or neglected as they age and retire (this may be the case in other industries as well). However, the rhetoric that surrounds the shifts in design purposes and strategies in the Indian context casts particular light on changes in both the film industry and its surrounding commercial and cultural environment.

## Fashion Critiques

Older designers need little encouragement to dismiss new designers as superficial arrivistes, and new designers need no more encouragement to castigate older designers as uninformed vulgarians. These are categorical rather than individual charges, involving grossly simplistic notions of how the other group designs. Thus, they are not to be taken as entirely factual statements about how film costume and fashion have evolved in the past twenty years or so. The intrinsic philosophies of design, as well as of what films are or should be, are valuable in the extreme, however. New designers pointed a finger at over-the-top costume mélanges they took to be ill-judged attempts at doing fashion on the part of amateurish designers with no idea at all about fashion. Their own role, as new designers see it, is to remake film fashion from the standpoint of professionals who wish to correct and improve what passed for fashion in older films. One important change is that contemporary stars have become more informed about dress and look. As a result, as one new designer put it, they can "relate to the clothes we are giving them." "Relatableness" also stems from the close connection of many stars to designers as people from the same social group and with many of the same tastes and interests. It is not at all uncommon for film costume designers to also have their own fashion retail and couture businesses; examples include Neeta Lulla, Abu-Sandeep (Abu Jani and Sandeep Khosla), Vikram Phadnis, and Manish Malhotra. Their film work is featured on their websites alongside seasonal collections and ready-to-wear lines.

In the North American industry, the integration of brands has become so standard in the provision of costumes that costume designers get a star's brand preferences along with his or her measurements when they are signed to a film. In India, personal designers already know the brands their stars prefer, and so, it is not necessary to formalize their use. However, when a star becomes a brand ambassador, the expectation is that the star will wear that brand's clothes whenever he or she can. For the appropriate credit, the company will provide clothes for a film; in turn, stars will expect that the brand will used in the costuming whenever possible, even if the brand is so costly that the characters wearing the clothing could never afford it. This is one way in which the ever-narrowing distance between the high-class brand and the cheap imitation can be superseded and a distinction asserted in the environs of the set and within the industry generally, particularly if the favored brands for a Bollywood star are still hard to obtain within India. As for the latest crop of designers, none denied that there is a distinct dissonance in a lower-middle-class character wearing Armani, for example, but with the renewed stress on the values of realism, the task then is to get the designer garment to submit to the overall characterization and not assert itself on screen autonomously, as couture can do (Bruzzi 1997).

These observations notwithstanding, older designers refuse to acknowledge that film costume design could legitimately use items already stitched and finished, arguing instead for the superior value of clothes made especially for a film—and for its stars. The arrival of ready-made and label clothing has led those who remember working before there were as many retail resources are there are now to grumble that design today is little more than throwing together a few articles of clothing, and "what's the design in that?" What older designers may not know is that contemporary designers do not

**Figure 17**  Inside the Infiniti Mall in suburban Mumbai, Indian chain stores cluster next to boutiques and global brand outlets. (Image courtesy of Clare Wilkinson-Weber.)

necessarily shop for a garment and put it "as is" on the star. Like the Hollywood designers interviewed by Miranda Banks (2009) in Los Angeles, several said they liked to play with the costume, adding patches or appliqué and, in general, modifying the original in distinct ways, as well as altering the garment to give a snugger and more flattering fit. For these purposes, ready-mades work particularly well. *Lisa*, the self-professed stylist explained:

> If I want a white shirt, I know it's readily available, and I won't get it stitched. Casual wear, T-shirts, maybe if after buying it I want to do something on it, to make it different, I will cut it or add sequins to it, do some patchwork. Stuff that is readily available, I would rather buy it than get it stitched. Stitching would cost me more.

The need to adapt and modify the clothes in order to become costume is, in the case of the American designers, intrinsic to the argument that costume is not fashion. It is also a way by which the designer asserts his or her own authorship against that of the designer of the purchased garment.

Old designers in Bollywood are unmoved by these arguments, mostly, I suspect, because of the close connection of ready-mades to Western and casual fashion that was common when these designers were in their heyday. In the present day, older designers' disdain for ready-mades could readily be channeled into a quasi-nationalist debate about the abandonment of Indian styles for now-ubiquitous Western clothes. New designers I interviewed, on the other hand, were concerned to bring themselves (and stars and audiences) into alignment with what they considered to be global norms of taste and behavior, elevating India from a position of unreflective mediocrity to one of equality and sophistication. Without being fully aware of it, both old and new designers are debating what it means to be Indian, with the kind of approach forged by the independence struggle being challenged by a new one that embraces corporatism, business, globalization, and the diminution of the state.

## What the Dressman Knows

Another probative area of differentiation and divergence is that between designer, stylist, or costume assistant and dressman. Previously, when dressmen were given more responsibility for sourcing costumes, it was a simple matter for them to engage tailors or visit menswear shops to get the suits, shirts, and trousers stars desired. However, when it comes to the delicate business of tracking down the brands with the most cultural capital or fashioning the most up-to-date look—complete with hairstyle and all necessary accessories—the dressman is at a distinct disadvantage. Few designers or their assistants would trust a dressman to exercise his own judgment in buying fashionable clothes in the marketplace; on the contrary, they regard dressmen as reluctant to change and irrationally devoted to old norms. To designers, dressmen are too inclined to render service to stars over doing what is best for the film, they lack imagination and willingness to change, and they spend too much time ironing. This last point is one on which designers and dressmen are unknowingly in complete agreement. In general, however, dressmen see their problem being not that they fail to understand the professional obligations of film costume; far from it. Instead, they are upset at their experience and knowledge being summarily dismissed.

The beginnings of this de-skilling of the dressman were apparent in 2002, but by 2010, several dressmen spoke in strikingly similar tones about what they saw going on around them. First, here is *Dev*, a dressman since 1985 on many top-tier film productions:

> Dressmen also had authority of designing and giving his viewpoints, also directors used to listen. They had creativity in their hands. Today, we can also do [such things], but now, every movie has a designer, and we are under them. We just

have to follow their instructions. We can do this [the things that designers do] but we don't have the authority. We get to earn under them.

Ravi, who entered the field 15 years before *Dev*, echoed the same sentiments:

We used to have meetings with the director, and they used to tell us about the script. In Indian style, our dresses are fixed—for example, the village girl or boy or *sarpanch* [head] of the village or the city girl. Now everything is handled by designers. The scope of dressmen has [been] reduced a lot.

For productions big and small, engaging a designer (with or without significant experience) has become practically a norm, leaving the dressman in an uncertain position. Since there has been no effort to create a costume department, as discussed in Chapter 1, no formal efforts seem to have been made anywhere in the industry to formalize a professional job description for dressmen. As a result, they are relegated to lower-status maintenance tasks, such as mending clothes, aging clothes, washing clothes, and so on, as opposed to the higher-status work of creation.

A class and linguistic divide prevents dressmen from finding ready ways to enhance and extend their position and responsibilities. Few dressmen speak English, and even fewer speak it well. The importance of speaking English had become clear to dressmen by 2010; as Ravi stated:

We don't have education, and so we are left behind. When we get our [association] card and come out to work in the industry, we are not able to talk properly to them [directors, actors], we're not able to convince [them] about our ideas, we can't speak English. All the fashion designers come in to the business after they finish their education and can speak very good English, and so they directly go close to the hero and heroine and can talk with them very nicely. Our dressmen are uneducated, and so they don't get ahead. They get scared to go and talk to big people on the sets. Not [being] educated is their weakness even if they know their work.

It is not only in limited educational qualifications and ignorance of English that dressmen fail to impress themselves upon the "creative" members of the film industry. I have argued elsewhere that the dressman's main disadvantage comes not from any deficiency as a worker, but rather from his deficiency as a consumer: the dressman does not participate in the practices of learning about brands, buying brands, and so on that are part and parcel of the dress designer's and the costume assistant's daily lives (Wilkinson-Weber 2010a). It is not that dressmen have failed to change at all: like other working men in the city, dressmen have moved away from a preference for neatly pressed, synthetic pants and a kurta top in favor of jeans and either a shirt or T-shirt. But subtle matters of fit and glaring matters of brand combine to mark the dressman's tastes as symptomatic of his class, and in an industry where design is predicated upon enlightened consumption, these tastes present themselves as a defect.

Informally, even covertly, however, dressmen continue to exert an influence on certain kinds of costuming. First, they still take the lead in dressing junior artists and actors in small character parts—actors and roles that the designer is not paid to envision and is often uninterested in, in any case. *Dev* explained that "only us dressmen know which trunk has which *patialas* (a variety of *salwar*) or skirts and so on, and also because it is old clothes and now neither the designer nor the star are interested in them, so we decide about what to do with them." Second, the dressman's reputation as a miracle worker who can fix problems at the last minute remains a source of considerable pride, and in speaking about these eventualities, dressmen emerge as figures full of subterfuge and trickery, quick thinking, and a certain disdain for those costume specialists who presume to know more than they do. Finally, opportunities still arise for dressmen to upstage their social superiors on the set and in exposing the vacuity of brand attachments. What dressmen have come to realize—or perhaps it is just that they are unconcerned to keep up a conceit they feel is hollow—is that a high-status brand can be called upon to pass as the dress of a street tough when a star demands it. Conversely, an article obtained from a street market or a local tailor can sometimes be used to do duty as a brand item. Dressmen use this knowledge (often in collusion with a producer) to make duplicates or replace costumes without having to pay designer-label prices. The entire scheme might unfold as follows, according to *Dev*:

> The producer is in charge of payment. He'll give 10,000 rupees and will say that you get ten T-shirts, two to three [should] come from the designer, but we need ten. If he [the actor] wants to wear all ten, let him. Then, we go to the market. We say to them that we might make an exchange later [taking items now and taking them back if both unwanted and unspoiled]. We show it to artist. We don't tell them that we've bought it [from the market] We tell them that the designer sent it. They look over the shirts; they say, give this back, give that back. . . . Some go back to the designer, others go back to the market. But some he keeps—and those will be designer *and* marketplace T-shirts, all in together.

In these stories, the dressman and producer are painted as the truly perceptive agents in the whole process, affording the dressman a connection to the upper levels of the filmmaking operation that circumvents the designer and actor altogether, as seen in this exchange, also with *Dev:*

> Q—The big brands, T-shirts or shirts like a Versace shirt and an ordinary shirt have no difference so do you interchange them?
>
> A—Yes (laughs).
>
> Q—The designers do that?
>
> A—Even some of the designers don't get to know. We worked for one producer, there was one particular shirt, for 3,000 rupees; it was a big star's, 3,500 to 4,000 rupees it was; he chose it. . . . Then, they sent word back to Gabbana's— what they needed they got from there, three to four of them. After that, the producer said to us, [if] you buy any more of that shirt, who would know if it was Gabbana's or someone else's? So we bought it in the market for 800 rupees.

The dressman and producer find common cause in a commitment to frugality and a respect for the ability to make do with whatever is available— qualities endorsed by dressmen (and older designers) time and again. While designers are busy bringing costume in line with the realities of a global fashion marketplace, which may mean incorporating real labels and designer outfits into their costuming, dressmen are essentially arguing for the continued validity of inscribing status on screen theatrically—that is, through performative sleight of hand.

Dressmen also have some acute observations about the ironies of branded clothing. A dressman on location in London described going to buy, at his wife's request, an umbrella to bring home with him. He found one for £4.50, but "it was marked 'Made in India.' Here, I could give you five umbrellas for that; there, it was four and a half pounds for just one." And following on from that observation, he continued, "A Christian Dior T-shirt, the people who have sewn this, they live in China. The T-shirt you get in the bazaar was made by people in India. If you get it here, the work stays in India."

Designers are not oblivious to these arguments, with many of them agreeing about the absurdity of demanding a foreign label or a particular item of clothing with a brand name on it when a perfectly good alternative can be purchased at home. Arguing along similar lines as the dressman, a young designer/stylist grumbled to me:

> If you go to London, there is H&M; the clothes say Made in India, but this star will say, I want clothes from H&M. But you are paying four times the price just because it is from H&M. But most stuff is made here!

Let us suppose that an illicit swap is to be done that must be concealed from the actor. It is usually the dressman who does it. After he visits a tailor or a cheap ready-made store, he then does some clever "faking" of a label (even going so far as to sew in a designer "tag"), he launches into an accomplished piece of verbal persuasion, and the garment finds its way on to the actor's body. By this stage, the costume is, if we take the notion of extended person-hood seriously, busy pretending to be a brand pretending to be an ordinary garment. Whether this is a harder trick to pull off than a designer shirt pretending to be one bought off the street at a bargain price cannot be decided separately from the ability of the actor to make the clothed character convincing.

Who knows or does not know about costume swaps, and what difference it makes whether they know or not, may be hard to determine. In the end, it is entirely possible that the actor is the only one kept purposely in the dark about illicit swaps in which a low-status manufactured garment takes the place of a more-vaunted one. This makes perfect sense, since a star's desire for labels is not simply a frivolous excuse to spend money, but, as I noted before, a sensitive measure of the star's prestige vis-à-vis other actors and

**Figure 18** Western global brands, both refined and comparatively mundane, have found a niche since the economic liberalization of the 1990s. Here is a Wrangler denim outlet in Bandra, Mumbai. (Image courtesy of Clare Wilkinson-Weber.)

other film personnel. If a small "con job" of persuasion is all one needs to keep the actors on an even keel, then filmmakers will reason that it is entirely worth it.

## Restyling the Traditional

Finally, dressmen confide that they are often approached by designers for advice on how to dress certain kinds of regional, historical, or working-class characters—what kind of kurta might they wear or how would their *pagdis* and dhotis be tied?—the very clothes for men that fashion in the form of Western menswear pushed to the margins. Filmmakers could go as well to dresswalas for their input on these questions, but the dressman is nearer to hand and tends to have some of the same knowledge. Ravi's complaint stands in well for others of this type:

> When they [designers] face problems, they come to us. They have no knowledge about mythological dresses, so they come to us for such a thing. They cannot make ready-to-wear dhotis, and we know how to wear around ten types of dhoti, so for such things they come to us. Even tying *pagdis* they are not having any knowledge of it.

The history of Hindi filmmaking, with its perennial interest in urbanism and fashion, would suggest that there may not be much of a future for films about the rural or urban working classes. At the same time, the arguments for realism mean that dramas are more likely to pay attention to a wider range of social groups represented in the cast, rather than dismissing working-class characters to be costumed from something out of a trunk. I was presented with an example of just this kind of thing in 2012, in an account of the costuming of lower-class, Muslim male characters in the recent film *Agneepath*. The film was set in the recent past, and, with this requirement in mind, the dressman found himself in his element, since this was a population and a time period he knew intimately. The designer was delighted to take advantage of his expertise, and the costuming was a great success. What this story reflects, in part, is that dressmen are probably more strongly associated with traditional costuming now than ever before, conforming once again to the perennial division of Western and Indian that still has the capacity to divide modernity from tradition and certain kinds of Indians from others. At the same time, it shows the particular benefits dressmen can bring to the realization of the new goal of realism in costuming, if only a dressman can get the attention of a motivated designer to use his expertise.

And so, after a detour into the construction of fashion in its narrower sense of style, change, and taste, we return again to fashion writ large, or fashion as the total sartorial expressions and engagements that we see in a community or society—the kind of fashion that is most completely realized with a single dress designer and a team of assistants working under him or her, whereas fashion as style or as spectacle has been relatively well served all these years by personal designers and favorite menswear shops. Notwithstanding that spectacle lives on in Hindi film in the self-consciously *filmi* song sequences, as well as via the use of CGI (computer-generated imagery), perhaps the most relentless use of spectacle comes in historical or period films, into which the rich material and commercial environment of metropolitan India is retrospectively projected. I turn to these concerns next, before concluding with a discussion of how costume filters out into the worlds of film viewers.

# –5–

# Dressing the Past

Open the website of any leading contemporary Indian designer and among the clothes most prominently displayed will be beautifully embroidered saris and *ghaghara cholis*, scarves, and plenty of well-burnished jewelry. Not for those with little means (though perhaps something to aspire to for a once-in-a-lifetime occasion, such as a wedding), the clothing items are heavy with *zardozi* (embroidery with metal wires), while men's *angarkhas* (long tunic-like coats) are covered with white-on-white *chikan* or other embroidery (Wilkinson-Weber 1999). Among the most captivating costume spectacles that Hindi film has to offer are its historical (and also mythological) epics, in which costumes not unlike the ones that appear on the designer websites—intricately decorated draped garments and meticulously embroidered and jewel-encrusted clothes—situate the viewer within past worlds enjoyed by the precolonial elite. These are spectacles not just for the sake of showcasing a breathtakingly extravagant and elaborate dress, but also for making the fabulous era of precolonial Indian wealth and autonomy come to life.

Like the assertive fashion garment discussed in the last chapter, the historical costume constantly threatens to overwhelm the star, ratcheting up the excitement and allure of the scene to intoxicating levels. Period costumes in several film industries frequently derive their fascination from attention to detail, as well as from the manifest value in the amount of skilled labor and special materials needed to make them. When Sarah Gilligan (2011, 9), writing about the English-language period films *Elizabeth* (1998) and *Marie Antoinette* (2006), remarks that "costume is placed at the forefront through an endless stream of costume changes and spectacular set pieces," she could as well be writing about a Hindi-language period film such as *Jodhaa Akbar* (2007) or *Devdas* (2002).

Period costume need not necessarily entail richness and splendor—there is more to Indian history than the Mughal Empire, after all. Even so, costume still manages to proclaim its own distinct value through other means—for example, its ability to conjure up a well-known historical figure via a set of distinct visual signs or, more importantly perhaps, its capacity to persuade the viewer of the action's "pastness." Notwithstanding that it is merely one among many persuasive devices, costume, with its unique power to stabilize conceptions of time as well as notions of character, is indispensable to the illusion of pastness in period films (Higson 2003; Sprengler 2009; Street 2001). In fact, the appeal to period correctness is part of a larger strategy of legitimizing and authorizing a film that recreates a historical context in its apparent entirety. In the realm of material culture, authenticating strategies take on enhanced significance in a world replete with copies, not so much to uncover an original as to offer reassurance that an object or performance issues directly and unaffectedly from what is, in essence, an idealized productive context (see, for example, Handler 1986; Spooner 1986). With film, audiences are willing to accept that appearances are contrived, but may expect instead a level of integrity in arriving at those appearances. All in all, however, disputes over what is authentic or how authenticity is to be gauged are, in effect, conflicts over present-day authority to interpret and control the past; the significance of the authenticated item resides in how it embodies the evaluative criteria and discerning faculties of the person whose claims win out.

Needless to say, some of the conflicts described in previous chapters in connection with films set in the present-day come to the fore in the production of costume for historical films as well. This time, though, the differences revolve around the sources of knowledge of India's past or, more specifically, the terms upon which compelling visual images of the past are created. More controversially, how are people to be constructed who inhabit a contemporary "past" (I am thinking here of villagers and tribespeople, in particular). In this chapter, we again meet the dresswala, or costume supplier, whose connection to the film industry goes back practically to its beginnings and who specializes still in providing paraphernalia such as turbans, shoes, flags, banners, and the like for historical films. The designer appears this time as a more intellectual figure, a researcher and aesthete, drawing on the cultural capital of taste and education to achieve "true" authenticity, with the most up to date designer elaborating his or her own variations upon certain historical themes (specifically, the extravagant and lavish clothes described at the beginning of this chapter) for a fashion market. And there are the artisans—jewelers and embroiderers—whose skill is particularly important for the recreation of royal spectacles from the high points of Indian history and who are themselves precariously positioned between what is coded old and what is new. This chapter, in sum, deals with the tricky matter of time and temporality—how it is made in films and how those who make the illusion of pastness may themselves be consigned to it.

## VIABILITY AND VERIDICTION

The demands of costuming for period films are, in some ways, comparable to those for contemporary films. At the same time, they are distinctly different, since the clothes must evoke in viewers a sense of a past of which they typically have little or no direct experience.[1] While I have never heard anyone hint that commitment to character is set in abeyance with historical costume, there is an equally strict imperative to be truthful to appearances in the time depicted. Intuitions and opinions about fashion or how a range of characters in a modern film might look are widely distributed, but period costume is the domain of a narrower set of experts. Character is thus elaborated within a narrow range of sartorial possibilities, subject to the consent of the viewer that this is, first and foremost, an acceptable version of a past reality (Bruzzi 1997, 28; Wilkinson-Weber 2010b, 128). Stars, too, must temper their demands with the realization that they must minimally conform to the dress conventions of the period. By extension, a great deal of power is deflected away from stars and designers, even directors, simply because they are not free to reinterpret the 1600s or the 1900s or even the 1970s in any way they wish.

At the same time, there is an apparent paradox at the core of historical costume design, since an exact replication of past styles, silhouettes, and fabrics is neither the intention nor the outcome of costume design for period films (Street 2001, 21). The audience's agreement that the film is true to the period does not rest on any particular expertise regarding the past; instead, it comes from recognizing critical signs and visual renderings of materials and movements that are deemed plausible. The most dramatic examples of this phenomenon come from portrayals of iconic historical figures, in which it is necessary to include certain irreplaceable signs to convince the audience that it is the life and times of this figure, in particular, that are being portrayed.

## Iconic Minimalism

Films that include figures from the Independence struggle take place at a time just barely within the memory of film viewers. Many of the most famous persons from this and more recent history entered the public visual imagination via iconic images and also caricature—a form of art that, via exaggeration, draws attention to and underscores certain notable facial and bodily features. Mohandas Gandhi, Bhagat Singh, and Subhas Chandra Bose are recognizable to audiences, before they even speak or act, via these compelling shorthands. To craft a Gandhi, one needs the spectacles, shaved head, and dhoti; for Bhagat Singh, the trilby or turban and the carefully groomed mustache; for Subhas Chandra Bose, the eyeglasses and the military uniform and hat. The effectiveness of these simple ensembles allows a far wider range of actors to take on roles, concealed as they are behind overdetermining signs.

This explains how the role of Bhagat Singh could be taken on by actors as physically distinct as Bobby Deol and Ajay Devgn in two films made about his life in 2002.[2]

It is worth pointing out, though, that as an art form that unfolds in real time and plays with time within its frame, film offers the possibility of a resolution of disparate forms of dress that are difficult to reconcile outside its purview—if, of course, the character is opened up to more narrative scrutiny. For example, the clothing choices of both the historical Gandhi and Bhagat Singh were not without considerable political and cultural import. Gandhi underwent several philosophical evolutions in his political career, each accompanied by experiments in dress (Bean 1989; Tarlo 1996). Bhanu Athaiya worked with John Mollo on the costume design for Richard Attenborough's biopic *Gandhi*, and she was responsible for creating costumes that captured the shifts in sartorial philosophy of the cinematic Gandhi. This involved investigation of the photographic record of Gandhi's life, an example of costume research about which I shall say more in a later section (Athaiya 2010, 153–64).

Bhagat Singh, meanwhile, is a trickier case, for even his iconic representation is a point of controversy. When the famous image of him wearing a felt hat and open-neck shirt was taken, Bhagat Singh was in disguise and on the run (Pinney 2004, 126). The whole point of the image was to frustrate the colonial authorities' search for a "turbaned, khaddar-clad fugitive" (Maclean 2011, 1078) by removing all sartorial signs of indigeneity, including cutting his hair. Like a good actor, Bhagat Singh passed as a Westernized Indian (Maclean 2011, 1074; Pinney 2004, 126). As this new image was copied, reproduced, and passed from hand to hand, the hat and shirt became both necessary and sufficient conditions to signify Bhagat Singh himself, setting up some complicated debates about Singh's real identity as man or symbol. Re-situating Singh as a Sikh by replacing his hat with a dastaar turban acknowledges the role of Sikhs in the struggle for independence (Maclean 2011, 1054), but it is an adjustment to his image that disrupts the clarity and immediacy of the familiar icon, more so than seeing Gandhi, say, in the suit and wing collar of a South African lawyer (his occupation before his return to India and recruitment to the Independence movement). Numerous films on Bhagat Singh have been made since Independence, of which the Devgn and Deol versions are merely among the most recent (Pinney 2004, 124). Another film, also made in 2002, starred Sonu Sood; earlier versions included one in 1963 starring Shammi Kapoor, and another, made in 1965, with Manoj Kumar. The solution adopted by these films was, as with Attenborough's Gandhi, to confine the sartorial sleight-of-hand to the film itself and all opted in their primary publicity material to depict Bhagat Singh with his distinctive mustache and hat, just as publicity for Gandhi mainly depicted his years as a dhoti-clad ascetic. Film's play with costume change does not extend necessarily to iconoclasm.

## Historical Re-creations

It is by now a cliché of period-film criticism that costume scholars will iden-tify errors in the characters' dress that render the films inauthentic, with some costumes being deemed less authentic than others (Maeder 1987). Few viewers are capable of bringing such a level of critical acuteness to film costume, of course, but to infer that the maker of the costumes must be ig-norant of clothing history is to miss the point of period film costume. Some designers, with the backing of the directors for whom they work, favor an ap-proach that involves dressing the actor in a way that simulates the histori-cal context as closely as possible, even to the extent of replicating unseen undergarments (Morris 2009), but this is by no means a hard and fast rule. For filmmakers, there is no great problem in using what are in essence cos-tume pastiches, since considerations of character, shifting notions of beauty and seemliness, and deference to the actor are not abandoned just because one wants to do an effective job of conveying a past era.[3] Besides, costume in period films, as in other kinds of films, is there to affirm certain moral and narrative contentions, not simply offer a lesson in dress scholarship. For ex-ample, writing about James Cameron's 1997 film *Titanic*, Sarah Street points out that Jack Dawson's stylishly cut clothes bear scant resemblance to the kinds of garments we see captured in photographs from the time period. The clothes perform the important narrative task of separating and elevating the character from his fellow third-class passengers; at the same time, the clothes reinforce the appeal and poignancy of his character arc via intertex-tual reference to actor Leonardo DiCaprio's fashionable and youthful persona (Street 2001, 21–3). In the same vein, Neeta Lulla adapted her costumes for *Jodhaa Akbar* to complement the looks and bodies of the two stars, Aish-warya Rai and Hrithik Roshan, as well as to illustrate the different factions in the story via variations in the color palette (rediff.com 2008).

Adaptation and modification are, in turn, possible only because costumes are all made new, at least for the main stars and character actors (unlike au-thentic props and settings that contain their own historical self-referentiality). This convention, by itself, invites the designer to expound upon the design process and the struggle for authenticity, as well as tally up the costs of ac-quiring jewelry, fabrics, accessories, and so on. When enumerated together, these tasks all speak powerfully of the designer's authorship of the designs and of his or her practical responsibility for deciding at what point faithfulness to period models ultimately concedes to other demands.

Given that it is possible, even desirable, to stray from the boundaries specified by clothing and textile scholars, how, then, can authenticity and truthfulness be claimed? Since most of the filmgoing audience lacks a sustained familiarity with primary historical materials, the power of historical costume to be convincing derives almost entirely from what viewers recognize as having been used before, making the very first designer for a historical film the de facto authority. Designers, too, cannot help but be influenced by the ways in which historical eras have been constructed via sets and costumes in previous films, whether they happily take in those influences or prefer to avoid them. Designers find themselves saddled with the creations of previous designers and even, ultimately, of the dresswalas that have been supplying mythological and historical costume for decades. At this point, we go to the dresswalas, the costume experts who first worked on historical films before designers had entered the scene and whose ideas have persisted in the industry to a greater extent than any designer is apt to admit.

## DESIGN AND THE DRESSWALA

The first dresswalas in Mumbai catered to theatrical troupes, to religious performers, and later to the film industry, once it established itself. Dresswalas were known to be adept at dressing up characters from folklore and mythology, as well as historical figures and regional archetypes; they had particular skills in tying turbans and draping dhotis. Once dresswalas had rooted themselves in the film industry, the knowledge they subsequently claimed to possess about historical or regional dress owed as much to the force of convention as it did to any personal or pseudo-ethnographic acquaintance with what people wore at different times in the past or in several parts of the country. Nevertheless, the immersion of dresswalas in producing many variants of Indian dress and in visualizing heroic figures from India's past helped cultivate enduring convictions concerning dresswala knowledge and acumen.

My assistant, Mona, and I made several visits to dresswalas in the Western Suburbs. Some premises were larger than others, but all contained the characteristic shelves and racks of brightly colored costumes, and somewhere in or out of sight, there was the constant whir of a sewing machine. A few establishments had installed a desk and shelves in one private, vigorously air-conditioned room, where the proprietor sat. Others merely stowed a desk in a back room or in the showroom itself. One interview in particular stuck in my mind for how the proprietor, seated at his desk, indicated the shelves of turbans, skirts, and dresses opposite him as he enumerated the different state and tribal costumes he had made, punctuating the recital with the repeated words "Kisko malum hai?" (Who knows this?). This pointed refrain drove home what many other dresswalas stated with somewhat less flair: that designers, directors, and other film personnel lacked the knowledge and appreciation of the distinctiveness of regional Indian costume that dresswalas possessed.

Some of the dresswala's knowledge undoubtedly has percolated down the generations from folk precedents. Eventually, as new generations took over and rival dresswalas entered the business, knowledge itself became circular, drawing on visual models already set in place by older films or stage productions. There were one or two dresswalas who were perfectly happy to say that their ideas came from watching old films and that they used little to no other design sources; the old films were considered authentic in themselves. Moreover, as with dressmen, a sureness of memory, built up over years of experience, was more valuable to dresswalas than a scant knowledge that required shoring up via other visual sources.

What dresswalas do not say or concede is that costumes in the past were themselves hybridized to some degree. Some of the most powerful sources of contemporary iconography and conventional costuming came from late nineteenth- and early twentieth-century innovations in art and chromolithography that introduced vivid and highly appealing visual models for dress (Dwyer 2006b, 17; Pinney 1995). In film as elsewhere, these compelling renditions of deities set a standard of beauty and correctness in the styling of saris, dhotis, and other garments. Dresswalas would have been as immersed in this vital visual environment as anyone else.

This is not to say that dresswalas use no external sources at all and simply produce their turbans and uniforms and military armor entirely from their imaginations. From time to time, scrapbooks and torn pages from books and magazines are provided by clients or are independently collected by dresswalas as an aide-mémoire to styles they may be called upon to create. These visual sources are treated as fact but, in actuality, are more equivocal. For example, a long-established dresswala whose specialty was making turbans kept among his reference pictures a reproduction from an old British publication with beautiful illustrations of middle-aged men wearing subtly different types of *pagdis* and jackets. Scholars today generally agree that exhaustive British efforts to document the natural and human resources of the subcontinent were not unconnected to the objectives of rule; the detailed compendiums of dress produced during the colonial era, complete with illustrations, were critical to demarcating and fixing identities territorially and materially. As Bernard Cohn has argued, explicating and authorizing the semiotic of the Sikh turban was one instance of British colonial efforts not simply to know, but also to define the colonized (Cohn 1989; Cohn 1998). Cohn astutely homes in on the British concern with defining difference in material forms such as dress, hairstyle, and characteristic personal possessions. Thus, the "proper" Sikh dressed one way, and the Pathan another, with no possibility for hybrids. In this way, the British sought not only to objectify and manage difference, but also to reinforce the mediating role of colonial authority amid this difference. The authenticity these pictures appear to guarantee is, therefore, an essentialist fiction.

Just the same, these icons of India's material and sartorial diversity, alongside less-tangible and less-formal influences, have filtered into the dresswala's repertoire. Whether dresswalas are talking about their grasp of historical costume or, secondarily, their insight into regional styles, typical clothing is often spoken of in connection with India's states or cities, with tribal costumes as a cross-state addendum. Dresswala *Rajan*, whose father started their costume business in the 1950s, gave the most compact example of this reasoning:

> I have done Rajasthan costumes, Assam, total tribal costumes, Tamil—that is totally different. So I should say, right from Karnataka to Kashmir, all traditions, all languages of India . . . you get different culture, different costume, different language. If you walk from Kashmir to Kanyakumari [the southernmost tip of India], how many cultures, how many costumes on people you will meet? We have got this stuff. All cultures. Particularly all the states, they have different culture, different language, different style.

Although no dresswalas made a point of being aligned either sympathetically or professionally with dressmen, similar tropes of unappreciated knowledge and ability featured in their conversations. Dresswalas and dressmen alike regard themselves as clear-eyed, plain-speaking men who are far more familiar with the habits and customs of ordinary Indians than are upper-middle-class and upper-class designers. More than a few sardonic jokes were proffered that featured impetuous, overconfident designers outfitting their casts in clothes that were all wrong. In one example, a production had put designer-made turbans on the heads of the cast, only for them to be roundly panned by a group of visitors who were descendants of the very people being portrayed. To be fair, there is no reason why the children and grandchildren of historical characters should know better how their ancestors looked if all they have to go on is the same stock of publicly shared images available to all. Careful research may well point out differences that are obscure to contemporary reminiscences. The larger point that is being made here, though, is that designers, directors, and producers are apt to overvalue their own assumptions about how a historical character should look, while neglecting to consult the authorities standing right in front of them—namely, the dresswala and the dressman. The dresswalas are not sidelined entirely, since they are still used for mass production of items such as ready-to-wear turbans (glued in place, not tied), uniforms, and other items for the background cast. However, the same emphasis upon expertise and taste to set designers apart is as evident here as in contemporary costume.

## EXPERTISE AND EXPERIENCE

Films have turned to experts on many occasions to provide skills and expertise that are hard to find within the industry itself. Important examples include foreign fight choreographers, stunt actors, and makeup artists. Looking over old promotional pamphlets and songsheets that list film credits, one can find "Muslim courtesan films" that employed a special costume authority (Bhaskar and Allen 2009; Dwyer 2006b). Most likely this authority would have been an inheritor of the courtesan (*tawa'if*) tradition in music and dance that filtered into the film world in Bombay in the industry's initial decades, helping shape much of its musical and linguistic character. Courtesan performance's exponents and their close descendants consulted on early films, to the extent that courtesan films seem, at once, part of the past and part of the film industry's present. By the time we get to later films, the critical precedents had been set, as in *Pakeezah* (1972) and *Umrao Jaan* (1981), whose costumes were designed, respectively, by star Meena Kumari and by director Muzaffar Ali's wife, Subhashini Ali.

Courtesan films exude a distinct sensibility that may be termed nostalgic, elegiac, and, certainly, melancholy. The *tawa'if* is a tragic figure—and counterintuitively chaste—who, despite her absolute loyalty to her beloved, is condemned to social disgrace because of her occupation. Admired and adored, she nevertheless remains distant and solitary, denied the support and consolations of a family (Dwyer 2006b, 118). Famous film *tawa'ifs* have all been celebrated actors known as well for their singular beauty: for example, Meena Kumari, Waheeda Rehman, Rekha, and Aishwarya Rai. Arguably, a subtle subtext in all these films is that the courtesan and the actor who

**Figure 19**   Meena Kumari plays a *tawa'if* in the gorgeously mounted film, *Pakeezah* (1972, directed and produced by Kamal Amrohi). Several scenes of her dancing give ample opportunity for her to wear beautiful clothes, designed (ostensibly) by Kumari herself. (DVD distributor, Shemaroo Entertainment.)

plays her are not so different from one another. Assuredly, heroines are not locked in *kothas* (the courtesan's dwelling and performance space, vulgarly brothels), forced to entertain men against their will; they marry, some have children, and they command respect in the social circles in which they reside. But the cost of celebrity, the ephemeral nature of fame, and the bartering of the body are all themes to which courtesans and actors can relate. For these reasons—the parallel with contemporary female heroines, the continuation of music and dancing via film—the temporal anchor points for courtesan films are sometimes ambiguous.

## THE CLAIMS OF RESEARCH

For the most part, until the mid-twentieth century, the choices for obtaining historical costumes were the same as for contemporary clothing: the dressman, the dresswala, or one's personal tailor. A key shift in historical costuming over the past half-century or so has been to draw it away from the dresswala and toward the same cadre of designers who now dominate what are called social or contemporary films. Differences of taste and aesthetic appreciation play as strong a role in the claims of designers to excel at historical-costume work as they do in other kinds of costuming. Here, though, to differentiate themselves from their predecessors, designers stress the intellectual labor of research and the practical work of exhaustive sourcing.

A few designers have built a reputation for themselves as particularly adept at period costume, sometimes taking on more than merely the responsibility for the lead hero or heroine's clothes. Bhanu Athaiya, whose name has already come up several times in this book, is best known for her designs for period films. Her reputation in this area stems mostly from her Oscar win (shared with John Mollo) for the costumes for *Gandhi* (Bhatkal 2002, 91), but over her career, she has designed for several period films, including *Sahib, Bibi, aur Ghulam* (1962), *Amrapali* (1966), and *Lagaan* (2001). Other designers have been hired via their star connections since the 1960s to oversee the clothing of actors in period films (as Leena Daru did for Rekha in her films *Umrao Jaan* and *Utsav*). On occasion, foreign designers have worked on productions (a Russian professor at a costume institute worked on the Indo-Soviet production *Pardesi*). In recent years, a few designers have found more success in gaining the sole credit and responsibility for historical films. Neeta Lulla was able to do so for *Jodhaa Akbar*, and Anna Singh for *Taj Mahal* (2005) and *Veer* (2010). Singh was also co-credited with Bindiya Goswami for J.P. Dutta's remake of *Umrao Jaan* (2006). As with contemporary costuming, the scale of a film and where it locates itself in film tradition make a considerable difference in who gets to design and manage costume: Pia Benegal has been the sole credited costume designer for the historical and contemporary films of her highly-respected director father, Shyam Benegal, since the 1990s. Still, old habits die hard: Sanjay Leela Bhansali's 2002 *Devdas* employed three sources of design—Neeta Lulla, the partnership known as Abu-Sandeep, and Reza Shariffi—to craft costumes for the three principals. A perfectly competent, even outstanding designer with strong period costuming skills may be required to defer, from time to time, to the star's personal designer, although the personal designer must stay within the overall historical brief of the film.

Costume scholarship and historical accuracy were watchwords in parallel and art films for many years, but now, even designers on big-budget epics lay claim to meticulous research. It is perfectly possible that the turban reference proffered by the dresswala that I described earlier had originated with a designer, such as Athaiya, for whom the dresswala had made a large number of *pagdis* for *Lagaan*. Designers speak in great detail about their consultation of extra-filmic visual or textual sources on costume, sources that are typically hard to find and expensive to buy. Some designers stress a preexisting interest in history. One of my interviewees, *Neera*, is a designer with strong theatrical roots who has worked on a few feature films as well as on period television serials. For her, the motivation to design period costumes was a desire to, in a sense, animate historical sources:

> My father was a history professor; my father did research in medieval India. So the family background is from history. So there's lots of research; this was in my blood. I wanted to see them [the historical characters] live, whatever was in the books.

Preeminent period costume specialists today, such as Neeta Lulla, have fashion backgrounds, but they have built up considerable film experience and use some of the same decorative elements (embroidery, for example) and silhouettes in their film work and their couture collections. The rhetorical commitment to research is fairly constant, no matter the previous activities and achievements of the designer.

## Sourcing Costume, Discerning Sources

Art and history books are what designers mention first when they discuss research, books the designers own or are given by the director and producers. For any film taking place in the late nineteenth or twentieth centuries, there are photographs and motion pictures, although access to these resources has become relatively easy only in recent years with the advent of the Internet (a resource that younger designers are very familiar with). Because of the ubiquity and power of late nineteenth-century art and chromolithographs, and because of their influence on film looks, designers are as apt to draw on these sources as are dresswalas. Finally, Orientalist fantasies originating from Hollywood historically provided rich visual inspiration for many films, with directors passing their enthusiasm for such spectacles to the star's designers (Dwyer 2006b, 110).

Historical periods before the advent of photography are accessed via museums, art books, and reproductions of portraits and other paintings. The resources for the Mughal era are among the most numerous and the most useful, particularly miniatures and other paintings of court life commissioned by the emperors and their aristocratic contemporaries. The compelling realism of films about the Mughal period comes in part from their being so visually familiar to a substantial segment of the audience, who have either seen previous films about the same historical era or imbibed their impressions of the period from the reproductions of Mughal art that have entered public culture. For the dress designer, the naturalistic conventions the Mughal elite explored following their exposure to sixteenth-century European painting permits the treatment of art as an unmediated source of information about costume. Miniatures and full size paintings are assumed to provide unambiguous guidance on matters of silhouette, color, jewelry, and decoration. Conveniently, bodies are usually shown with the head in profile (depicting the tie of the turban) and the torso comparatively straight with respect to the viewer (displaying the cut and decoration of the clothing). The faces and hands, as well as other uncovered parts of the body, are rendered with a precision and naturalism that is not replicated in the clothing, whose design

**Figure 20**    Like other historical epics, lavish costume is a key part of the mise-en-scène of *Jodhaa Akbar* (2008, directed by Ashutosh Gowarikar, produced by Ashutosh Gowarikar and Ronnie Screwvala). There are many shots of Aishwarya Rai Bachchan as Jodhaa enigmatically concealed behind a gauzy veil—an old Bollywood standby in the visual language of romance, as well as a fair copy of the kinds of diaphanous clothing seen in Mughal paintings. (DVD distributor, UTV Home Entertainment.)

is stylized to the point that a print pattern is repeated like a tiny portion of wallpaper. Strangely enough, this draws the source closer to the kind of illustrative sketch that designers make as they compose designs.

Yet, what we know about Mughal art and the philosophies of dress of the time tell us that paintings should not be read simply as descriptive documents; instead, they open up a window upon how power and status were enacted via what Dani Cavallaro and Alexandra Warwick (1998, 29) term "vestimentary codes and theatricality of power." Clothing was worn, but it was also exchanged, displayed, and appraised as a uniquely rich and multifarious materialization of political and social life (Cohn 1989, 312–16). Visually speaking, the treatment of dress in Mughal art as pattern and texture, when set against the more naturalistic depiction of the face, effects a fragmentation of the body, whose parts seem strangely at odds with the clothing. Whether the designer is aware of these facts or not, the ironic outcome of putting Mughal-inspired costumes on celebrity actors is that it does not just recall the miniatures to mind (for those viewers who know them), but it also enhances the stars' charismatic appeal in ways that bear comparison with the historical originals. For example, the precise fit, detailing, and crispness of the costumes—tight-waisted *sherwanis*, jeweled turbans, richly embroidered *cholis*—in Ashutosh Gowarikar's 2007 film *Jodhaa Akbar*, with costumes designed by Neeta Lulla, produce the uncanny impression that they have been literally lifted from the paintings that inspired them. There is little to no aging of the costumes to create the impression of wear; everything is immaculate.

Absent the naturalistic inclinations of the Mughal painters, evidence for period costume any earlier than the sixteenth century is somewhat more problematic. Repeated forms and detailing of dress and adornment on Hindu and Buddhist sculpture suggest a set of conventions that the costumemaker can follow. However, the degree of stylization complicates any attempt at direct transposition into film costumes. Designers with an arts background like to stress that their training not only informs their understanding of color and form, but also gives them insight into historical dress via their acquaintance with India's art history. The affirmations of Bhanu Athaiya and Leena Daru to have made close observations of dress in temples or museums through sketching have been presented already.

For color and texture, the wall paintings of Ajanta and Ellora provide clues to the dress of the elite in the fifth century CE. Bhanu Athaiya describes Vyjayantimala as *Amrapali* in the 1966 film of the same name making her entrance for the *mahurat*, held in the Ajanta caves east of Mumbai, dressed in an orange draped garment Athaiya had designed using the wall paintings as influences. In her book *The Art of Costume Design*, Athaiya writes: "It is believed that the monks who lived there dyed their robes orange from the *parijat* flowers found on the many bushes dotting the hillside. Vyjayanthimala looked exactly like a picture from that era" (Athaiya 2010, 93). The flower story strikes a romantic tone, but Athaiya's later remark that "a renowned historian . . . had excitedly exclaimed that she [the character Amrapali] appeared just like how the actual Amrapali must have looked" adds the unusual (and definitive) authorization of an academic source (Athaiya 2010, 97).

Immersion in textual sources is equally indicative of serious research on costume. Designer Lovleen Bains, whom we met in Chapter 1, worked as a costume associate on Mira Nair's *Kama Sutra* (1996), a film about love and jealousy in the royal courts of sixteenth-century India. Here, she gives an example of how the textual approach might work:

> [It] was very difficult, I must confess, because this is a pre-Mughal era in which *Kama Sutra* is set. It's just before the advent of the Mughals into India. It's fifteenth- to sixteenth-century India [the Mughals came to power in the 1520s], so that was an age where there is very little pictorial reference, so we had go to the Bhandharkar Institute in Pune, and there are some Sanskrit texts with descriptions. So we had to translate from Sanskrit, read the descriptions, and we created our own world.

The costume team that immerses itself in Sanskrit documents has come some distance from merely referencing chromolithographs to inform a vision of the distant Indian past. One may note that Nair's films are not typically included in the corpus of Hindi cinema, although several of her actors and a good proportion of her production team in India have worked on both small-budget and large-budget films that are solidly aligned with the Mumbai industry. Yet, the authorizing details of research are becoming as normative in mainstream films as in films that are identified with an art ethos. Neeta Lulla is described as having picked up eighty antique shawls in her scouring of the Kolkata landscape for materials for Sanjay Leela Bhansali's *Devdas*, which is set somewhat indeterminately in the early 1900s (Times Internet Limited 2002); meanwhile, Mumbai's Chor Bazaar has become a gold mine of finds for film fans and filmmakers alike concerned with tracking down authentic props and costumes (Dubey 2011). Both forays into the hustle and bustle of such markets bring to mind the fortuitous discoveries by connoisseurs of African art related by Christopher Steiner (1994), in which the expert's purported superior discernment enables him or her to see the value in things that would otherwise have come to the end of their commodity career. Steiner's examples feature traders who cannily exploit these assumptions to stage the very contexts that connoisseurs imagine they control. I do not claim that dress designers do not know exactly what they are looking at or that they are being hoodwinked, only that we can be sure that the story of finding treasures in unexpected places is useful for underwriting the designer's authority.

## THE PARADOXES OF HERITAGE

Summing up internal Indian diversity via costume remains compelling to filmmakers today, alongside stereotyped demeanor, food choice, language and accent, and so on. The well-etched divisions and demarcations of the peoples of India have a firm grip on the film imagination, not simply because they appear true but also because they facilitate a speedy process of design, as well as an equally rapid identification on the part of the audience. The dresswalas encountered earlier in this chapter tended to gather up period costumes and regional costumes into a single category, most likely an outcome of their having to supply a range of costumes that included all these possibilities. Regionalisms are cemented in caricature (Dwyer 2006b, 105) and the distinctness of each state given intellectual credence by tourist policy and literature from state to state, as well as the handicraft outlets and emporia that populate every large city in India. Inside these shops, the material signs of regional and state identity are laid out for the acquisitive gaze of foreign tourists, as well as affluent Indians.

The typicality of dress is repeatedly invoked in reference to regional costume, so as to shore up both the designer's acumen in being able to recreate it and the spectacle of its detailing (with accessories and jewelry). Thus, Mala Sinha is said to have worn "a typical *pahadi* [a Himalayan ethnic group] dress" in 1970's *Geet* (Athaiya 2010, 70), and Sunil Dutt was a "traditional Rajasthani groom" in 1972's *Reshma aur Shera* (Athaiya 2010, 77). Even populations living practically in the shadow of Film City in Mumbai don't escape this pigeonholing. Mumbai's Warli tribal groups, explains William Elison (2010, 212), dress in "full-length saris of mill cloth and the men wear shirts, pants, and lungis like everyone else." As he notes, this will not do for film portrayals of rural or tribal people, which are normally set within arcadias "where life is simple and peaceful, based on an abundance provided by nature" (Inden 1999, 45). In film, rural and tribal peoples may be contemporary, but they are assuredly not modern: the overall effect, then, is to assert the truth of backwardness as a condition and assert that certain ways of life are continuations of past ones (Fabian 2002). These visions align comfortably with ideas about the Indian population held by the middle and upper classes, as well as by diasporic Indians, and are only slightly more stereotyped than the customary depictions found in coffee-table books and tourist literature. So compelling are these images that film's recycling of them in its sets and backdrops appears, like the *filmi* Warli hamlet observed by Elison, to be more real than the homes people actually inhabit.

To the urban dwellers who make up the normative audience from the filmmaker perspective, villagers, tribal peoples, folk performers, and artisans embody the archaic. Yet, ethnography and history belie these preconceptions, revealing instead the hybridity of sartorial choice among rural and tribal populations, ranging from experiments in jewelry and adornment to innovation in choice of fabric (Gell 1986; Tarlo 1996; Wadley 2008). This is, indeed, exactly what we should expect, given the paradox at the heart of authenticity—that the nonreflexive, genuine object or practice has, in fact, to be manipulated in order to seem real. People in all corners of the country have, for many years, been confronted with choices that go far beyond what might be deemed authentic to their age, their caste, or their location.

Re-viewing history via film frequently (perhaps always?) signals an explicit or implicit absorption in a contemporary question to which the historical materials seem relevant. Literally dressing up questions in an apparently disinterested re-creation of a past era permits a certain deflection of the most contentious disputes that might surround them. Thus, in a curious reversal of the consignment of some people's present to the past just described, images of the past can be marshaled in service of commentary on the

**Figure 21**  In *Lagaan: Once Upon a Time in India* (2001, directed by Ashutosh Gowarikar, produced by Aamir Khan and Mansoor Khan), the varied identities of India are shrunk into a single
Gujarati village and take form in the characters' clothes. (DVD distributor, Eros International.)

present, further illustrating the slipperiness of history in the mounting of period drama.

The 2001 film *Lagaan*—an Oscar-nominated film in which nineteenth-
century Indian villagers living in the environs of Champaner, Gujarat, enter
into a perilous wager to escape onerous tax burdens imposed by the British—
nicely exemplifies the perceived atemporality of contemporary Indians by a
double sleight of hand. A motley group of fractious villagers unites to form a
cricket team to play the British colonial officers. Bhanu Athaiya (2010, 180)
writes that each character in the village team was "dressed traditionally according to his profession," effectively reinforcing a notion of Champaner as
an ecumenical haven and potentially ideal community based on *jajmani* exchange (or a system of intercaste exchanges of labor and materials) and
presided over by a benevolent ruler (Raja Puran Singh, played by Kulbhushan
Kharbanda). Athaiya also declared that the villager extras would require no
additional work, since, as Satyajit Bhatkal (2002, 91) reports, she deemed
their clothes to be "naturally period." At the same time, the village setting
serves as an imagined microcosm of the (yet to be created) nation, containing representatives of several contemporary Indian communities (Muslim,
Hindu, Dalit), alongside a Sikh ex-sepoy and a feudal king. With Champaner
standing in for India, the lesson is, of course, that it behooves the country to
strive for the kind of unity that not only wins cricket matches, but (by implication) also helped defeat colonialism (Farred 2004, 100). Unspoken is the
premise that unity is inevitably built upon marked and undiminished difference that is projected from the present.

Similar concerns to *Lagaan*'s regarding tolerance and cooperation reverberate in Gowarikar's later film *Jodhaa Akbar*, whose borrowing of Mughal

visual conventions has already been discussed. Shahnaz Khan (2011) situates the film within present-day anxieties about religious radicalism, arguing that the film makes Muslim identity its core concern and predicates Akbar's realization of the ideal of religious toleration upon the domesticating and moderating influence of a good Hindu wife—saris on her body, *ghunghat* (veiling) on her face, *sindhoor* (red powder symbolic of wifehood) in her hair. Meanwhile, Akbar's people are divided between those Muslims who are willing to adapt to Indian ways and those who press for a more exclusivist, purified Islamic rule. His religious advisers are dressed in sober, clerical garb, and his powerful nurse, Maham Anga, wears her *hijab* (headscarf) pulled tightly around her hairline and behind her ears. A contemporary portrait of Maham Anga depicts her wearing the same colors and unostentatious clothes of her film equivalent; the difference, however, is that the more sinuous, flowing lines of the clothes in the miniature are replaced, in the film, by angles that are markedly more severe. The historical Muslim that Akbar stands for—dutiful but sensual, in love with beauty—is, the film argues, preferable to the severe traditionalist, a figure the film suggests is an ahistorical, perennial threat in its adherence to asceticism, rigidity, and intolerance.

## HEIRS OF A TIMELESS TRADITION

I have talked about the way in which the rendering of the past in film is about the present—an observation that other scholars have definitively made with regard to period films in other industries (Bruzzi 1997; Cook 2004; Gilligan 2011; Higson 2003; Sprengler 2009). A peculiar distinction of the Indian film industry is the employment of artisans in the creation of historical costumes who are regarded by craft advocates as living antiquities, working in the same ways, with the same skills and materials, as craftspeople serving royal courts, or the precolonial urban bazaar, or the local village community over the course of decades or even centuries. Paul Greenough (1995), in his account of the ethos of Delhi's Craft Museum, draws attention to the irony of supporting craftwork and craft lifestyles but forbidding hybridity and innovation, as well as the degree of praise given to craftsmanship that draws equal to the past via its impersonation of it. Craft, in this view, is automatically presumed to be debased from its former glories and acquires value only to the extent that it conforms to a set of decontextualized ideals.

Fatalism about craft notwithstanding, in the austere decades following Independence, craft work was the one area in which pleasure in material goods was not just tolerated but actively encouraged. Government patronage of small-scale weavers, embroiderers, dyers and printers helped steer craft goods into emporia and tourist shops frequented as much by Indian travelers as foreign visitors. In spite of a distrust of fashion as ephemeral and inauthentic, official policies of craft preservation and a devotion to native textiles ultimately produced their own fashion market sutured to an ideology of nationalism by the compelling theme of craft revival and preservation (Tarlo 1996; Wilkinson-Weber 2004b). Such objects were marketed as touchstones of Indian heritage and authenticity, and they incidentally provided an escape valve for a fashion sensibility by rendering it morally acceptable. This support for crafts began to wane once neo-liberal economic policies were introduced, although the moral imperative of saving handicraft industries continues to be articulated by culture critics, designers, and artists (Greenough 1995; Wilkinson-Weber 2004b). The example par excellence is arguably ethnic chic, a design sensibility that came to the fore in the 1980s and reached its commercial apogee in the present-day Fabindia chain. Ethnic chic comprises Indian-style clothing in a distinctly "peasant" vein—typically intensely dyed cottons along with chunky accessories. The designers who presided over the rise of ethnic chic and orchestrated its production and marketing appear, with hindsight, to be the forerunners of the far-more-numerous and diversified fashion designers of the present day (Tarlo 1996). Contemporary designers have co-opted some of the same rhetoric, professing their commitment to reviving crafts that, at a conservative estimate, have been targets of revival every generation for more than one hundred years.

An unexpected outlet for the finest craft work, that would not have been anticipated by the nationalist boosters of handicrafts who abhorred cinema, is in fact film costume, specifically those costumes described at the beginning of this chapter that feature lavish embroidery and dazzling arrangements of colors. The kinds of clothes crafted by embroiderers and jewelers for historical costumes employ the layering of sensory pleasures—the dress's texture and thickness, its noise (jangling jewelry, rustling skirts)—heightening further the "haptic" dimensions of audience experience. It is these demonstrative attributes of the period or traditional costume that compete with the star who wears it, either because they are overtly designed to be spectacular or because the weight they contain, the particular limitations they place upon movement, mean that they distract the viewer from focusing singularly upon the star's face and body.

In recent years, young designers immersed in both fashion and film have turned more and more toward integrating crafts into their fashion designs, playing deliberately and creatively with various craft forms as they create the kinds of hybrids that, on a lesser scale and in relative anonymity, are effected by ordinary people. Contemporary designers use the work of artisans to fashion clothes, interior decorations, and accessories that happily fuse forms, functions, and materials (DeNicola 2005; Greenough 1995, 238; Tarlo 1996; Wilkinson-Weber 2004b). However, I have never heard the embroiderer, jeweler, or tailor working on costumes for films such as *Taj Mahal* or *Jodhaa Akbar* being described as "heirs of a timeless tradition" (Greenough 1995, 225). Whoever is directing the design—designer, dresswala, dancer—wants artisans to reproduce the work of the past not as the fulfillment of a set of ideals about India and its craft identity (Greenough 1995, 241), but in service of the ideal of verisimilitude. The value of artisans comes less from their ability to tap a deep cultural current of style and design than from their professional ability to do exactly what the designer requires of them. The standards are exacting, the visual attention to the work is intense, and the rewards are undeniably greater than churning out average goods at average cost for middle-class consumers.

As to the intangible rewards, the contrast is stark. In the craft and fashion markets, the artisan confronts the almost impossible task of living up to the vaunted standards of past work while producing goods within economic and social frameworks whose demands are rarely compatible with such expectations. The film artisan, on the other hand, is tasked with making historical fakes whose authenticity is contingent upon a host of other filmmaking considerations, but for which the designer, not the artisan, takes both the credit and (where appropriate) the blame. Together, the artisans and designers are producing a vision of India eminently suitable both for internal consumption and for overseas admiration, much as the 1851 Great Exhibition at Crystal Palace in London displayed royal treasures and artifacts as the essence of India more than one hundred years ago (Breckenridge 1989). The high production values of historical films are one way in which Hindi filmmakers strive to assert their credibility and professionalism on a global stage (Wilkinson-Weber 2010b), a goal for which craft artisans are indispensable.

Creating the visible signs of Indian history for period films is not all the artisans are asked to do, however. Overseas designers have sourced fabrics and had work done in India, including Janty Yates for the Ridley Scott films *Gladiator* (2000), *Kingdom of Heaven* (2005), and *Robin Hood* (2010) (Gloss 2013), and Catherine Martin and Angus Straithie for their Oscar-winning costumes for *Moulin Rouge* (2001) (Powerhouse Museum 2013). And when John Bright, the designer for *Jefferson in Paris* (1995), wanted to reproduce eighteenth-century embroidery and prints on his costumes, replicas were made by Indian craftsmen. The same slippage I noted before is evident in these cases, since it seems that whatever the craft worker makes can easily be slipped into a historical context without dissonance. Only as time goes by do the implicit anachronisms of such an approach become evident, as for example in the beautifully mounted 1978 film *Junoon*, set during the Uprising of 1857. The male characters' transparent muslin kurtas with spare *chikan* embroidery conform to prevailing conventions of *chikan* design in the 1970s and undoubtedly reflect what the filmmakers were able to obtain in Lucknow. *Chikan* today is more likely to feature generously applied embroidery, emphasizing relief and texture over translucence and subtlety. In effect, *chikan* has its own peculiar film history that is indexed to the ebb and flow of preferences in the marketplace at the time a film was made.

The perceived obligation of the middle and upper classes to inform and uplift their fellow citizens has not abated, even with the diminution of government leadership in craft production and preservation. The crafts museum saw, and still sees, its mission as, in part, didactic—to inform the consumer of the proper value and quality of Indian craft (Greenough 1995, 224). Film, too, has its didactic function, directed as well at the consumer. Film and fashion designers tack between the various "stages" on which their work appears (the movie theater, the runway, the magazine spread, and so forth) to resurrect fashion ranges from the lush *chikan*-embroidered clothes of Abu-Sandeep, to the lavish trousseaux of major fashion and film designers such as Neeta Lulla and Manish Malhotra. Taking their cue from these high-end designers, local boutiques engage their own tailoring and embroidery workshops to make knockoffs.

From the perspective of the artisan, designers have directly or indirectly provided for the craft worker a community of knowledgeable users, albeit not the ones that craft scholars and activists of the post-Independence era had in mind. When I last visited Mumbai in 2012, the owner of an embroidery workshop, whom I and my assistant, Mona, had met in 2002, told us that while the work he was commissioned to do for film costume designers remained satisfying, he was becoming increasingly frustrated with the designers' wish to intervene directly in the actual process of embroidery, to the point of, in effect, telling this man how to do his job. This comment may reflect a growing confidence in the designer's mind that he or she can begin to direct the artisan, while the artisan properly concedes to the designer the privilege of directing the minutiae of the stitched design. It is a little premature to draw too many conclusions from this one remark, but it would seem to fit the general pattern noted in this book so far of the elevation of one kind of film worker to the level of decision making, while others are pushed culturally and linguistically toward the margins. It remains to be seen how long the allure of doing the finest work available in the country will incline artisans toward accepting commissions even from designers who intrude too much upon their well-established areas of expertise.

# –6–

# Beyond the Screen

Who ever saw his old clothes—his old coat, actually worn out, resolved into its primitive elements, so that it was not a deed of charity to bestow it on some poor boy . . .

Henry David Thoreau, *Walden*

The trends of fashion in most of Asian countries follow the Bollywood outfits style. Even if we talk about the present fashion and style, it is not wrong in saying that Bollywood outfits are up to the mark. In other words, we can say that Bollywood outfits represent the fashion of modern age.

Kaneesha.com

## COSTUME BIOGRAPHIES

In his essay "The Cultural Biography of Things," Igor Kopytoff (1986) proposed that objects tack between "singularity" and "commodity" as they slip into or out of milieus of exchange. Things set out on paths that may detour into sequestration or exchange, as historical and cultural circumstances dictate. In complex societies, such as India's, numerous systems of value coexist and sometimes conflict: a commodity at one moment is withdrawn from exchange the next, and vice versa; what defies commoditization for some is ripe for it from the point of view of others. The fortunes of the costume after a film is completed are complicated by the fact that it is, by this point, both material object and nonmaterial image. The possibilities it contains are distinct to each form. Is the material costume reused, discarded, or entered into exchange networks as an object transvalued by its connection to a film and to a star? Does the image stimulate the production for exchange of many duplicates?

The biography of the physical costume ends, for the most part, in ignominy. Its use finishes with the conclusion of the shoot, and unless it has to be resurrected for reshoots, it is packed away inside a trunk and carted off to the production-house *godown* (warehouse). Warehouse is an extravagant word for some of these storage places. The one I visited in the Mumbai suburb Goregaon was in a row of shops, its internal space open and undivided for metal trunks to be piled one on top of the other from floor to ceiling, leaving a narrow path in between to get from the front to the back. To secure the premises, a rolling metal door, like one on a garage or the back of a truck, was pulled down and padlocked. Only the dresswalas keep used costumes formally as stock. If designers or dressmen want to use something from a completed film to dress a junior artist, they have to wade through the trunks in the godown and fish out what they want. Costumes are not kept according to any kind of system that would allow for easy location and identification; at most, the name of the film in which the costumes were used is painted on the side of the trunk, along with the name of the star who wore them and, perhaps, some details of what the particular costumes are. In any case, the humid climate is not conducive to good costume preservation, meaning that only the most recent stock is likely to be of any use. Said Ravi, the dressman cited earlier in the book, "Two films back you can use stuff from trunks, but after that you cannot use anything. Like leather will rot. It's the moisture; things get spoiled."

I would routinely ask designers if they were bothered by where costumes went after they were delivered to the set or after a film was done. None seemed particularly perturbed that the costume would be destined for a post-filming "retirement" moldering in a trunk in an obscure godown. Ashley Rebello, a designer who had come into the business in the late 1990s and had built up a portfolio in both big and small budget films, explained:

> That particular dress has got its due on screen for whatever value or whatever worth it is at that point of time. Then, it doesn't really bother me as to what happens to the dress because you learn to detach yourself, because otherwise, you know, every outfit that you make you'd be running around telling your clients, "Don't spill anything on it!"

Costume assistants and ADs talk about the potential of old film costumes, and some describe having trawled through them in the company of dressmen. But currently, there is no one in the film-production team with responsibility for maintaining costume stock. One studio has preserved its costumes: RK Films in the Mumbai suburb of Chembur, where Raj Kapoor's films were made in the 1940s, 1950s, and 1960s. As of 2013, the studio was not open for filming, but the costume collection is still intact, although not as a source of stock but rather as a museum-in-waiting, so to speak, containing many of the iconic costumes of Kapoor's films. RK Films is alone in its concern for conserving these fragments of film history; so indifferent is the industry as a whole to its material history that the dress Parveen Babi wore for her famous 1976 cover portrait in the European edition of *Time* was, in 2002, kept in a designer's desk drawer—and not even the designer who made it in the first place.

In recent years, fresh prospects for commoditizing costumes have arisen, as the value of film memorabilia begins to be realized. Auctioning costumes has become popular: one example that attracted considerable attention was the sale of Deepika Padukone's skirt from a *Dum Maaro Dum* (2011) item number (Express Features Service 2011). Other auctions launched or rumored included those for costumes from Sanjay Leela Bhansali's *Devdas* (*Times of India* 2002) and from *Ra.One* (*Indian Express* 2011). In 2002, the London department store Selfridges hosted a month-long Bollywood-oriented extravaganza, including a display of film costumes (Robson 2002). What will happen later to auctioned costumes—whether any may be conserved, displayed, or resold—is simply unknown at this stage. With rising interest in the memorabilia of Bollywood, however, the likelihood of at least some costumes attaining a value far in excess of what it took to make them is considerable.

While the life of the costume as artifact seems destined to end either in a trunk or as a personal souvenir, the costume as image is limited only by the quality of its visual reproduction and by how many people see it and keep it in their memory. The crisp details of costume in old films become indistinct as the film's visual qualities deteriorate; without careful restoration, their visual impact is inexorably compromised. But costumes enjoy another, qualified reprieve through being inscribed in viewers' memories. Memory can nowadays be continually nourished via reproduction of film stills in print or digital form, or through re-viewing films on video or DVD or via online streaming. Even absent these aides-mémoire, however, film costumes form a part of audience discourse about movies, allowing people to collaboratively reproduce the visual sensations of film viewing in conversation. I noted this in interviews, when my research assistant, Mona, a woman who had seen many, many more films than I had, would strive to recall a costume that our interviewee (a dressmaker, a dressman, occasionally a designer) mentioned from a more-obscure-than-average film. As Mona closed in mentally on the film and the scene in question, recognition spread over her face, the interviewee would smile, and the two of them, replaying a few seconds of the film in their minds, had something in common to talk about. The most remarked way in which costumes enter into the lives of viewers is, however, through their being co-opted and copied for personal wear.

## FASHIONABLE EDUCATIONS

The didactic purposes of film, particularly with respect to how to act in modern society, are by now widely acknowledged. In reference to the United States and Europe, Richard Dyer (2003, 17) writes that film stars act as models for film viewers of what a person in a capitalist social formation should act or look like. At a more pragmatic and mundane level, film executives in the United States have needed little convincing that seeing fashionable clothes, accessories, decor, appliances, gadgets, and so forth would encourage the film viewer to become a potential commodity buyer. Although Janet Staiger (1990) questioned whether this might simply be wishful thinking on the studios' part, work by Sarah Berry (2000), Charles Eckert (1990), and Jackie Stacey (1994) soon confirmed what had hitherto been simply assumed. Stacey, in particular, marshaled copious interview and ethnographic data to show that female filmgoers in the post-World War II period in Britain actively sought out and emulated the styles worn by their preferred stars onscreen. The mutual reinforcement of fashion and stardom in the Hollywood (and European) film industries is another industry truism that is often given short shrift in studies of celebrity, although Church Gibson (2012), Moseley (2005), Studlar (1990), and Vincendeau (2000) have provided important correctives.

The evidence for film influencing audience dress choices, as well as for an intimate relationship between style and celebrity, is arguably even more direct and unequivocal in India than in the United States. Academic and popular literature flesh out the many anecdotes of copying and borrowing. Erik Barnouw and Subrahmanyam Krishnaswamy (1980, 80) quote a 1939 magazine article about the appeal of a cap worn by P.C. Barua in *Mukti* (1937) and the influence of Lila Desai's sari in *Didi* (1937) on fashion-conscious denizens of Calcutta. Young women eager to dress like Sadhana and Sharmila Tagore in the 1965 film *Waqt* paid for their tailors' film tickets, so these tailors could see for themselves the clothes they were to copy (Athaiya 2010). In the following decade, a shirt worn by Rajesh Khanna in a film releasing on a Friday would be duplicated and ready for sale by the following Monday (Grimaud 2003). In the 1990s, Madhuri Dixit's red dress and purple *lehenga* from *Hum Aapke Hain Koun . . . !* were eagerly copied (Wilkinson-Weber 2005), and Urmila Matondkar's dresses designed by Manish Malhotra for *Rangeela* "could be found in every city street stall almost immediately after the film's release" (Pinto 2012a).

Film's pervasive influence on the clothing of viewers is clear in direct copies of star outfits, and some film fans take their impersonations extremely seriously. Only after many years did I realize that I had witnessed a devoted Shammi Kapoor fan in Rajkot, Gujarat, in 1986. He was a waiter in the restaurant of a small hotel, a 35–40-ish man who had adapted his waiter's coat to look as much like a tuxedo jacket as possible, had teased his quiff into an extravagant pompadour, and liked to strike poses before a mirror in the corridor leading toward the kitchen. Even at the time, I thought the possibility of his being an Elvis impersonator in Rajkot was a little slim, but after watching a few of Shammi Kapoor's famous films, such as *Junglee* (1961) and *Teesri Manzil* (1966), I knew exactly whom the waiter was copying. However, film also steers fabric choices, draping styles, and decisions on how to dress for a wedding—or for a simple walk in a city park. Potential consumers of costume are themselves extremely diverse; what may be an almost inconsequential innovation of dress for one set of consumers is so bold and unimaginable for others that they can only borrow small components of the dress so as to incorporate some of its alluring power.

Speaking about what sets viewers to thinking that here is a costume they can make their own, Bollywood designers commonly use the word "identification," referring to the extent to which Indian viewers can glimpse themselves in portrayals onscreen and can imaginatively project themselves into the dress and behaviors of another person. Jackie Stacey's account of British female audiences appropriating style cues from wartime and post-war Hollywood stars takes identification to encompass an assortment of relationships between spectator and star. The nature of identification varies with the perception of similarity versus difference between the viewer and the viewed; the kinds of acts that the identification in question leads to vary as well (Stacey 1994, 128). As a result, the kinds of impersonation can range from borrowing a few sartorial signs to a more exact replication.

We know already that dress is a powerful mediator of self and the world, and so, it should come as no surprise that identification, the drawing near of viewer to star, might take the form of acquiring the same dress. To go to the length of copying a costume implies that some similarity has been detected, a similarity predicated (for most) on being able to translate film appearances into one's own quotidian experience. *Seema*, the owner of a hair salon catering to several stars and other fashionable clients in suburban Bandra, elaborated:

> You have to have understanding of Indian culture, because it's an Indian cinema, Indian public, you're talking about someone who is driving a rickshaw, talking about someone who is sitting in Bhopal in the market. He has to be able to identify with his hero, you know, to kind of put him up there. So you've got to find a very fine balance of incorporating some part of the fashion part, of what's happening globally and now in Bombay, at the same time . . . finding a safe way whereby it's not too radical, to kind of identify with their hero.

## Stars and Emulation

With the growth of the fashion industry in India, more fashion models are becoming known in public culture. Previously, there were few alternatives to actors for populating India's fashion scene. Designers like Anna Singh, whom we met in Chapter 2 discussing character, freely admit that Indian movies have been the most influential source of new dress ideas.

> [I]n India, basically, the trends for the people do not come from the fashion [industry], they come from the Indian movies. That's where people look at their respective actors and actresses. That's why actors and actresses are so huge in India, and nearly like demigods for the people, because that's what they emulate and that's what they look at all the time. So then, you have particular people who get followed very seriously, you know, where the women perhaps watch a particular woman, and they know this is the way to be, this is the way to dress. So they become icons in terms of trendsetters, in the way they have to look, and those actors and actresses have a far more serious responsibility because they are the ones who come into the category of setting the trends.

Few will argue that an engagement with fashion has been a critical component of a leading actor's success (whether the actor is male or female) throughout the history of Hindi film. Designers regard it as self-evident that some audience members want to "dress up like the star." With few other sources for determining what to wear, audiences have looked to stars almost exclusively for guidance. *Sonu*, whose career has directly coincided with economic liberalization, put it this way:

> [With fashion] there is a much bigger influence happening from the movie stars, because when they wear it and the movie releases, all around India at least the masses follow the movie stars, blindly. They like Hrithik Roshan; they've seen this outfit worn; they will just follow it.

Heroes and heroines are valuable commercial assets who have for decades publicized and popularized other kinds of products and services offscreen. In light of the realization that actor personae interpenetrate film and real life, Indian advertisers and manufacturers (like their counterparts in other parts of the world) concluded early that film celebrities were exemplary "movers" of consumer goods. Devika Rani promoted Palmolive soap in print advertisements in 1939 (Weinbaum et al. 2008, 35), and heroine after heroine, from Leela Chitnis to Hema Malini, and even vamp figures such as Shashikala, appeared in advertisements for Lux soap from 1941 onward (Gadihoke 2010).

Why, though, does the wearing of a costume while playing a character exert so powerful a grip on the public imagination? Following Sarah Gilligan, we might say that the importance of costume in these transactional realms is to effect the conversion of the incorporeal into the physical, or as Gilligan puts it, "enabling the formation of 'tactile transmediality' for the spectator by bridging the gap between the virtual 'worlds' on screen and the lived material body" (Gilligan 2011, 25). In an analysis of femininity and fashion in Hollywood's golden age that resonates in the Indian context, Sarah Berry (2000, xvii) argues that star costumes arouse "fantasies of self-transformation" in viewers. The abstraction of the costume, in other words, is not a permanent reimagining but instead works side by side with viewers' memories of the dressed actor's character. Costume changes and the identity shifts they embody or effect draw the attention of the viewer again and again to the possibility of transcending oneself. Even knowing that they could not, or would not, look exactly like the stars and their characters, viewers could carry away the hope and desire that an equivalent costume might, via a similar mediation with the world, enrich their experience. To wear the costume without taking on some gestural and behavioral attributes of the body that wore it first would strip it of much of its significance. In this way, character is reinserted into acts of wearing, and the star, via a sequence of events of copying, enters materially into the lives of his or her fans through their distinct characterizations. An upmarket dressmaker interviewed in 2002 described how she had been approached by an NRI customer who wanted an entire series of replicas of dresses worn by Rani Mukherjee in a song sequence (the dressmaker, sadly, did not remember the film in question). The unbridled replacement of one costume by another in song sequences is, in part, a realization of the character's self via material signs; clearly, it is entirely possible for audience to take the same view with respect to themselves.

Significantly, perhaps, all the examples of copied costumes are described as garments worn by the *actor*, not by the character. Rarely, if ever, does one hear of someone copying "Nisha's" outfits from *Hum Aapke Hain Koun . . . !*, which would imply that emulation is focused on re-creating, via dress, a semblance of the character. Instead, the talk is of "Madhuri's sari" or "Madhuri's *lehenga*." That a garment can be, at the same time, joined to a celebrity body and separable from it (to be worn by someone else) speaks to the ability of the audience to engage in the film's imaginary elements while recognizing that these elements derive from a material, physical reality that can be appropriated. The costume to be copied is already imaginatively lifted out of its narrative context, and its ties to the character's trajectory are loosened, before the actual copying is done. The desirable costume, once copied, enters into the interactions in which the wearer is engaged, but one could argue that the peculiar power of the copied costume resides not just in how it serves the aims and desires of the wearer, but also in its extending the reach of the star and character into new social scenarios.

Recognizing the clothing item's film origin is critical to its effectiveness in this regard, so that the magic inherent in bringing a costume image to life in a physical garment empowers anew the star-as-character—what we might describe as, to use Alfred Gell's terminology, an example of "distributed personhood," or the extension of the agency of the original wearer with the object as mediator (Gell 1998). This is not to say that there cannot be identifications with characters as opposed to actors: a memorable characterization can mean that the star shares top billing with his or her character, so that it's possible to hear remarks like the following offered to me by a young designer, *Nandini*, who had just started her career in film: "They [the audience] love to dress like actors; even people from abroad, they get in touch: we want to look like Don, just send us outfits that look like that" (where the "Don" in question is the title character from the 2006 remake of a 1978 original). Interestingly enough, *Don* is a film about impersonation, in which masquerade is used as a plot device, which might explain the shift from actor to character in this particular case.

## Media Reinforcements

When Sarah Gilligan (2011) describes the heightened importance of the Hollywood star as a linchpin of numerous media environments—film, television, digital—in which brands and media texts circulate, she could as easily be talking about stars in Bollywood, as well. Film stars exist offscreen as well as onscreen, as do film artifacts (at least until the arrival of the green screen and computer graphics). Film star images have for years populated extra-filmic media such as magazines, posters, postcards, and greeting cards (Dickey 1993, 41). Sometimes, these images come from a film; other times, they capture stars as "themselves" in other areas of their lives. The accelerated growth of consumerism since the early 1990s has multiplied the opportunities for brand endorsements by actors, and hardly any of them appear to be reluctant to have their names associated with consumer goods. Unlike their Western counterparts, Indian actors have needed little encouragement to "rac[e] to meet the corporations halfway in the branding game . . . developing and leveraging their own brand potential" (Klein 2000, 30). The potential income from endorsements is vast, and even for the top ranks of Bollywood actors, it easily equals or exceeds the paydays from starring in films. Carefully

**Figure 22**  Heroine Priyanka Chopra's image hovers over the Levi's outlet in Bandra. Shortly before her, Akshay Kumar was the featured star on this larger-than-life billboard. (Image courtesy of Clare Wilkinson-Weber.)

designed and managed campaigns reflect the emerging sense among affluent Indians of being fully integrated into global mediascapes. A prominent designer active since the 1990s, *Rohan* put it this way:

> There is an exposure, there is TV, there's media. You travel the world today, just sitting in your drawing room. There is a very, very huge exposure to English films, to what is happening all over the world. People are getting house proud; people are getting very conscious of where they live, what they do.

The theme of transcending a previous state of blissful ignorance came up again in a conversation with a scriptwriter, *Ashis*:

> Earlier, people lived in a more closed world; [they] did not travel so much and go outside. There was no cable TV; they did not know what was outside. They were happy with their own rules.

The visual environment of Mumbai (and no doubt other cities) is striking for the ubiquity of advertisements containing celebrity endorsements for particular brands of cell-phone service, washing machines, clothes, potato chips, banks, soft drinks, and countless other goods and services. Images of stars with endorsed products pop up on billboards, on the sides of buses, and in front of shops and are plastered on the sides of buildings. Brand endorsement is now a lucrative and entirely expected aspect of a star's professional activity, and it takes on considerable importance in a relatively new consumer economy. The brands include both foreign and Indian ones. Thus, Shah Rukh Khan endorses Tag Heuer, Nokia, and Tata Tea; Aamir Khan is the "brand ambassador" for Coca-Cola, Samsung, and Parle (Bhushan 2010). Even lesser stars, such as John Abraham, are linked with major brands, including Wrangler and Bombay Dyeing. Among women, Kareena Kapoor has promoted Garnier, Head & Shoulders, Alpenliebe chocolate, and Limca soda (*Economic Times* 2012). Stars with a modeling or beauty pageant background (such as Aishwarya Rai Bachchan), or a distinct fashion sensibility (for example, well-known fashionista Sonam Kapoor), come with additional professional credentials to endear themselves to advertisers. It is no accident that Christian Dior and Chanel were prominently featured in Sonam Kapoor's 2010 starring features *Aisha* and *I Hate Luv Storys* (Shah 2011). Increasingly, however, almost every actor in the top tiers has had some experience working both in film and in the fashion and advertising business.

The star's own distinct brand identity, cultivated in films, to be sure, but tempered in media work outside film, grows as a result of the elaboration of his or her persona through these interconnected realms (a realization that is particularly acute to Shah Rukh Khan, who is accustomed to making gnomic statements about the fractured nature of his person into father, actor, brand, and so on) (Wilkinson-Weber 2010a, 15). The conventions of Hindi film have been well suited to producing a relatively stable star persona; this, in turn, stabilizes and enriches the actor brand and makes for an unusually apt and productive convergence of the interests of manufacturers, advertisers, actors, and—because of the intensification of the effect of star recognizability—film producers.

Film magazines have played a critical role in connecting films and film personalities to consumption, particularly of fashion (Dwyer 2008). Advertisements have been carried in film periodicals for decades, but the arrival of color publications such as *Filmfare*, and later *Stardust* and *Cine Blitz*, raised advertising to new heights. The English-language versions of these magazines are riveted to consumption, either as demonstrated by stars in elaborate fashion shoots, in which hairstylist, makeup artist, and clothes designer are all credited, or via the pages upon pages of advertisements for a surprising

**Figure 23** A display of *filmi* postcards—often sold together with posters of stars, deities, and animals—presumably for buyers to use in various kinds of interior decoration. (Image courtesy of Clare Wilkinson-Weber.)

range of products, both glamorous and mundane (Dwyer 2008, 248). Reports of gossip, sniping, and backbiting give the magazines a certain zest (Dwyer 2008, 252), but far from cutting the stars down to size, stories of intrigue, envy, and bad behavior tend to reinforce the impression of stars as somehow apart from mundane experience in India. The absence, until recently, of the paparazzi shots capturing unwary stars disheveled, without makeup, or out of control has compounded the effect of star exceptionalism. In general, print media have opted for uninterrupted coverage of stars as beautiful, stylish, and blessed people, although paparazzi shots are increasing with the ubiquity of camera phones, and stars command less of the reverence they have hitherto enjoyed. In 2012, an unauthorized photograph of Aishwarya Rai Bachchan in which she appeared to have retained the weight she gained during pregnancy was the subject of much controversy in India (*Hindustan Times* 2012).

## Modes of Imitation

Viewers who would like to obtain a copy of an outfit they see in a film have several options. Astute businesses anticipate demand and flood the market as soon as they can with knockoffs that approximate, as far as possible, the main colors and stylistic features of the favored costumes. It is not inconceivable that the buyers of obvious rip-offs of film costumes sold by street vendors are drawn solely by the formal features of the dress. It is far more likely, however, that they are attracted by the handwritten signs above the clothes racks with the actor and film names (such as "*Bunty aur Babli* women's kurtas, as worn by Rani Mukherjee"—kurtas that were widely copied), or a photograph from the film itself, or simply a recognition that this is the outfit that they saw quite recently in a film. The implications for film viewing are that audiences engage with a film in several ways, collaborating in the elicitation of a narrative while hatching ideas about how to co-opt elements of the mise-en-scène into their own daily lives. In addition, these responses are not restricted solely to the most affluent of viewers; they can be seen widely distributed across class, caste, and regional boundaries, for when (as a theater actor once told me): "Rajesh Khanna wore a Gandhi kurta, the entire country wore it, the entire country, everybody wanted to wear that kurta. Everyone wore it. Every youngster went to the shop and got a kurta. Amazing! Amazing the effect on a common person."

For the film viewer, the association of the hero and heroine with virtue, even through tribulation and setbacks, makes the stars' costume choices, even those that push the boundaries of fashion, potentially acceptable. Only potentially, however, for the precise silhouette, the cut, and the fabric may all be unacceptable for reasons of expense or propriety. The time-honored procedure for getting a costume copied to one's own, highly personal specifications involves going to a tailor, not a roadside stall. Consulting with a master in his shop allows for the client to fine-tune colors, textures, cut, and cost. Buyers of ready-made garments can sometimes make use of a tailor sitting inside the shop (or on the pavement outside) to make adjustments. In contrast, making a genuine made-to-measure dress is a far more precise, as well as a more lengthy, procedure. Tailors and clients both describe detailed negotiations that start with a photograph taken from a magazine or newspaper of the costume (or if the costume has already acquired a reputation, the tailor may not need a visual reference). As direct a replica as possible is the goal of some clients, but in many cases, the outfits that are generated from film models are adaptations rather than precise replicas of what is seen on-screen, perhaps combining elements from a couple of outfits or substituting a different neckline, hemline, collar style, or the like. The range of experimentation suggests that films have made certain innovations thinkable and acceptable, particularly an expansion of silhouettes, colors, and textiles for women, whether a sleeveless *choli* with a sari or the color white in a *salwar kameez* (Dwyer and Patel 2002, 88). Film costumes also engender creative interactions between client and tailor in which bits and pieces of film images can be literally stitched together to make a unique garment. In these cases, film styles spread unevenly and idiosyncratically, with authorship sufficiently dispersed that it may be hard to decide whether finished garments reflect the vision and tastes of the original designer, or rather those of the dressmaker, the client, or even the tailor tasked with transposing flat designs and a series of conversations into an actual garment (Wilkinson-Weber 2005).

Buying a cheap knockoff or getting a more precise and fitted version of a film costume is commonplace for many Indian film fans, mostly in the lower-middle classes. Film is, in essence, their window into capitalism, introducing forms and uses that they can adapt as they see fit. This is not an approach much favored by contemporary designers, however, since it does not engage the most sophisticated tastes and determinations in India's contemporary fashion scene. Among other concerns, designers point to the large proportion of "masses" who get costume copies made, who have little capacity for introspection and reflection about their looks, and who "have no taste" to boot. Conventionally, the prolonged shooting schedule for most films militates against being able to use very up-to-date fashion. What looks cutting edge in one month will be stale several months later. Designers with excellent fashion credentials, like *Amir*, echoed remarks made by others like *Sonu*:

> All the outfits which you're making in a film, they're not fashion. Basically, you can use just the colors which are in, and the movie is released around six months later, that fashion changes. So what ultimately you see on screen is old outfits.

Another reason why the contemporary designers I interviewed were skeptical about whether film costume could ever be an exemplar of cutting-edge fashion was that they regarded audiences as tentative and risk-averse in their tastes. In part, their arguments bolstered their point about the importance of designing for character rather than fashion as a goal. Also, as previously noted, the fleeting nature of fashion and the tedious process of most Hindi filmmaking caused anything fashionable in a film to be unfashionable by the time it was released: the people who found it fashionable at that point were, in the temporal metaphor so common to discourse about modernity, behind the times. The most cynical view that I heard of the path beaten by costume to fashion was articulated by *Sunil*, who spoke from a position of confidence borne out of his interest in moving into mass-market apparel:

> So basically, when these film outfits become trendsetters, it's not sold in like a high-profile place or whatever. Mostly, what trendsetter means [is that] you'll see

[the costume] mostly selling on the roads, pavements, or vendors, or in smaller shops, because that's when, for the villagers or for the people in out of state, they're more fashion-conscious outfits.

The willful copying of costumes was also viewed somewhat askance by designers when it involved co-opting certain *filmi* elements that were clearly decent but, for everyday wear, tasteless. A glimpse into this attitude can be obtained from a scene in *Rangeela* that I already alluded to in an earlier chapter, where lower-class hero Munna (Aamir Khan) escorts Urmila Matondkar as Mili (his friend and the woman he secretly loves) to the foyer of a five-star hotel dressed in a loud, very *filmi* bright yellow shirt and trousers. As in many fish-out-of-water scenarios, the humor of the situation derives as much from Munna's inability to recognize the absurdity of his dress and behavior as from the dress and behavior itself (see Mazumdar 2007, 62, for a discussion of this scene). A man whose idea of dressing up is what film tells him is a somewhat sorry figure, although it cannot be argued that Munna derives a level of confidence from his suit that emphasizes the magical effects of Bollywood-style costume on those who copy it.

## Retail Innovations and Designer Interventions

With the acceleration of economic reforms, the middle class has grown markedly. Estimates as to its size are variable, perhaps because of the difficulty of precisely defining what the middle class actually is. For example, the National Council of Applied Economic Research estimated it had grown from 6 percent of the population in the decades following Independence to 18 percent by the turn of the millennium (Virdi 2003, 201). In 2010, however, the *Economic Times* put its lower limit at 13 percent and its upper end at 20 percent (2011). Either way, though it is numerically vast the middle class remains a minority within the country as a whole. In response to an ideological shift that has reconciled Indianness with the enjoyment of commodities and consumerist lifestyles (Ganti 2012, 17; Ludden 2012, 582, 596; Mazzarella 2005, 98; Mehta and Pandharipande 2011, 4–5), members of the middle class have come to share an interest in consumption, although the capacity to consume varies considerably from the top to the bottom of the ranking (Fernandes 2000). At its upper reaches, the middle class's collective purchasing power and thus contribution to India's consumer capitalism is immense (see also Deshpande 2003). The prevailing wisdom in financial and economic circles is that the middle class will continue to grow extremely rapidly in the immediate future (Saxena 2010, 2) and be the source of new markets (*Economic Times*

2011). The mushrooming of boutiques and stores selling brand-label cloth-ing in the suburban areas where I have done most of my research is a use-ful index of the growth of a consumer market for ready-mades. Global brands with substantial retail spaces along Linking Road in Bandra include Benetton, Levi's, and Nike. Shopper's Stop, with several branches throughout Mumbai, offers a department store experience to shoppers, while Indian chains such as Globus and Westside give over extensive floor space exclusively to the display of clothes. In among these colossuses are numerous small fashion boutiques and shoe stores. There are also, of course, a number of shopping malls in the city and its suburbs, complete with air-conditioning, food courts, small supermarkets, and, at the entrance of every single one, an airport-like security checkpoint through which every visitor must pass.

The newer retail spaces have little in common with the old-style shops in which clothes are folded and compacted on shelves, pulled out, and tossed in front of a buyer in a selection process that owes much to trial and error—and where the proprietors' tailors whip up costume copies on a few days' no-tice. Bright and airy, with clothes arranged on racks for ease of viewing, and with a striking preference for American pop or rock music in the background—in the larger stores, in any case—the newer businesses entail a different re-lationship between customer and seller. Sales associates include both men and women, who are themselves fashionably dressed, and while they are (to this customer anyway) more intrusive than their European or North American equivalents, nevertheless, the disposition of articles in the space of the shop hands over far more choice (and responsibility) to the buyer in deciding what to purchase—and, therefore, what to wear. While these newer businesses are important, and highly visible, additions to the retail scene in cities such as Mumbai, they have by no means replaced tailoring and dressmaking shops that cater to those consumers who have neither the means nor the inclina-tion to visit malls and brand-name stores. There are also plenty of shops that are filled with fake label clothes at bargain prices, the source of stylish clothing for buyers without any hope of buying authentic brand-name clothes. Jeans, those most ubiquitous of items, can range from 200 rupees for cheap Indian brands or global-brand knockoffs all the way up to 3,000 rupees or more for premium brands, depending upon where one looks. The 200-rupee jeans sometimes are obviously inferior to the brands being copied; other times not. One of the curious features of jeans is, in fact, the relative lack of overt distinction between a genuine premium-label pair and a cheap alterna-tive (Miller and Woodward 2007, 338).

With potential markets expanding, for designers of the immediate postliber-alization era, such as Manish Malhotra, Neeta Lulla, Rocky S, and Anna Singh, make film work just one part of their professional activities, alongside fashion design and, increasingly, fashion retailing in a variety of forms. Fashion designers with one foot in the film world and one outside are focused on the upper layers of Indian society, the very people who can afford (like their film avatars) the best and most expensive of everything. Catering to what are termed "the classes" (as opposed to "the masses") presents a unique opportunity for designers to become part of the global fashion scene. Film is as compelling an entertainment for them as for previous generations; their exposure to film is of a very different nature, however. Within India, they mostly see films at multiplexes with high prices, plush seats, and a more-decorous ambience than old-style theaters with balcony and orchestra seating. Their demands regarding plot, acting, and mise-en-scène, are shaped, to a great extent, by international filmmaking ideals. Some designers are now celebrities in their own right, their own fame fed by and feeding the stardom of actors. Stars insists on certain designers creating their film costumes, their event couture, and their promotional outfits. Designers, meanwhile, use their associations with stars to promote their other fashion and style activities, and it has become practically the norm for a movie star to be the showstopper when fashion collections are showcased in runway shows, such as the Lakmé Fashion Week (Pinto 2012a). In 2013, Hindi film heroine Vidya Balan was a juror at the Cannes Film Festival; prominent in the coverage of her presence at Cannes was mention of her favorite designer, Sabyasachi Mukherjee, who designed all the outfits she wore at the event and traveled with her to preside personally over her "look" (Mehta 2013).[1]

Complaints by designers about the poor quality of copies that are sold by street vendors or made to order by ordinary tailors are often balanced by accounts of how authorized copies (supervised by the designer) are being developed for sale in higher-status retail outlets. Over the past decade, designer websites have appeared that include promotional material for seasonal collections, bridal trousseaux, advertisements, and film. Designers' work for film is widely discussed in film magazines, in newspapers, and on online entertainment sites. In 2002, Neeta Lulla worked with Biba Apparels to prepare a range of clothes based on films such as *Taal* (1999), *Pardes* (1997), and *Badhaai ho Badhaai* (2002). A decade later, some of Lulla's costumes from the 2011 film *Devdas* were displayed in the Crossroads mall in Mumbai. In 2011, Manish Malhotra produced a line of clothing linked to the release of the film *Bodyguard*, starring Salman Khan and Kareena Kapoor. The clothes, which sold briskly, were modeled on the pastiche of looks created for Kapoor—"*kurtas*, mismatching ensembles and lots of oxidised jewellery" (Pinto 2012b). Designer websites belonging to Manish Malhotra, Neeta Lulla, Vikram Phadnis, Sabyasachi

Mukherjee, and others include links to film work as well as couture and prêt collections.

Older designers I spoke with lamented that ordinary people would ask for *filmi* clothes, not realizing that they would never look as good as a professional actor in the kinds of clothes that film designers made. Even with adjustments for modesty, the dictum was that most Indians did not having the body for Western clothes and would be disappointed in how they looked in a film outfit. Younger designers are more sanguine, realizing that a relentless focus on the bodies of actors validates and perhaps helps stimulate a growing interest among rich, young Indians in getting the same kinds of treatments—cosmetic, surgical, medicinal—to perfect their own frames. Men are not immune from these pressures; I have seen entire shelves of upscale department stores given over to muscle-mass protein powders and other weight-training aids. While wearing Western clothing (T-shirts, blouses, jeans, and so on) in public is still confined to the young and the affluent, no one I have met who habitually wears these kinds of clothes (women in particular) has expressed even a moment's discomfort or unease wearing them (unless this was an unease produced by the adverse reactions of men—which is, of course, a significant problem).

A final area in which we see designers—now in the sense of high-status, global labels—implicated in film is the rising popularity of product placement and product tie-ins. Shatrujit Singh, adviser to the chairman of Louis Vuitton, quoted in the *New York Times*, stated: "India has a young population. Movies are an important messenger of change, style and sophistication. . . . Bollywood has become like Hollywood, in terms of its emphasis on appearance, and as a fashion brand, it's important to align ourselves with this change" (Shah 2011). Louis Vuitton permitted a bag to be featured in 2003's *Kal Ho Na Ho*, and a Hermès bag took center stage in *Zindagi Na Milegi Dobara* (2008). Anecdotally, the appearances led to spikes in consumer interest in the brands, although spokespeople were coy as to whether the films actually could be said to have increased sales of any items (Shah 2011).

More mass-market brands also make use of opportunities to connect their names with films. When, in 2006, Pepe Jeans launched a collection of clothes inspired by *Dhoom: 2*, a press release on the Yash Raj Films website quoted Chetan Shah, the national head of Pepe Jeans London, as saying: "The exciting and explosive content of the movie encapsulates everything that the Pepe Jeans brand stands for—young, cool, trendy, hip, fashionable and innovative. The *D:2* tie-up will go a long way in enabling millions of Indian youth to connect with an aspirational jeanswear brand like Pepe" (Yash Raj Films 2006). The same year, menswear brand Louis Phillippe agreed a tie-in with the film

*Don*; it then offered a *Don* clothing line in its stores, launched by none other than "Don" himself, star Shah Rukh Khan (*Hindu Business Line* 2006). An essential part of the appeal of such a clothing line, besides its being directly associated with a film (and, therefore, well suited to the desires of filmgoers to copy costumes), is that the number of images of the star wearing the outfit that inspired it is greatly magnified by the sheer fact of the costume being part of a film and film marketing.

The rough-and-ready copying that packed shelves and racks with knockoffs is giving way, at least in the practices of more discriminating consumers, to more deliberative assessments of the impact of film costume on sartorial tastes. Writing about a coat worn by Preity Zinta in *Kal Ho Naa Ho*, Kanika Gahlaut opined that the success of versions that soon appeared in North Indian stores during an unusually cold winter meant that "Bollywood is finally influencing the upmarket, trendy youth" (Gahlaut 2004, 72). In 2010, an article in the *Hindustan Times* surveyed the potential of two 2010 films, *Harry Potter and the Deathly Hallows* and *Guzaarish*, for fashion consumers. Responses were gleaned from two designers, one a co-owner of a Mumbai boutique, and the emphasis was on assisting readers in fashioning their own versions of costumes they saw through astute shopping choices—for example, looking for "jackets in light cotton or silk weaves [that] can replace the heavier varieties worn abroad." Putting Bollywood costumes into the context of wider fashion trends, one interviewee said: "Scarves were always a hot trend, and now that Bollywood's picked it up, you see everyone wearing it. In fact, it's become more of a man's accessory than a woman's. . . . We over did the whole *kurti* [short *kurta*] phenomenon so you see everyone, even stars like Vidya Balan, moving towards longer silhouettes" (Pinto 2010).

It is striking to note the print articles and media interviews that make reference to film realism in the same breath as that familiar term, identification. Designer Shubhra Gupta, who worked on Anurag Kashyap's *Dev D* (2009) and *That Girl in Yellow Boots* (2010), is quoted in a 2011 article as saying: "With cinema changing its course, the need to connect with people has become much more prominent than to show them the glamorous side. I guess the realistic approach has come in now where a layman can feel or identify with the character through clothes" (Indo-Asian News Service 2011). An essay in the *Times of India* in 2004 discusses actors' new "freedom to dress in a more realistic fashion," citing Rani Mukherjee's comment on her film *Hum Tum* (2004): "I observed a lot of 12–21-year-olds, the way they talk, the way they dress. I wanted them to identify with me" (Bamzai 2004). The inference is that as spectators are presented with costumes that are more fashionable, more wearable, and less *filmi*, identification and its corollary, desire, will magically take root among the more sophisticated dressers in the audience. There is a relentless circularity in operation here. Films now draw upon a world of fashionable commodities, the same world in which versions of these commodities are becoming available to more and more consumers. Once a costume seizes the public imagination, copying it has always taken place very quickly. The goal of retailers, in collaboration with the film and advertising industries, is to shrink the time between viewing and buying as far as possible by starting up corporate-controlled machinery of impersonation even earlier than in the past. Let the roadside vendor continue to produce his cheap knockoffs; the choosy buyer can go instead to a reputable store and buy a "certified" copy.

There is another advantage in going for the "authorized" copies or, at least, the more upscale replications of film costumes, rather than going to a street vendor or even to the stalwart tailor: this is that whatever the customer gives up in fit or in cost is made up for in the level of reliability in the finished product. Standardization removes from the process of copying all the risks of a dress not coming out as one expected, as well as giving the prospective wearer the opportunity to get the outfit as soon as possible. A friend told me that an acquaintance of hers had paid for her tailor to see *Bunty aur Babli* with her, so that he would be able to copy Rani Mukherjee's outfits. Unfortunately, all the *kameezes* and kurtas came out far too short, and a long and hitherto satisfactory business relationship came to an abrupt end. Whether the tailor's apprehension of the costumes was in some way flawed, or whether the customer failed to anticipate how the clothes would look on her body without a more drawn out process of consultation and fitting, I do not know. Had she gone to buy ready-made items, trial and error would have allowed her to avoid such an expensive and upsetting result.

## THE LIMITS OF FILM INFLUENCE

The ever-closer ties between the film industry and the advertising and fashion industries are a result of a realignment of how costume is designed and understood in the filmmaking process. Bollywood costume fantasy can still reach into heady realms too daring for most viewers to follow, whether the difficulty is expense, everyday expectations of proper dress and behavior, or scenarios that are, to a greater or lesser extent, unreal or absurd. But Bollywood excess does not now root itself in the idiosyncratic approaches to fashion that are relentlessly mocked by contemporary designers; rather, the *filmi* is either displaced onto history, pastiche, and dreams (the latter always a suitable arena for the expression of desire) or domesticated within intrinsically fantastic events that everyone understands: weddings, festivals, and the like. The push toward greater realism to balance fantasy means there is a proportionately greater influence of film on the exploration of a modern identity that coincides with a range of acquired tastes in interior decoration, music, lifestyle, and so on—all practices to which easy familiarity with consumer settings is crucial. This is only in part the domain of runway, couture fashion; it better reflects, instead, the domain of street fashion—of young, middle-class, urban style. Designer Vikram Phadnis's decision to dress a college student (played by Aishwarya Rai Bachchan) not in the elite label Juicy Couture but in a (supposedly) mundane T-shirt and jeans in *Kyun! Ho Gaya Na* (2004) reflects this philosophy perfectly (Bamzai 2004, 62).

As mundane as these clothes seem to the uppermost layers of Indian society, they are assuredly not taken for granted by the majority. As I have already noted, Steve Derné (2005) and Shakuntala Rao (2007) have pointed out that most Indians have not accepted, still less adopted, the kinds of relationships and behaviors films depict. Men are most likely to have altered their clothes choices in response to film, while women's responses are, for the most part, comparatively muted, particularly with regard to the more daring kinds of outfits. Entrenched convictions about dress and morality, specifically in the relationship between certain kinds of clothing and degrees of body exposure, are still quite robust among the lower-middle and working classes. Additionally, the new kinds of retail outlets are accessible only to the very affluent, urban fractions of India's population, and off-the-rack clothes can be extremely expensive (Fernandes 2000). There is no doubt, however, that acute emotional responses to films are very much present across classes and communities. Stacey's work on English film viewing and costume reception in the materially diminished climate of wartime and rationing describes how her subjects were engaged in a complex negotiation of the boundaries of self and other as they thought through, and even acted out, the similarities as well as the differences between themselves and the stars they admired. Many of her subjects described intense emotional responses to films, alternately acknowledging the sheer distance of their own lives from those depicted onscreen or imagining themselves within the action. As the 1950s went on, the opportunities to buy commodities—dresses, hats, shoes, and so on—became more plentiful, and women who had already entertained fantasies of being like the stars they saw onscreen could now begin to realize them (Stacey 1994, 220). For a particular swath of Indian society, this process is repeating itself as consumer goods multiply.

Film also now faces competition for influence over dress choices from television, where many women (and men) see clothes that they like and feel they can reasonably wear, without succumbing to the global fashion trends and edgy looks found in film. Even consumers with fewer inhibitions have new places to look for fashion inspiration. Media industry events, red-carpet appearance, fashion shows—all provide fodder for the wealthy to augment their own wardrobes. In 2012, I visited a small shop that sold heavily embroidered saris, *lehenga cholis*, and *ghaghara cholis* for special events such as weddings. The proprietors drew their inspiration, in part, from film outfits, but also from what they could find on the web or in newspapers about appearances by celebrities at a variety of public events. The tailoring and embroidery the store had done on their goods came from the same category of *darzis* and embroidery *karigars* who might otherwise work on film costumes. The selling point of this shop's goods was that they were not a mere approximation of the clothing of the stars; they were, to all intents and purposes, the same thing. Another interesting trend is the growth of businesses catering to the fashionable inclinations of pious Muslim women. Film is perhaps one of the last places one might look for different fabrics, decorative elements, and so on to use for burqas, but women who want and can afford to "style" these concealing garments now have international Islamic clothes websites to consult, as well as information from friends and relatives who have traveled overseas. I once passed a shop (sadly closed at that hour) in the Seven Bungalows area in suburban Mumbai that had the name Variety Hijab (in reference to veiling

**Figure 24**  For sale here are beautiful embroidered clothes for special-event wear, many of them inspired by film, as well as TV and fashion shows. (Image courtesy of Clare Wilkinson-Weber.)

practices among Muslim women that connote modesty) and that purported to supply all manner of wants and desires for weddings.

Is India, therefore, at the point where the kinds of copying described by Stacey, and evident to date in India, are extended preludes to phases when consumer goods become sufficiently abundant and affordable that not only does a vast swath of society become avid and reliable buyers of commodities, but films (and stars) lose their unique position as arbiters of style? For some, yes it is; for most people, it is not. The prevailing mores and limited means of the majority of the Indian population keep these people out of the modern shops, with their novel ways of displaying goods and treating their customers. The more long-established sources of clothes are likely to linger for some time, in other words.

## FILM COPYING FILM

Although not an example of clothes escaping film to be appropriated and re-created in material form as the dress choices of ordinary Indians, nevertheless, the use of costume pastiche in films that purport to take place in the relatively recent past (*Om Shanti Om, Once Upon a Time in Mumbaai*) merits a few words, since it does represent a species of copying that, like the copying of everyday consumers, has its own distinct patterns and priorities. In both films, the audience's collusion is invited in producing "past worlds" (in this case, the 1970s) that are informed by film models. *Once Upon a Time in Mumbaai* (2010) features Kangna Ranaut as heroine Rihana wearing a succession of trouser suits, evening gowns, saris, and *churidar* kurtas—each time with a new hairstyle. In fact, Ranaut's hairdresser, Maria Sharma, put her own past experience to use, re-creating hairstyles she had originally done in the 1970s for stars such as Rehana Sultan and Hema Malini. In one of the film's most striking references to past films, Emraan Hashmi and Prachi Desai, as lovers Shoaib and Mumtaaz, recreate some of the magic of the 1973 film *Bobby*, starring Dimple Kapadia and Rishi Kapoor. After viewing the film together, Shoaib urges Mumtaaz to wear an exact copy of the famous miniskirt and polka-dot waist-tied blouse that Kapadia wore. The film hereby situates itself within a historical context that is defined by film viewership, and it compounds this by dressing Mumtaaz in a costume that is a copy of a copy of the original costume.

*Om Shanti Om* takes this one step further by insulating the 1970s to which it refers almost wholly inside a film frame. Even the hero, junior artist Om Prakash (Shah Rukh Khan), who longs to become a film star, lives entirely under the shadow of a vast billboard from which the heroine of his dreams, Shantipriya, smiles down on him. The political upheavals of the 1970s (border wars and the Emergency) evaporate completely, and life is retrospectively cast as the dream that film constructs. The costumes in the film's first half are ingeniously made to elicit memories of a 1970s genre of costumes without ever being a copy of any one of them. Director Farah Khan was emphatic that she did not want so much to bring the 1970s back to life as to interpret them, providing enough leeway for them to become items in promotional apparel sold in Shopper's Stop (Wilkinson-Weber 2010b, 140). With the industry heavily invested in what Tejaswini Ganti (2012, 95) terms "gentrification," remakes represent one tactic for turning the base metal of Hindi film trash and flash into something far more refined. Redoing the costume is part and parcel of this restorative project, which, given that it involves at least a modicum of research, overtly projects an impression of care and reflectiveness that might not have clung to the very films upon which these remakes are based. Other films, such Salman Khan's recent *Bodyguard* and *Dabangg*, are not remakes or even period films per se, but they co-opt characterization, camerawork, and dramatically extended and exaggerated fight scenes from 1970s and 1980s precedents. Costume, too, is enhanced through the creation of character looks, as well as by being displayed on more-disciplined bodies. Bollywood's own capacity for self-parody is now so well honed that Western film and television pastiches (in American shows as diverse as *Sesame Street*, *Dancing With the Stars*, and the unsuccessful TV musical series *Smash*), drawing on what they imagine Bollywood to be, are surprisingly amateurish and unpolished in comparison. If Hindi film dress designers and directors were once considered to be wide of the mark in their renditions of Western clothes, lifestyles, and locations, now it seems that the *chappal* (sandal) is on the other foot.

## LOOKING BACK

In the ten years since I began this piece of research, the field of costume production has shifted in some significant ways. In 2002, the personal designer as fashion emissary was uppermost; by 2012, the costume designer as a branch of a design enterprise that included production design and art direction was far more pronounced, at least in certain large-budget films, as well as in small, *hatke* (non-mainstream) films. With the designers active in the 1980s largely retired, the designers whose careers took off in the 1990s after economic liberalization were at their peak in the early 2000s. These designers are very much still around, but there is now an even newer wave of designers, arriving from around 2005, who are singularly dedicated to film costume design as their primary professional calling and with fewer simultaneous engagements in the fashion world. Everyone in 2002 said they designed for the character, and everyone does so now. What has changed is the kinds of films, the resources available to make them and to make costume, and the division of labor through which costume comes into being, finds its way onto an actor body, and then goes along whatever visual or material path is laid out for it.

Various issues present themselves at this new point of departure. First, there is the impact of film costume in a style environment that is characterized by discrepancies in wealth, taste, and morals, that is now thoroughly inundated with material goods, and that is increasingly opened up to new visual influences from television and the web (largely via handheld devices). There is the future of film costume in itself, with the aesthetic of realism becoming mainstreamed in production design and the *filmi* being carefully sectioned off (while simultaneously marked and celebrated). Still, the issues I find most interesting relate to the organization of labor, the nurturing of skills, and the integration of people involved with costume at all levels and all stages into collaborative (or competitive) frameworks. To date, there is still no costume department within which all the costume functions are subsumed, and there is no coherent plan that I know of to include dressmen and other craftspeople involved in costume in the massive project of professionalization that the industry says it is instituting. A few costume assistants and designers have described taking particularly talented dressmen under their wings to train them as competent costumers, but the impression that most costume assistants and designers give is that the dressman with a genuine thirst to do or learn more is the exception rather than the rule. Tailors and other craftspeople are formally acceded respect on the basis of their highly developed skills, but differences of class and education, and sometimes of gender, raise barriers that divide dressmen and artisans from designers and their assistants. Those on the "creative" side see complacency and limited horizons among dressmen and artisans; the latter, for their part, see arrogance and favoritism among the designers. The result is a certain obliviousness to the reality of the social characteristics that structure the situation and that make it harder to remake the business of film costume in its entirety from top to bottom. For now, the system canters along, quite well in fact, but it is, in essence, a set of new conventions, personnel, and goals dropped rather clumsily upon a foundation that is unchanged and comparatively ignored.

**Figure 25**  At this turn in the road on the way to Juhu, there is a rank of billboards that are always showing the latest in fashion, accessories, and films. This particular display was up in 2005 and included posters for hit films *Don* (2006) and *Kabhi Kushi Kabhie Gham . . .* (2001). (Image courtesy of Clare Wilkinson-Weber.)

Another area in which change is merely rerouting rather than uprooting existing patterns is the phenomenon of film stardom. Where once stars were important to sell films and a few select commodities, now they are the centripetal force that holds together several industries—advertising, fashion, media, public relations—with film as the industry that connects them all. New forms of industrial practice and expertise related to film are becoming commonplace (for example, talent agencies, professional management, brand development and design), coexisting with activities that are constantly adapted (but not revolutionized) to cope with new demands (tailoring, embroidery, jewelry-making). A key source in the future, with respect to how costume production develops, will be the film industry in its own reflections upon itself. DVD extras, such as "The Making of [name of the film]," are giving way to YouTube mini-features, but the facts they reveal are much the same. "The Making of . . ." features involve the industry's invasion of its own Goffman-esque backstages and the rendering of them as frontstages, subject to all the same molding and polishing that the mainstream products (that is, the films themselves) of the film industry require (see Goffman 1959). But in the very process of making practices such as costume production known, the messiness of its procedures, the details of sourcing, the struggle to create certain impressions and to simulate reality all become known. Perhaps there will be little ill effect of these revelations on the audience's willingness to enter into the proper spirit of spectatorial compliance. At the same time, however, the evident gap between what is made and what is seen opens a small window into dress manipulations and remediations that are cognates of what we all do in daily life.

Meanwhile, anthropologists, historians, and media scholars can continue to turn the anthropologist's "jeweler's eye" (Marcus and Fischer 1999, 15) onto the production of costumes, documenting more precisely the negotiations and manipulations that make up day-to-day practice in the industry. Another direction to take might be to reconstruct (using one or two films as examples) memories of costume from a variety of angles, including people from the dressman all the way to the director, in part to elicit the texture of a working culture from the past, but also to tease out variations in the narratives that are the surface signs of deeper fissures in making contextual sense of costume. A very obvious gap exists in what we know about how film viewers choose a costume to copy and go about obtaining that copy. Ethnographic work on this question would be a valuable contribution to research already ongoing in consumption; what would be essential, however, would be to link consumption practices to the productive endeavors of the people who do the copying. Finally, inviting commentaries from overlooked film personnel on a given film—drawing out, for example, the hairdresser's commentary or the dresswala's commentary as a film unfolds and the costume is in movement—will be important to elicit memories, as well as to observe the way in which recognition and viewership feed into this process. Acknowledging the significance of costume means accepting not just that dress materializes struggles over social mores and cultural identities, or even that it is capable of authoring its own semi-autonomous narrative in collusion with the actor's body. It means accepting that costume stamps on perception and memory the culmination of the work and imagination of many social agents, perhaps not least the viewer of the film himself or herself.

# Notes

## INTRODUCTION

1. Bombay was renamed Mumbai in 1995; however, Bombay is still popularly used in conversation, particularly by film personnel. I have retained Bombay when the name was used in an interview, as well as in reference to the city in the pre-Independence era, but I have otherwise used Mumbai to reflect current political realities.
2. The Hindu concept of *darsan* (a powerful, mutual gaze between god and worshipper) undergirds this interpretation, but the active, penetrative power of vision is well understood in Islamic tradition as well (Lutgendorf 2006, 231–2).
3. For in-depth discussions of the history of Indian cinema, and Hindi cinema in particular, see Ganti (2004), Majumdar (2009), Rajadhyaksha (1996a; 1996b), and Virdi (2003).
4. *Chikan* and *zardozi* embroideries are North Indian, urban craft products, and both have featured in Hindi film costumes over the years; handlooms are woven cotton fabrics championed by Mohandas Gandhi and other figures of the Independence movement and post-Independence era who put great stress upon encouraging indigenous handicraft production.

## CHAPTER 1 THE PEOPLE AND PLACES OF COSTUME PRODUCTION

1. I have used italicized pseudonyms for interviewees with a reasonable expectation of confidentiality and a position in the industry that carries with it greater vulnerability to those in power. Where the speaker is a well-known film figure and where written consent was obtained before press time, real names have been used. Elsewhere, and in particular with respect to remarks that might entail embarrassment to the speaker or those their speech refers to, italicized pseudonyms have been used.
2. The issue of credit is a complicated one. There do not seem to be any clear rules governing who is named where in the film's credits—sometimes costume/dress designers are in the opening credits, sometimes they are not. Categories to do with costume are also highly fluid. A given film might list names in the final credits under "costume," "dress," or "wardrobe." What is important about the

films cited here is that one designer is distinctly credited, rather than a ragtag of names being tossed into the credits.

3. Job titles can be the subject of intense negotiation between filmmaking sites in North America. Categories recognized in Vancouver, B.C. where I have done some comparative research, include costumer supervisor, set supervisor/key costumer, and truck, set, and prep costumers (Jane Still and Anthea Mallinson, personal communication). No such classification exists in Mumbai.

# CHAPTER 2  COSTUME AND CHARACTER: WEARING AND BEING

1. *Hum Dil De Chuke Sanam's* director, Sanjay Leela Bhansali, is noted for his attention to the design of his films and fits the definition of a director with a sufficiently strong vision to repel the tendencies toward costume fragmentation.
2. Among the best known examples of the repeated use of a name to drive home the identification of actor with a persona is the association of Amitabh Bachchan in the earlier part of his career with characters named "Vijay." Additionally, the case of Raj Kapoor is described in Chapter 4.
3. Figures 8, 10–16, and 19–21 are screen captures chosen to reflect film "moments" that merit special analysis.
4. A "star" director can have considerable sway over an actor, as well as over the visual coherence of the film project as a whole. So, too, can an influential art director or, even more so, a production designer, who coordinates all aspects of the film's look.

# CHAPTER 3  COSTUME AND THE BODY

1. *Spot boy* is the term given to the male or female lead's assistant paid for by the production to assist the artist during the course of filming. The spot boy is always male, and does assorted tasks the actors set him, including any kind of fetching and carrying.
2. These remarks echo Christopher Breward's essay on the importance of the tailor's skill in crafting the custom-made suit in the late nineteenth century (Breward 2001).
3. For a detailed and incisive analysis of the song "Chole ke peechay kya hai?" (What's beneath my blouse?), see Monika Mehta (2011, 159–84).
4. Some caricatures of women are clearly informed by the performative traditions of *hijras* (eunuchs), whose preference for female attire is dictated in part by desire but also in part by their lacking "entitlement" to men's clothing (Nanda 1998).

## CHAPTER 4  FASHION AND SPECTACLE

1. Often stars play characters who are lower in social status than their clothes would seem to imply (a phenomenon observable in other film industries as well, including the American). In other words, the engagement of fashion is considered to be more important in characterization than conforming to the tastes and capacities of real members of the middle and lower-middle classes.
2. Raja Ravi Varma was a prominent Indian painter of the late nineteenth century, whose portraits of Indians and depictions of Indian deities had an incalculable impact on the visual culture of contemporary India (Guha Thakurta 1991; Pinney 1995).

## CHAPTER 5  DRESSING THE PAST

1. This is the "veridiction contract" (Calefato 2004, 92), which refers to the production of "truth" within constrained social and historical circumstances. In other words, not only must what is considered to be true conform to certain expectations about knowledge and verification, but truth itself is produced within the framework of these expectations. Calefato's usage derives from Algirdas Greimas, Frank Collins, and Paul Perron (1989), and the concept of veridiction itself comes from Michel Foucault.
2. *The Legend of Bhagat Singh*, Devgn's film, fared better than Deol's—*23rd March 1931: Shaheed*. After the rush of Bhagat Singh biopics, there was a lull in films specifically about the more-contentious Independence fighters—although Bhagat Singh did make a shadowy appearance in the 2006 film *Rang De Basanti*.
3. Thus, in the film *Utsav*, based on the second-century BCE story of courtesan and dancer Vasantsena, it was necessary to stitch the costumes of star Rekha, even though it was clearly understood that clothes of the time were draped, not sewn. The explanation was that the dance scenes would have been far more difficult and challenging for the star had she not had outfits that were stitched and fitted to withstand vigorous movement.

## CHAPTER 6  BEYOND THE SCREEN

1. At the 2013 Cannes Film Festival, Vidya Balan's and Amitabh Bachchan's clothes were generally criticized, while Aishwarya Rai (now Aishwarya Rai Bachchan) was reviewed favorably. Even now, Rai Bachchan is considered the best fashion ambassador for India at events like these.

# Bibliography

Appadurai, A. 1990. "Disjuncture and Difference in the Global Cultural Economy." *Public Culture* 2 (2): 1–24.

Athaiya, B. R. 2010. *The Art of Costume Design*. Noida: HarperCollins India.

Bamzai, D. 2004. "Bollywood's Coolest Summer: The Trendspotter's Guide to 2004." *India Today* (April 19). Available at: http://archives.digitaltoday.in/indiatoday/20040419/cover.html. Accessed August 27, 2013.

Banerjee, M., and D. Miller. 2003. *The Sari*. New York: Oxford University Press.

Banks, M. 2009. "Gender Below the Line: Defining Feminist Production Studies." In *Production Studies: Cultural Studies of Media Industries*, ed. V. Mayer, M. Banks, and J. T. Caldwell, 87–98. New York: Routledge.

Barber, K. 2003. *The Generation of Plays: Yoruba Popular Life in Theater*. Bloomington: Indiana University Press.

Barnes, R., and J. B. Eicher. 1992. *Dress and Gender: Making and Meaning*. New York: Berg.

Barnouw, E., and S. Krishnaswamy. 1980. *Indian Film*. Vol. 2. New York: Oxford University Press.

Barthes, R. 1990. *The Fashion System*, trans. M. Ward and R. Howard. Berkeley: University of California Press.

Bayly, C. A. 1986. "The Origins of Swadeshi (Home Industry): Cloth and Indian Society, 1700–1930." In *The Social Life of Things: Commodities in Cultural Perspective*, ed. A. Appadurai, 285–322. New York: Cambridge University Press.

BBC IndiaFM. 2008. "Ayesha Takia Won't Wear a Bikini for Hollywood." Available at: http://entertainment.oneindia.in/bollywood/gupshup/2008/ayesha-takia-no-bikini-080108.html. Accessed August 30, 2013.

Bean, S. S. 1989. "Gandhi and Khadi, the Fabric of Independence." In *Cloth and Human Experience*, ed. A. B. Weiner and J. Schneider, 355–76. Smithsonian Series in Ethnographic Inquiry. Washington, DC: Smithsonian Institution Press.

Becker, H. S. 1982. *Art Worlds*. Berkeley: University of California Press.

Bernard, M. 2002. *Fashion as Communication*. 2nd ed. New York: Routledge.

Berry, S. 2000. *Screen Style?: Fashion and Femininity in 1930s Hollywood*. Minneapolis: University of Minnesota Press.

Bhaskar, I., and R. Allen. 2009. *Islamicate Cultures of Bombay Cinema*. New Delhi: Tulika.

Bhatkal, S. 2002. *The Spirit of Lagaan*. Mumbai: Popular Prakashan.

Bhaumik, K. 2005. "Sulochana: Clothes, Stardom and Gender in Early Indian Cinema." In *Fashioning Film Stars: Dress, Culture, Identity*, ed. R. Moseley, 87–97. New York: Routledge.

Bhushan, R. 2010. "Aamir Khan Bags Biggest Endorsement Deal with Etisalat." *Economic Times* (January 21). Available at: http://articles.economictimes.india times.com/2010-01-21/news/28390738_1_indian-advertising-endorsement-vikram-mehra. Accessed August 30, 2013.

Bhutia, P. D. 2011. "Clause & Effect Game of Bollywood." *Times of India* (June 30). Available at: http://articles.timesofindia.indiatimes.com/2011-06-30/news-inter views/29717776_1_bikini-emraan-hashmi-clause. Accessed August 30, 2013.

Booth, G. D. 1995. "Traditional Content and Narrative Structure in the Hindi Commercial Cinema." *Asian Folklore Studies* 54 (2): 169–90.

Bourdieu, P. 1977. *Outline of a Theory of Practice*. New York: Cambridge University Press.

Bourdieu, P. 1993. *The Field of Cultural Production*, ed. R. Johnson. New York: Columbia University Press.

Breckenridge, C. A. 1989. "The Aesthetics and Politics of Colonial Collecting: India at World Fairs." *Comparative Studies in Society and History* 31 (2): 195–216.

Breward, C. 2001. "Manliness, Modernity and the Shaping of Male Clothing." In *Body Dressing*, ed. J. Entwistle and E. Wilson, 165–82. New York: Berg.

Bruzzi, S. 1997. *Undressing Cinema?: Clothing and Identity in the Movies*. London: Routledge.

Caldwell, J. T. 2008. *Production Culture?: Industrial Reflexivity and Critical Practice in Film and Television*. Durham, NC: Duke University Press.

Calefato, P. 2004. *The Clothed Body*. New York: Berg.

Calhoun, J. 2008. "Modern Mode: Film Costume Design in the Here and Now." Available at: http://livedesignonline.com/mag/show_business_modern_mode_film. Accessed August 30, 2013.

Cavallaro, D., and A. Warwick. 1998. *Fashioning the Frame: Boundaries, Dress and the Body*. London: Berg.

Chakravarty, S. S. 1993. *National Identity in Indian Popular Cinema, 1947–1987*. Austin: University of Texas Press.

Church Gibson, P. 2012. *Fashion and Celebrity Culture*. New York: Berg.

Cohn, B. S. 1989. "Cloth, Clothes, and Colonialism: India in the Nineteenth Century." In *Cloth and Human Experience*, ed. A. B. Weiner and J. Schneider, 303–54. Washington, DC: Smithsonian Institution Press.

Cohn, B. 1998. "The Past in the Present: India as Museum of Mankind." *History and Anthropology* 11 (1): 1–38.

Cook, P. 2004. *Screening the Past: Memory and Nostalgia in Cinema*. New York: Routledge.

Craik, J. 1994. *The Face of Fashion?: Cultural Studies in Fashion*. London: Routledge.

DeNicola, A. O. 2005. "Working through Tradition: Experiential Learning and Formal Training as Markers of Class and Caste in North Indian Block Printing." *Anthropology of Work Review* 26 (2): 12–16.

Derné, S. 2005. "The (Limited) Effect of Cultural Globalization in India: Implications for Culture Theory." *Poetics* 33 (1): 33–47.

Deshpande, S. 2003. *Contemporary India: A Sociological View*. New Delhi: Penguin India.

Dickey, S. 1993. *Cinema and the Urban Poor in South India*. Cambridge: Cambridge University Press.

Doane, M. 1991. *Femmes Fatales?: Feminism, Film Theory, Psychoanalysis*. New York: Routledge.

Douglas, M. 2002. *Purity and Danger: An Analysis of Concepts of Pollution and Taboo*. New York: Routledge.

Dubey, B. 2010. "Bhanu Athaiya Fumes over Tailor Remark." *Times of India* (July 8). Available at: http://articles.timesofindia.indiatimes.com/2010-07-08/mumbai/2828 2112_1_fashion-designer-tax-exemption-tarun-tahiliani. Accessed August 30, 2012.

Dubey, B. 2011. "Playing at Chor Bazaar, the Director's Special." *Times of India* (November 13). Available at: http://articles.timesofindia.indiatimes.com/2011-11-13/special-report/30393773_1_chor-bazaar-film-industry-milan-luthria. Accessed August 20, 2013.

Dudrah, R. 2008. "Queer as Desis: Secret Politics of Gender and Sexuality in Bollywood Films in Diasporic Urban Ethnoscapes." In *Global Bollywood?: Travels of Hindi Song and Dance*. ed. S. Gopal and S. Moorti, 288–307. Minneapolis: University of Minnesota Press.

Dwyer, R. 2000a. *All You Want Is Money, All You Need Is Love?: Sexuality and Romance in Modern India*. New York: Cassell.

Dwyer, R. 2000b. "Bombay Ishtyle." In *Fashion Cultures*, ed. S. Bruzzi and P. Church Gibson, 178–90. New York: Routledge.

Dwyer, R. 2000c. "The Erotics of the Wet Sari in Hindi Films." *South Asia: Journal of South Asian Studies* 23 (2): 143–60.

Dwyer, R. 2002. *Yash Chopra*. London: British Film Institute.

Dwyer, R. 2006a. "The Saffron Screen: Hindu Nationalism and the Hindi Film." In *Religion, Media, and the Public Sphere*, ed. B. Meyer and A. Moors, 273–90. Bloomington: Indiana University Press.

Dwyer, R. 2006b. *Filming the Gods: Religion and Indian Cinema*. New York: Routledge.

Dwyer, R. 2008. "The Indian Film Magazine: Stardust." In *Global Bollywood*, ed. A. P. Kavoori and A. Punathambekar, 240–67. New York: New York University Press.

Dwyer, R., and D. Patel. 2002. *Cinema India?: The Visual Culture of Hindi Film*. New Brunswick, NJ: Rutgers University Press.

Dyer, R. 2003. *Heavenly Bodies: Film Stars and Society*. New York: Routledge.

Eckert, C. 1990. "The Carole Lombard in Macy's Window." In *Fabrications: Costume and the Female Body*, 100–21. New York: Routledge.

*Economic Times*. 2011. "India's Middle Class Population to Touch 267 Million in 5 Yrs." February 6. Available at: http://articles.economictimes.indiatimes.com/2011-02-06/news/28424975_1_middle-class-households-applied-economic-research. Accessed August 30, 2013.

*Economic Times*. 2012. "Coke Ropes in Kareena Kapoor to Endorse Limca for Rs 2.5 Cr a Year." April 13. Available at: http://articles.economictimes. indiatimes.com/2012-04-13/news/31337556_1_coke-ropes-limca-rival-pepsico. Accessed August 30, 2013.

Eicher, J. B. 2001. "Dress, Gender, and the Public Display of Skin." In *Body Dressing*, ed. J. Entwistle and E. Wilson, 233–52. New York: Berg.

Eicher, J. B., S. Evenson, and H. Lutz, eds. 2000. *The Visible Self?: Global Perspectives on Dress, Culture, and Society*. New York: Fairchild.

Elison, W. 2010. " 'Bonafide Tribals': Religion and Recognition among Denizens of Mumbai's Forest Frontier." *Journal for the Study of Religion, Nature, and Culture* 4 (2): 191–212.

Entwistle, J. 2000. *The Fashioned Body: Fashion, Dress and Modern Social Theory*. Malden, MA: Blackwell Press.

Entwistle, J. 2001. "The Dressed Body." In *Body Dressing*, ed. J. Entwistle and E. Wilson, 33–58. New York: Berg.

Entwistle, J., and E. Wilson. 2001. "Introduction: Body Dressing." In *Body Dressing*, ed. J. Entwistle and E. Wilson, 1–12. New York: Berg.

Evans, C. 2003. *Fashion at the Edge: Spectacle, Modernity, and Deathliness*. New Haven, CT: Yale University Press.

Express Features Service. 2011. "The Skirt Is Haute Property." *Indian Express* (April 22): Available at: http://www.indianexpress.com/news/the-skirt-is-haute-property/779728/. Accessed August 30, 2013.

Fabian, J. 2002. *Time and the Other: How Anthropology Makes Its Object*. New York: Columbia University Press.

Farndale, N. 2009. "Slumdog Millionaire Star Dev Patel: An Underdog No More." *The Telegraph* (February 6). Available at: http://www.telegraph.co.uk/culture/film/4524146/Slumdog-Millionaire-star-Dev-Patel-an-underdog-no-more.html. Accessed August 30, 2013.

Farred, G. 2004. "The Double Temporality of Lagaan: Cultural Struggle and Postcolonialism." *Journal of Sport & Social Issues* 28 (2): 93–114.

Faulkner, R. R. 2002. *Hollywood Studio Musicians*. Lanham, MD: University Press of America.

Fernandes, L. 2000. "Restructuring the New Middle Class in Liberalizing India." *Comparative Studies of South Asia, Africa, and the Middle East* 20 (1–2): 88–112.

Gadihoke, S. 2010. "Selling Soap and Stardom: The Story of Lux." *Tasveer Ghar: A Digital Archive of South Asia Popular Visual Culture*. Available at: http://www.tasveergharindia.net/cmsdesk/essay/104/index_2.html. Accessed August 30, 2013.

Gahlaut, K. 2004. "Style It Like Bollywood." *India Today* (September 6): 60.

Gaines, J., and C. Herzog. 1990. *Fabrications?: Costume and the Female Body*. New York: Routledge.

Ganti, T. 2004. *Bollywood?: A Guidebook to Popular Hindi Cinema*. New York: Routledge.

Ganti, T. 2012. *Producing Bollywood: Inside the Contemporary Hindi Film Industry.* Durham: Duke University Press.

Gell, A. 1986. "Newcomers to the World of Goods: Consumption among the Muria Gonds." In *The Social Life of Things*, ed. A. Appadurai, 110–40. Cambridge: Cambridge University Press.

Gell, A. 1998. *Art and Agency: An Anthropological Theory.* New York: Oxford University Press.

Gilligan, S. 2011. "Heaving Cleavages and Fantastic Frock Coats: Gender Fluidity, Celebrity and Tactile Transmediality in Contemporary Costume Cinema." *Film, Fashion & Consumption* 1 (1): 7–38.

Gledhill, C. 1991. "Signs of Melodrama." In *Stardom: Industry of Desire*, ed. C. Gledhill, 207–29. London: Routledge.

Gloss. 2013. "Interview with Hollywood Costume Designer, Janty Yates." Available at: http://www.gloss.co.nz/Entertainment/Film/Interview-with-Hollywood-Costume-Designer-Janty-Yates.html. Accessed June 18, 2013.

Goffman, E. 1959. *The Presentation of Self in Everyday Life.* Garden City, New York: Doubleday.

Gopal, S., and S. Moorti. 2008. "Introduction: Travels of Hindi Song and Dance." In *Global Bollywood: Travels of Hindi Song and Dance*, ed. S. Gopal and S. Moorti, 1–62. Minneapolis: University of Minnesota Press.

Govil, Nitin. 2008. "Bollywood and the Frictions of Global Mobility." In *The Bollywood Reader*, ed. R. Dudrah and J. Desai, 201–15. New York: Open University Press.

Greenough, P. 1995. "Nation, Economy, and Tradition Displayed: The Indian Crafts Museum, New Delhi." In *Consuming Modernity: Public Culture in a South Asian World*, ed. C. A. Breckenridge, 216–48. Minneapolis: University of Minnesota Press.

Greimas, A. J., F. Collins, and P. Perron. 1989. "The Veridiction Contract." *New Literary History* 20 (3): 651.

Grimaud, E. 2003. *Bollywood Film Studio?: Ou Comment Les Films Se Font à Bombay.* Paris: CNRS Éditions.

Guha Thakurta, T. 1991. "Women as 'Calendar Art' Icons: Emergence of the Pictorial Stereotype in Colonial India." *Economic and Political Weekly* 26 (43): 91–99.

Hallpike, C. R. 1969. "Social Hair." *Man* 4 (2): 256.

Handler, R. 1986. "Authenticity." *Anthropology Today* 2 (1): 2–4.

Hansen, K. T. 2002. "A Different Desire, a Different Femininity: Theatrical Transvestism in the Parsi, Gujarati, and Marathi Theatres, 1850–1940." In *Queering India: Same-Sex Love and Eroticism in Indian Culture and Society*, ed. R. Vanita, 163–80. New York: Routledge.

Hansen, K. T. 2003. "Languages on Stage: Linguistic Pluralism and Community Formation in the Nineteenth-Century Parsi Theatre." *Modern Asian Studies* 37 (2): 381–405.

Hansen, K. T. 2004. "The World in Dress: Anthropological Perspectives on Clothing, Fashion, and Culture." *Annual Review of Anthropology* 33: 369–92.

Hastrup, K. 1998. "Theatre as a Site of Passage: Some Reflections on the Magic of Acting." In *Ritual, Performance, Media*, ed. F. Hughes-Freeland, 29–45. ASA Monographs 35. New York: Routledge.

Higson, A. 2003. *English Heritage, English Cinema?: Costume Drama since 1980*. New York: Oxford University Press.

*Hindu Business Line*. 2006. "Louis Philippe Unveils New Don Collection." October 23. Available at: http://www.thehindubusinessline.com/todays-paper/tp-marketing/louis-philippe-unveils-new-don-collection/article1749700.ece. Accessed August 30, 2013

*Hindustan Times*. 2012. "Aishwarya Rai Criticised for Post-baby Figure." May 17. Available at: http://www.hindustantimes.com/Entertainment/Fashion/Aishwarya-Rai-criticised-for-post-baby-figure/Article1-857304.aspx. Accessed August 30, 2013.

Inden, R. 1999. "Transnational Class, Erotic Arcadia, and Commercial Utopia in Hindi Films." In *Image Journeys: Audio-visual Media and Cultural Change in India*, ed. C. Brosius and M. Butcher, 41–66. New Delhi: Sage.

*Indian Express*. 2011. "SRK, Kareena to Attend Dubai Premiere of 'Ra.One.'" October 20. Available at: http://www.indianexpress.com/news/srk-kareena-to-attend-dubai-premiere-of-ra.one/862762. Accessed August 30, 2013.

Indo-Asian News Service. 2011. "Fashion Changing in Bollywood, Connecting with People." *BollywoodWorld* (September 15). Available at: http://www.bollywoodworld.com/bollywood-news/fashion-changing-in-bollywood-connecting-with-people-116393.html. Accessed August 30, 2013.

Indo-Asian News Service. 2012. "Sonakshi Sinha Says No to Bikini." *Hindustan Times* (May 23). Available at: http://www.hindustantimes.com/Entertainment/Bollywood/No-bikini-for-Sonakshi-Sinha/Article1-859516.aspx. Accessed August 30, 2013.

Jha, S. K. 2011. "Karisma Brings Manish Malhotra on Board for Dangerous Ishq." *Bollywood Hungama* (July 28). Available at: http://www.bollywoodhungama.com/moviemicro/news/type/view/id/1353287. Accessed August 30, 2013.

Kabir, N. 2001. *Bollywood?: The Indian Cinema Story*. London: Channel 4 Books.

Kavi, A. R. 2000. "The Changing Image of the Hero in Hindi Films." In *Queer Asian Cinema: Shadows in the Shade*, ed. A. Grossman, 307–12. Binghamton, NY: Haworth.

Kesavan, M. 2008. "No One Writes to the Prison Doc Anymore." *Outlook India* (May 19). Available at: http://www.outlookindia.com/article.aspx?237463. Accessed August 30, 2013.

Khan, S. 2011. "Recovering the Past in Jodhaa Akbar: Masculinities, Femininities and Cultural Politics in Bombay Cinema." *Feminist Review* 99 (1): 131–46.

King, B. 1985. "Articulating Stardom." *Screen* 26 (5): 27–50.

Klein, N. 2000. *No Logo?: Taking Aim at the Brand Bullies*. New York: Picador.

Kopytoff, I. 1986. "The Cultural Biography of Things: Commoditization as Process." In *The Social Life of Things*, ed. A. Appadurai, 64–94. New York: Cambridge University Press.

Landis, D. 2006. "Costume Designers, Costumers & Fashion Designers." Available at: http://costumedesignersguild.com/wp-content/themes/costumedesignersguild/downloads/costume-designers-costumers-fashion-designers.pdf. Accessed August 30, 2013.

Lave, J., and E. Wenger. 1991. *Situated Learning?: Legitimate Peripheral Participation*. Cambridge: Cambridge University Press.

Ludden, D. 2012. "Imperial Modernity: History and Global Inequity in Rising Asia." *Third World Quarterly* 33 (4): 581–601.

Lutgendorf, P. 2006. "Is There an Indian Way of Filmmaking?" *International Journal of Hindu Studies* 10 (3): 227–56.

Maclean, K. 2011. "The Portrait's Journey: The Image, Social Communication and Martyr-Making in Colonial India." *Journal of Asian Studies* 70 (4): 1051–82.

Maeder, E. 1987. *Hollywood and History: Costume Design in Film*. London: Thames and Hudson.

Majumdar, N. 2009. *Wanted Cultured Ladies Only!: Female Stardom and Cinema in India, 1930s–1950s*. Urbana: University of Illinois Press.

Marcus, G. E., and M.M.J. Fischer. 1999. *Anthropology as Cultural Critique: An Experimental Moment in the Human Sciences*. Chicago: University of Chicago Press.

Marx, K.F.B. [1867] 1976. *Capital: A Critique of Political Economy*. Vol. 1. New York: Vintage.

Mazumdar, R. 2007. *Bombay Cinema: An Archive of the City*. 1st ed. Minneapolis: University of Minnesota Press.

Mazzarella, W. 2005. *Shoveling Smoke: Advertising and Globalization in Contemporary India*. Durham, NC: Duke University Press.

McDonald, T. J. 2010. *Hollywood Catwalk: Exploring Costume and Transformation in American Film*. London: I. B. Tauris.

Mehta, M. 2011. *Censorship and Sexuality in Bombay Cinema*. Austin: University of Texas Press.

Mehta, R. B., and R. V. Pandharipande, eds. 2011. *Bollywood and Globalization: Indian Popular Cinema, Nation, and Diaspora*. New York: Anthem Press.

Mehta, S. 2013. "Sabyasachi Mukherjee Defends His Cannes Creations for Vidya Balan." *Hindustan Times* (June 20). Available at: http://www.hindustantimes.com/Entertainment/Fashion/Sabyasachi-Mukherjee-defends-his-Cannes-creations-for-Vidya-Balan/Article1–1079511.aspx. Accessed August 30, 2013.

Miller, D. 1997. *Material Culture and Mass Consumption*. 1st ed. New York: Wiley-Blackwell.

Miller, D. 2005. "Introduction." In *Clothing as Material Culture*, ed. S. Kuchler and D. Miller, 1–20. New York: Berg.

Miller, D., and S. Woodward. 2007. "Manifesto for a Study of Denim." *Social Anthropology* 15 (3): 335–51.

Mishra, V., P. Jeffery, and B. Shoesmith. 1989. "The Actor as Parallel Text in Bombay Cinema." *Quarterly Review of Film & Video* 11 (3): 49–67.

Mohsini, M. 2010. "Becoming an 'Asli Karigar': The Production of Authenticity among Old Delhi's Muslim Artisans." PhD Thesis, School of Oriental and African Studies, London.

Monks, A. 2010. *The Actor in Costume*. New York: Palgrave Macmillan.

Morris, R. C. 2009. "The Costumes That Made Them Stars." *New York Times* (August 11). Available at: http://www.nytimes.com/2009/08/11/fashion/11iht-ftirelli.html. Accessed August 30, 2013.

Moseley, R. 2005. *Fashioning Film Stars?: Dress, Culture, Identity*. London: British Film Institute.

Nanda, S. 1998. *Neither Man nor Woman: The Hijras of India*. 2nd ed. Belmont, CA: Wadsworth.

Naremore, J. 1988. *Acting in the Cinema*. Berkeley: University of California Press.

Nielsen, E. 1990. "Handmaidens of the Glamour Culture: Costumers in the Hollywood Studio System." In *Fabrications: Costume and the Female Body*, ed. J. Gaines and C. Herzog, 160–79. New York: Routledge.

Obeyesekere, G. 1984. *Medusa's Hair: An Essay on Personal Symbols and Religious Experience*. Chicago: University of Chicago Press.

Ortner, S. B. 2009. "Studying Sideways: Ethnographic Access in Hollywood." In *Production Studies: Cultural Studies of Media Industries*, ed. V. Mayer, M. Banks, and J. T. Caldwell, 175–89. New York: Routledge.

Patel, A., and D. Dugar. 2011. "Bal Thackeray's Fashion Designer, in the House." *CNN Travel* (August 9). Available at: http://travel.cnn.com/mumbai/shop/bal-thackerays-fashion-designer-house-515261. Accessed August 30, 2013.

Pattison, S. 2011. *Seeing Things: Deepening Relations with Visual Artefacts*. London: SCM Press.

Pinney, C. 1995. " 'An Authentic Indian "Kitsch" ': The Aesthetics, Discriminations and Hybridity of Popular Hindu Art." *Social Analysis* 38: 88–105.

Pinney, C. 2004. *Photos of the Gods: The Printed Image and Political Struggle in India*. London: Reaktion Books.

Pinto, J. 2006. *Helen: The Life and Times of an H-Bomb*. New Delhi: Penguin Books.

Pinto, R. 2010. "Aishwarya's Dresses, Emma's Jackets." *Hindustan Times* (November 25). Available at: http://www.hindustantimes.com/Entertainment/Fashion/Aishwarya-s-dresses-Emma-s-jackets/Article1-628752.aspx. Accessed August 30, 2013.

Pinto, R. 2012a. "Lakme Fashion Week: Ready, Set, Go." *Hindustan Times* (March 4). Available at: http://www.hindustantimes.com/Entertainment/Fashion/Lakme-Fashion-Week-Ready-set-go/Article1-820629.aspx. Accessed August 30, 2013.

Pinto, R. 2012b. "Costume Count." *Hindustan Times* (April 6). Available at: http://www.hindustantimes.com/Books/LiteraryBuzz/Costume-count/Article1-898263.aspx. Accessed August 30, 2013.

Powerhouse Museum. 2013. "2008/199/2 Film Costume, Black Diamonds, from the Movie, 'Moulin Rouge,' Various Materials, Designed by Baz Luhrmann/

Catherine Martin/Angus Strathie, Sydney, New South Wales, Australia, 2000." Available at: http://www.powerhousemuseum.com/collection/database/?irn=3 83691&collection=Baz+Luhrmann+Movie. Accessed June 18, 2013.

Prasad, M. M. 1998. *Ideology of the Hindi Film?: A Historical Construction*. Delhi: Oxford University Press.

Rabine, L.W., and S. Kaiser. 2006. "Sewing Machines and Dream Machines in Los Angeles and San Francisco." In *Fashion's World Cities*, ed. C. Breward and D. Gilbert, 235–50. Oxford: Berg.

Rajadhyaksha, A. 1996a. "Indian Cinema: Origins to Independence." In *The Oxford History of World Cinema*, ed. G. Nowell-Smith, 398–409. New York: Oxford University Press.

Rajadhyaksha, A. 1996b. "India: Filming the Nation." In *The Oxford History of World Cinema*, ed. G. Nowell-Smith, 678–89. New York: Oxford University Press.

Ramamurthy, P. 2008. "All-Consuming Nationalism: The Indian Modern Girl in the 1920s and 30s." In *The Modern Girl around the World*, ed. A. E. Weinbaum and the Modern Girl around the World Research Group, 147–73. Durham, NC: Duke University Press.

Rao, R. R. 2000. "Memories Pierce the Heart: Homoeroticism, Bollywood-style." In *Queer Asian Cinema: Shadows in the Shade*, ed. A. Grossman, 299–306. Binghamton, NY: Haworth.

Rao, S. 2007. "The Globalization of Bollywood: An Ethnography of Non-Elite Audiences in India." *The Communication Review* 10 (1): 57–76.

rediff.com. 2008. "Dressing up Jodha & Akbar." Available at: http://specials.rediff.com/movies/2008/feb/12sd1.htm. Accessed August 30, 2013.

Reuben, B. 1979. *The Shalimar Adventure*. New Delhi: Vikas.

Robson, J. 2002. "All Set for an Indian Summer." *The Telegraph* (May 21). Available at: http://fashion.telegraph.co.uk/news-features/TMG3299784/All-set-for-an-Indian-summer.html. Accessed August 30, 2013.

Sahlins, M. 2000. "Notes on the American Clothing System." In *American Cultural Studies: A Reader*, ed. J. Hartley, R. E. Pearson, and E. Vieth, 96–105. New York: Oxford University Press.

Sassatelli, R. 2007. *Consumer Culture: History, Theory and Politics*. Thousand Oaks, CA: Sage.

Saxena, R. 2010. "The Middle Class in India: Issues and Opportunities." *Deutsche Bank Research* (February 15). Available at: http://www.dbresearch.de/PROD/DBR_INTERNET_DE-PROD/PROD0000000000253735.pdf. Accessed August 30, 2013.

Schechner, R. 1985. *Between Theater & Anthropology*. Philadelphia: University of Pennsylvania Press.

Screen Weekly. 2007. "Anaita Shroff—The Stylist for *Dhoom 2*." *Oneindia Entertainment* (January 1). Available at: http://entertainment.oneindia.in/bollywood/features/2007/dhoom2-010107.html. Accessed August 30, 2013.

Shah, G. R. 2011. "Bollywood Takes Some Style Cues." *New York Times* (October 4). Available at: http://www.nytimes.com/2011/10/05/fashion/bollywood-takes-some-style-cues.html. Accessed August 30, 2013.

Shiekh, M. 2008. *The Making of Om Shanti Om*. New Delhi: Om Books International.

Spooner, B. 1986. "Weavers and Dealers." In *The Social Life of Things: Commodities in Cultural Perspective*, ed. A. Appadurai, 195–235. New York: Cambridge University Press.

Sprengler, C. 2009. *Screening Nostalgia?: Populuxe Props and Technicolor Aesthetics in Contemporary American Film*. New York: Berghahn Books.

Stacey, J. 1994. *Star Gazing?: Hollywood Cinema and Female Spectatorship*. London: Routledge.

Staiger, J. 1990. "Announcing Wares, Winning Patrons, Voicing Ideals: Thinking About the History and Theory of Film Advertising." *Cinema Journal* 29 (3): 3–31.

Steiner, C. B. 1994. *African Art in Transit*. New York: Cambridge University Press.

Street, S. 2001. *Costume and Cinema?: Dress Codes in Popular Film*. New York: Wallflower Books.

Studlar, G. 1990. "Masochism, Masquerade, and the Erotic Metamorphoses of Marlene Dietrich." In *Fabrications: Costume and the Female Body*, ed. J. Gaines and C. Herzog, 229–49. New York: Routledge.

Synnott, A. 1987. "Shame and Glory: A Sociology of Hair." *British Journal of Sociology* 38 (3): 381–413.

Tarlo, E. 1996. *Clothing Matters?: Dress and Identity in India*. Chicago: University of Chicago Press.

Taussig, M. T. 1993. *Mimesis and Alterity: A Particular History of the Senses*. New York: Routledge.

Team MissMalini. 2013. "Exclusive Interview: Manish Malhotra Reveals His Favorite Bollywood Show Stopper!" *MissMalini.com* (February 21). Available at: http://www.missmalini.com/2013/02/21/exclusive-interview-manish-malhotra-reveals-his-favorite-bollywood-show-stopper. Accessed August 30, 2013.

Thomas, R. 1989. "Sanctity and Scandal: The Mythologization of Mother India." *Quarterly Review of Film and Video* 11 (3): 11–30.

Thomas, R. 1995. "Melodrama and the Negotiation of Morality in Mainstream Hindi Film." In *Consuming Modernity: Public Culture in a South Asian World*, ed. C. Appadurai Breckenridge, 157–82. Minneapolis: University of Minnesota Press.

Times Internet Limited. 2002. "Costumes That Speak." *Official Site of the Hindi Film Devdas*. Available at: http://devdas.indiatimes.com/costumes.htm. Accessed August 30, 2013.

*Times of India*. 2002. "*Devdas* Costumes to Be Auctioned in UK." July 24. Available at: http://timesofindia.indiatimes.com/entertainment/bollywood/news-interviews/Devdas-costumes-to-be-auctioned-in-UK/articleshow/16848855.cms. Accessed August 30, 2013.

Turner, V. W. 1982. *From Ritual to Theatre?: The Human Seriousness of Play*. New York: Performing Arts Journal.

Vasudevan, R. 1989. "The Melodramatic Mode and the Commercial Hindi Cinema: Notes on Film History, Narrative, and Performance in the 1950s." *Screen* 30 (3): 29–50.

Vedwan, N. 2007. "Pesticides in Coca-Cola and Pepsi: Consumerism, Brand Image, and Public Interest in a Globalizing India." *Cultural Anthropology* 22 (4): 659–84.

Vincendeau, G. 2000. *Stars and Stardom in French Cinema*. 1st ed. New York: Continuum.

Virdi, J. 2003. *The Cinematic Imagination?: Indian Popular Films as Social History*. New Brunswick, NJ: Rutgers University Press.

Wadley, S. S. 2008. *Wife, Mother, Widow: Exploring Women's Lives in Northern India*. New Delhi: Chronicle Books.

Weinbaum, A. E., L. M. Thomas, P. Ramamurthy, U. G. Poiger, M. Y. Dong, and T. E. Barlow. 2008. "The Modern Girl around the World: Cosmetics Advertising and the Politics of Race and Style." In *The Modern Girl around the World: Consumption, Modernity, and Globalization*. Durham, NC: Duke University Press.

Wilkinson-Weber, C. M. 1999. *Embroidering Lives: Women's Work and Skill in the Lucknow Embroidery Industry*. SUNY Series in the Anthropology of Work. Albany, NY: State University of New York Press.

Wilkinson-Weber, C. M. 2004a. "Behind the Seams: Designers and Tailors in Popular Hindi Cinema." *Visual Anthropology Review* 20 (2): 3–21.

Wilkinson-Weber, C. M. 2004b. "Women, Work and the Imagination of Craft in South Asia." *Contemporary South Asia* 13 (3): 287–306.

Wilkinson-Weber, C. M. 2005. "Tailoring Expectations: How Film Costume Becomes the Audience's Clothes." *South Asian Popular Culture* 3 (2): 135–59.

Wilkinson-Weber, C. M. 2010a. "From Commodity to Costume: Productive Consumption in the Production of Bollywood Film 'Looks.'" *Journal of Material Culture* 15 (1): 1–28.

Wilkinson-Weber, C. M. 2010b. "A Need for Redress: Costume in Some Recent Hindi Film Remakes." *BioScope: South Asian Screen Studies* 1 (2): 125–45.

Wilkinson-Weber, C. M. 2011. "Diverting Denim: Screening Jeans in Bollywood." In *Global Denim*, ed. D. Miller and S. Woodward, 51–68. Oxford: Berg.

Wilkinson-Weber, C. M. 2012. "Making Faces: Competition and Change in the Production of Bollywood Film Star Looks." In *Working in the Global Film and Television Industries*, ed. A. Dawson and S. Holmes, 183–98. New York: Bloomsbury Academic.

Wilson, E. 1987. *Adorned in Dreams: Fashion and Modernity*. Berkeley: University of California Press.

World Bank. 2011. "India Country Overview—September 2011." Available at: http://www.worldbank.org.in/WBSITE/EXTERNAL/COUNTRIES/SOUTHASIAEXT/INDIAEXTN/0,,contentMDK:20195738~menuPK:295591~pagePK:141137~piPK:141127~theSitePK:295584,00.html. Accessed August 30, 2013.

Yash Raj Films. 2006. "Dhoom: 2 Fashion Apparel Now Available in India." November 11. Available at: http://www.yashrajfilms.com/News/NewsDetails.aspx?newsid=66b728d3-1421-4436-a91d-bdb2b960116f. Accessed August 30, 2013.

# Filmography

*23rd March 1931: Shaheed*, 2002. Directed by Guddu Dhanoa. India: Vijayta Films.

*Agent Vinod*, 2012. Directed by Sririam Raghavan. India: Illuminati Films, Eros Entertainment.

*Agneepath*, 2012. Directed by Karan Malhotra. India: Eros Entertainment.

*Aisha*, 2010. Directed by Rajshree Ojha. India: Anil Kapoor Films, PVR Pictures.

*Amar Akbar Anthony*, 1977. Directed by Manmohan Desai. India: Hirawat Jain and Company, M.K.D. Films, Manmohan Films.

*Amrapali*, 1966. Directed by Lekh Tandon. India: Eagle Films.

*Andaz*, 1949. Directed by Mehboob Khan. India: Mehboob Productions.

*Anhonee*, 1952. Directed by Khwaja Ahmad Abbas. India: Naya Sansar.

*Awaara*, 1951. Directed by Raj Kapoor. India: All India Film Corporation, R. K. Films.

*Baazi*, 1995. Directed by Ashutosh Gowarikar. India: Aftab Pictures.

*Badhaai ho Badhaai*, 2002. Directed by Satish Kaushik. India: Mukta Arts.

*Bandit Queen*, 1994. Directed by Shekhar Kapur. India: Kaleidoscope Entertainment.

*Bobby*, 1973. Directed by Raj Kapoor. India: R. K. Films.

*Bodyguard*, 2011. Directed by Siddique. India: Funky Buddha, Reel Life, Reliance Entertainment.

*Bunty aur Babli*, 2005. Directed by Shaad Ali. India: Yash Raj Films.

*C.I.D.*, 1956. Directed by Raj Khosla. India: Guru Dutt Films.

*Chandni*, 1989. Directed by Yash Chopra. India: Yash Raj Films.

*Chupke Chupke*, 1975. Directed by Hrishikesh Mukherjee. India: Mohan Studios.

*Coolie*, 1983. Directed by Manmohan Desai and Prayag Rai. India: Aasia Films, M.K.D. Films.

*Dabangg*, 2010. Directed by Abhinav Kashyap. India: Arbaaz Khan Productions, Shree Ashtavinayak Cine Vision.

*Dancing With the Stars*, 2005–present. United States: BBC Worldwide Americas.

*Dangerous Ishhq*, 2012. Directed by Vikram Bhatt. India: BVG Films, DAR Motion Pictures, Reliance Entertainment.

*Deewaar*, 1975. Directed by Yash Chopra. India: Trimurti Films.

*Dev D*, 2009. Directed by Anurag Kashyap. India: UTV Motion Pictures.

*Devdas*, 1955. Directed by Bimal Roy. India: Bimal Roy Productions, Mohan Films.

*Devdas*, 2002. Directed by Sanjay Leela Bhansali. India: Mega Bollywood.

*Dhoom*, 2004. Directed by Sanjay Gadhvi. India: Yash Raj Films.

*Dhoom: 2: Back in Action*, 2006. Directed by Sanjay Gadhvi. India: Yash Raj Films.

*Didi*, 1937. Directed by Nitin Bose. India: New Theatres.

*Dil Chahta Hai*, 2001. Directed by Farhan Akhtar. India: Excel Entertainment.

*Do Bigha Zamin*, 1953. Directed by Bimal Roy. India: Bimal Roy Productions.

*Don*, 1978. Directed by Chandra Barot. India: Nariman Films.

*Don*, 2006. Directed by Farhan Akhtar. India: Excel Entertainment.

*Dum Maaro Dum*, 2011. Directed by Rohan Sippy. India: Cheyenne Enterprises, Fox STAR Studios, Louverture Films, Ramesh Sippy Entertainment.

*Elizabeth*, 1998. Directed by Shekhar Kapoor. United Kingdom: Polygram Filmed Entertainment, Working Title Films, Channel 4 Films.

*Gandhi*, 1982. Directed by Richard Attenborough. United Kingdom: International Film Investors, NFDC, Goldcrest Films, Indo-British Films, Carolina Bank.

*Geet*, 1970. Directed by Ramanand Sagar. India: Sagar Art International.

*Ghulam*, 1998. Directed by Vikram Bhatt. India: Vishesh Films.

*Gladiator,* 2000. Directed by Ridley Scott. United States: Dreamworks SKG, Universal Pictures, Mill Film, C&L, Dawliz, Scott Free Productions.

*Guide*, 1965. Directed by Vijay Anand. India: Navketan International Films.

*Guzaarish*, 2010. Directed by Sanjay Leela Bhansali. India: Prime Focus, Sanjay Leela Bhansali Films, UTV Motion Pictures.

*Harry Potter and the Deathly Hallows*, 2010. Directed by David Yates. United States: Warner Brothers, Heyday Films.

*Hum Aapke Hain Koun . . . !*, 1994. Directed by Sooraj R. Barjatya. India: Rajshri Productions.

*Hum Dil De Chuke Sanam*, 1999. Directed by Sanjay Leela Bhansali. India: Sanjay Leela Bhansali Films, Jhamu Sughand Productions.

*Hum Tum*, 2004. Directed by Kunal Kohli. India: Yash Raj Films.

*I Hate Luv Storys*, 2010. Directed by Punit Malhotra. India: Dharma Productions, UTV Motion Pictures.

*Jefferson in Paris*, 1995. Directed by James Ivory. United States: Touchstone Pictures, Merchant Ivory Productions.

*Jewel Thief*, 1967. Directed by Vijay Anand. India: Navketan.

*Jodhaa Akbar*, 2007. Directed by Ashutosh Gowarikar. India: Ashutosh Gowarikar Productions, UTV Motion Pictures.

*Junglee*, 1961. Directed by Subodh Mukherji. India: Subodh Mukherji Productions.

*Junoon*, 1978. Directed by Shyam Benegal. India: Film-Valas.

*Kabhi Kushi Kabhie Gham . . .* , 2001. Directed by Karan Johar. India: Dharma Productions.

*Kal Ho Naa Ho*, 2003. Directed by Nikhil Advani. India: Dharma Productions, Dillywood.

*Kama Sutra: A Tale of Love*, 1996. Directed by Mira Nair. India: Mirabai Films, NDF International.

*Kaminey*, 2009. Directed by Vishal Bhardwaj. India: UTV Motion Pictures.

*Khalnayak*, 1993. Directed by Subhash Ghai. India: Mukta Arts.

*Kingdom of Heaven*, 2005. Directed by Ridley Scott. United States: 20th Century Fox, Scott Free Productions.

*Kyun! Ho Gaya Na*, 2004. Directed by Samir Karnik. India: Narsimha Enterprises.

*Laawaris*, 1981. Directed by Prakash Mehra. India: Prakash Mehra Productions.

*Lagaan: Once Upon a Time in India*, 2001. Directed by Ashutosh Gowarikar. India: Aamir Khan Productions, Ashutosh Gowarikar Productions, Jhamu Sughand Productions.

*Lakshya*, 2004. Directed by Farhan Akhtar. India: Excel Entertainment.

*Luck by Chance*, 2009. Directed by Zoya Akhtar. India: Excel Entertainment, Reliance Big Picture.

*Mangal Pandey: The Rising*, 2005. Directed by Ketan Mehta. India: Kaleidoscope Entertainment, Maya Movies.

*Marie Antoinette*, 2006. Directed by Sofia Coppola. United States: American Zoetrope.

*Mother India*, 1957. Directed by Mehboob Khan. India: Mehboob Productions.

*Moulin Rouge*, 2001. Directed by Baz Luhrmann. Australia: Bazmark Films.

*Mr India*, 1987. Directed by Shekhar Kapur. India: Narsimha Industries.

*Mukti*, 1937. Directed by P. C. Barua. India: New Theatres.

*Omkara*, 2006. Directed by Vishal Bhardwaj. India: Big Screen Entertainment, Shemaroo.

*Om Shanti Om*, 2007. Directed by Farah Khan. India: Red Chillies Entertainment.

*Once Upon a Time in Mumbaai*, 2010. Directed by Milan Luthria. India: Balaji Motion Pictures.

*Pakeezah*, 1972. Directed by Kamal Amrohi. India: Mahal Pictures, Sangeeta Enterprises.

*Pardes*, 1997. Directed by Subhash Ghai. India: Mukta Arts.

*Pardesi*, 1957. Directed by Khwaja Ahmad Abbas, Vasili Pronin. India: Mosfilm, Naya Sansar.

*Ra.One*, 2011. Directed by Anubhav Sinha. India: Red Chillies Entertainment, Eros International, Prime Focus, Tata Elxsi Visual Computing Lab, Winford Productions.

*Ram Tera Ganga Maili*, 1985. Directed by Raj Kapoor. India: R. K. Films.

*Rang De Basanti*, 2006. Directed by Rakeysh Omprakash Mehra. India: Romp, UTV Motion Pictures.

*Rangeela*, 1995. Directed by Ram Gopal Varma. India: Varma Productions.

*Reshma aur Shera*, 1972. Directed by Sunil Dutt. India: Ajanta Arts.

*Robin Hood*, 2010. Directed by Ridley Scott. United States: Universal Pictures, Scott Free Productions, Imagine Entertainment, Relativity Media.

*Rowdy Rathore*, 2012. Directed by Prabhudheva. India: SLB Films, UTV Motion Pictures.

*Sahib, Bibi, aur Ghulam*, 1962. Directed by Abrar Alvi. India: Guru Dutt Films.

*Satyam, Shivam, Sundaram*, 1975. Directed by Raj Kapoor. India: R. K. Films.

*Sesame Street*, 1969–present. United States: Children's Television Workshop, Jim Henson Productions, Sesame Workshop.

*Shalimar*, 1978. Directed by Krishna Shah. India: Judson Productions.

*Shanghai*, 2012. Directed by Dibakar Banerjee. India: PVR Pictures.

*Sharaabi*, 1984. Directed by Prakash Mehra. India: Prakash Mehra Productions.

*Sholay*, 1975. Directed by Ramesh Sippy. India: United Producers, Sippy Films.

*Shree 420*, 1955. Directed by Raj Kapoor. India: R. K. Films.

*Silsila*, 1981. Directed by Yash Chopra. India: Yash Raj Films.

*Slumdog Millionaire*, 2008. Directed by Danny Boyle. UK: Celador and Film4 Productions.

*Smash*, 2012–2013. United States: Dreamworks Television, Madwoman in the Attic, Universal Television.

*Taal*, 1999. Directed by Subhash Ghai. India: Mukta Arts.

*Taj Mahal*, 2005. Directed by Akbar Khan. India: Mashreq Communications, Trilogy Entertainment Group.

*Talaash*, 2012. Directed by Reema Kagti. India: Aamir Khan Productions, Excel Entertainment.

*Teesri Manzil*, 1966. Directed by Vijay Anand. India: Nasir Hussain Films, United Producers.

*That Girl in Yellow Boots*, 2010. Directed by Anurag Kashyap. India: Anurag Kashyap Films, NFDC, Sikhya Entertainment.

*The Legend of Bhagat Singh*, 2002. Directed by Rajkumar Santoshi. India: Tips Film.

*Titanic*, 1997. Directed by James Cameron. United States: Lightstorm Entertainment, 20th Century Fox, Paramount Pictures.

*Umrao Jaan*, 1981. Directed by Muzaffar Ali. India: Integrated Films.

*Umrao Jaan*, 2006. Directed by J. P. Dutta. India: J. P. Films.

*Utsav*, 1984. Directed by Girish Karnad. India: Film-Valas.

*Veer*, 2010. Directed by Anil Sharma. India: Eros International, Vijay Galani Moviez.

*Waqt*, 1965. Directed by Yash Chopra. India: United Producers, B. R. Films.

*Zindagi Na Milegi Dobara*, 2011. Directed by Zoya Akhtar. India: Eros International, Excel Entertainment, Kanzaman, UTV Motion Pictures.

# Index